Comparative Literature East and West:
Traditions and Trends

Comparative Literature East and West: Traditions and Trends

Selected Conference Papers

Edited by
Cornelia N. Moore
Raymond A. Moody

Stafford Library
Columbia College
10th and Rodgers
Columbia, MO 65216

Published by
the College of Languages, Linguistics and Literature
University of Hawaii
and the
East-West Center

Copyright © 1989 by College of Languages, Linguistics and
Literature, University of Hawaii, Honolulu, Hawaii, 96822

All rights reserved.
Manufactured in the United States of America.

Library of Congress Cataloging-in-Publication Data

Comparative literature--East and West.

    (Literary studies--East and West ; v. 1)
    1. Literature, Comparative--Oriental and Occidental--
Congresses. 2. Literature, Comparative--Occidental and
Oriental--Congresses. I. Moore, Cornelia Niekus,
1938-   . II. Moody, Raymond A., 1936-   .
III. Series.
PN858.C64   1989   809   89-9132
ISBN 0-8248-1247-6

Manufacture of this book was through the production services program of the
University of Hawaii Press.

Distributed by
University of Hawaii Press
Order Department
2840 Kolowalu Street
Honolulu, Hawaii 96822

TABLE OF CONTENTS

Acknowledgements   vii
Introduction by *Daniel Stempel*   ix

I. CRITICAL THEORY

Walter Cohen, Cornell University
The Concept of World Literature   3

Eugene Eoyang, Indiana University
Polar Paradigms in Poetics: Chinese and Western Literary Premises   11

Carl Freedman, Louisiana State University
The Transformation Problem and Cultural Theory   22

II. WEST COMES EAST

Daniel Stempel, University of Hawaii
Lafcadio Hearn's Translations and the Origins of Imagist Aesthetics   31

Arnold Edelstein, University of Hawaii
The Lessons of Misreading   38

Evelyn Ellerman, University of Alberta
Intertextuality in the Fiction of Camus and Wendt   43

P. Joseph Cahill, University of Alberta
Style and Substance: Two Instances of Cross-Cultural Hermeneutics   51

Nobuko Miyama Ochner, University of Hawaii
Robert Louis Stevenson through a Japanese Eye: The Silkworm Image in
   Light, Wind, and Dreams   58

Jean Y. Toyama, University of Hawaii
Intertextuality and the Problem of Translation: A Study of Two
   Translations of Verlaine's "Chanson d'Automne"   65

III. EAST COMES WEST

Herbert Knust, University of Illinois
East-West Encounters in Brecht's Szechwan Play ... 73

Mark Heberle, University of Hawaii
Pagans and Saracens in Spenser's *The Faerie Queene* ... 81

IV. EUROPEAN INTERACTIONS

Ulrich Weisstein, Indiana University
Giovanni Verga's "Cavalleria Rusticana": A Translator's Nightmare? ... 91

Maria-Regina Kecht, Hamilton College
The Victim as Oppressor: Mirror Structures in Mother-Daughter Relations in Recent German Women's Fiction ... 107

Anna Makolkina, University of Toronto
Temporality as a Fictional Device in Biography: Some Pushkin and Byron Biographies ... 117

Judith L. Kellogg, University of Hawaii
Christine de Pizan and Boccaccio: Rewriting Classical Mythic Tradition ... 124

Svetlana Boym, Harvard University
Politics of Mis-translation: The Aragon Affair ... 132

Susan L. Wing, University of Hawaii
Something about Emilia: Woman as Love Object in Boccaccio, Chaucer, Anne de Graville, and Shakespeare and Fletcher ... 139

V. ASIAN INTERACTIONS

Joseph Chadwick, University of Hawaii
Allegories of the Novel in Albert Wendt's *Pouliuli* ... 155

Victoria Vernon, Hamilton College
The Mold of Force: Maternal Transformations of Submission into Aggression in Modern Japanese Women's Literature ... 162

Contents

Lucy Lower, University of Hawaii
Poetorii and New-Style Poetry in the *Shintaishishō*   170

Arthur H. Thornhill III, University of Hawaii
Typology in Traditional Japanese Poetics: The Reception of
   Chinese Buddhist Models   177

John T. Dorsey, Nihon University
National and Comparative Literature in Japan   184

VI. DOMINATION, DECOLONIZATION, AND DICHOTOMY

Marilyn Randall, Queen's University
   The Context of Decolonization and the Poetics of Plagiarism   193

K. J. Phillips, University of Hawaii
Salman Rushdie's *Midnight's Children*: Models for Storytelling, East
   and West   202

Deborah Weiner, University of Hawaii
"Difference that Kills," / Difference that Heals: Representing Latin
   America in the Poetry of Elizabeth Bishop and Margaret Atwood   208

ACKNOWLEDGEMENTS

The editors would like to thank the following people for their help in the always laborious process that accompanies the publication of conference proceedings. We thank the Conference Committee members, Cristina Bacchilega, Ruth Dawson, Robert Huey, Kathleen Falvey, David McGraw and Arthur Thornhill of the University of Hawaii, Laurence Kitching, formerly of the University of Hawaii, and Wimal Dissanayake of the East-West Center for their careful reading and their many helpful suggestions. We thank Janet Heavenridge of the University Press of Hawaii for her expert advice and assistance. We are especially grateful to Steven Bradbury, graduate student in the Department of East-Asian Languages. His editing and computer skills and his many helpful insights during the preparation process were essential ingredients for the successful completion of this volume.

The Editors
Cornelia N. Moore
Raymond A. Moody
College of Languages,
  Linguistics and Literature
University of Hawaii

INTRODUCTION

Daniel Stempel, University of Hawaii

It is customary, when introducing a collection of papers on diverse topics, to begin with a hearty benediction by echoing Dryden's preface to *The Canterbury Tales*: "Here is God's plenty!" To which I would add that the divine plenitude, being infinite, must surely have room for an occasional comment by a devil's advocate. For this reason I shall occasionally depart from a scrupulous neutrality to suggest that there may be another side to the question under discussion.

The usual procedure is to line the papers up in review and pass down the line, shaking hands and pinning a verbal medal on each in turn. These papers, however, refuse to stand meekly at attention, although the editors have arranged them in a manageable order. Perhaps it would be preferable to classify them as "lambs" or "tigers," on the model of Blake's division between innocence and experience.

"Lambs" are papers that use the topics and methodology of traditional comparative literature: genre study, historical periods, movements, source and influence studies, myth and themes, literature and the arts and sciences, literary history, literary criticism, and—the broad rubric of this conference—cross-cultural relations. "Tigers" are those who, as Blake would have put it, are (like Milton) of the "Devil's party," the rebel angels who break free of the restraints of traditional scholarship. Of course, the distinctions here are far from clear-cut: the lambs sometimes growl and the tigers can roar you as gently as any sucking dove.

The influx of Continental literary criticism and philosophy since the early seventies has prompted rereadings of familiar texts. Structuralism introduced a new formalism that spread beyond linguistics to the reading of all possible constellations of signs. Deconstruction followed on its heels, pushing formalism beyond its breaking point by an ontological *reductio ad absurdum* of the elements of language and metaphor that murdered reason ("logocentrism") to dissect.

Under the influence of the revolution of the irrational, even Marxism and psychoanalysis, both avowedly scientific disciplines, have shifted toward losing themselves in an "O Profundo!" of ineffability. Nevertheless, the "tigers" (those of Yale, not Princeton) have, from the point of view of a historian, performed a valuable service in stirring up controversy about the value of all disciplines, academic, political, and cultural. As an old Spenglerian and a new Foucauldian, I am quite willing to listen to prophecies of the imminent decline of the West, especially since I do not expect to be around to witness it.

The most original and productive of these new revisionist disciplines is, beyond question, feminist literary history and criticism, whose transformation of traditional scholarship is visible in every journal as well as in the papers of this conference. It is far from monolithic—feminism draws on all sources and uses the theories and methods of every modern and post-modern approach. The extreme positions which sometimes shock more traditional scholars are less characteristic of its work than a flexible eclecticism and pragmatism which any intelligent reader will find persuasive. But before turning to papers on specific topics, I would like to look at the three theoretical papers that introduce this collection.

Our broad topic, as the title of this collection indicates, is not merely comparative literature, but comparative literature, East and West. As Walter Cohen urbanely points out in his paper on "The Concept of World Literature," despite the paradoxes of living on a sphere, we accept the traditional attribution of "East" as everything east of Western Europe, although Asia is, in fact, to the west of the New World. (Perhaps the resurgence of fundamentalism will solve this paradox by banning the teaching of spherical geometry as well as evolution.) Professor Cohen traces the development and spread of the idea of world literature through the successive dominance of centers of power in the West and through the spread of colonialism in the wake of an aggressive and expanding world economy. As he emphasizes, the encounter between cultures is as much dialogical as hierarchical.

Although some of the papers see this encounter as destructive to the politically and economically weaker cultures, there is a complexity in this relationship which defies all simple dichotomies of good and evil. As T. S. Eliot reminds us, "Think now / History has many cunning passages, contrived corridors / And issues, deceives with whispering ambitions, / Guides us by vanities." He adds, "Virtues / Are forced upon us by our impudent crimes." I am thinking of the changing attitudes since F. S. C. Northrup's book, *The Meeting of East and West* (1946), appeared in the immediate aftermath of World War II. Northrup analyzed and categorized the differences between cultures, as he saw them, and looked forward to mutual understanding. It was a time when those of good will dreamed of One World, not three. But only a few years ago one of our local Hawaiian poets wrote: "East / I'm afraid / Does not / Meet West— / they COLLIDE!" The truth, as always, probably falls somewhere between these dramatic extremes. My own experience, based on early *Wanderjahre* in exotic places, as well as a lifetime spent teaching on the frontier, is that East and West neither meet nor collide; they pass by each other, pursuing their own illusory expectations. Even the Pacific War was merely a clumsy sideswipe.

John T. Dorsey, whose paper on "National and Comparative Literature in Japan" takes a hard look at the present state of comparative literature in Japan, would, I think, agree. Professor Dorsey points out the difficulty of finding a common ground for any kind of comparison when, as in Japan (and, to a lesser degree, in the West), the national literature is privileged as the model by which other literatures are analyzed and judged. He proposes to limit the scope of East-

West comparative literary studies to carefully qualified discussions of genre and other traditional topics without regard to the priority of any national literature, always keeping in mind that apparent similarities may be deceptive. Professor Dorsey would rule out any extension of these literary studies into the area of cross-cultural influences and differences; comparatists cannot be experts in everything without losing the sharp focus of their scholarship.

Nevertheless, if we return to Professor Cohen's argument for studying non-literary exchanges between cultures, we can support it with an actual example, the mission of Father Matteo Ricci (and other Jesuits) to China, which Professor Cahill describes as a mutual conversion in his gracefully written paper, "Style and Substance: Two Instances of Cross-Cultural Hermeneutics." These missionary scholars first introduced the West to the use of Chinese characters. From Leibniz, who read their works, to Pound, who read Fenollosa, the West has pursued the search for a written language whose meaning would be clear to all, free of all linguistic variations, with as much zeal as the alchemical quest for the Philosopher's Stone. Alas, the closest we have come to it is the telephone book, with its lists of Arabic numerals which can be read in Tibet or Timbuktu with equal ease.

Professor Eugene Eoyang's paper, "Polar Paradigms in Poetics: Chinese and Western Literary Premises," is, to some degree, the kind of traditional comparative scholarship recommended by Professor Dorsey, but it steps boldly beyond the limits of literature to broad cultural comparisons and contrasts. He carefully distinguishes four types of paradigmatic presuppositions in both East and West and shows how they differ and how those differences must be recognized and accepted. His points are well-taken and worth noting, although as a Blake scholar I must protest that poet-painters are not unknown in the West. Blake's stylus was not merely a pen, it was the engraver's tool that traced what Blake called "the wiry bounding line" essential to all art. (The engraver's burin, in fact, created the model for nineteenth century "copperplate" calligraphy.) Professor Eoyang's comments on the enviable lack of "dissociation of sensibility" in Chinese literature, that is, a separation between intellect and emotion, are reinforced by Arthur H. Thornhill's paper "Typology in Traditional Japanese Poetics: The Reception of Chinese Buddhist Models," which shows how the subtle permutations of *kokoro* and *kotoba,* content and language, are used to define a nine-fold hierarchy of critical evaluation that would be applauded by any Aristotelian.

The third paper on theory, Carl Freedman's "The Transformation Problem and Cultural Theory" is far more abstract and, at first glance, appears to be unrelated to the theme of the conference. But Professor Freedman's conclusion, after examining apparent inconsistencies between theories of value in the first two books of Marx's *Capital,* is that the problem is resolved in the third book by the Marxist concept of totality, as defined by Louis Althusser. It is this concept of totality which Professor Freedman proposes to apply to cultural problems, such as the unity of the Romantic movement in Europe. If I understand him correctly, he sees in Althusser's concept of Marxist totality the possibility of dealing with a unified complexity in which no single factor can be isolated as a structuring principle. The structure is defined only by its effects. Since both Professor Freedman's paper and this introduction are prologues to larger topics, this is not the place to argue the question. I merely wish to note that a New Historian (or an old historian) might protest that Althusser's genealogy of totality from Spinoza to Marx confuses distinctly different paradigms, somewhat like tracing modern astrophysics to Giordano Bruno. Perhaps Darwin's "entangled bank" in the closing pages of the *Origin of Species* might come closer to Marx's overdetermined totality. It is this anti-historical structural approach that has been criticized by Marxists and non-Marxists, including Raymond Aron, Michel Foucault, Bertell Ollman, and, most forcefully, by Adam Schaff, the brilliant Polish Marxist, whose lectures on alienation I attended at the University of Vienna in 1977.

Nevertheless, Professor Freedman's paper, like the other theoretical papers, gives us an intimation of the complexity of criticism, cultural and literary, in the main body of papers in this collection. I should like to consider the papers on translation as a group, beginning with Ulrich Weisstein's magisterial "Giovanni Verga's 'Cavalleria Rusticana': A Translator's Nightmare?" One of the most difficult tasks for a translator, as Professor Weisstein demonstrates, is the translation of a dialect in one language into an effective equivalent in another language. In "Cavalleria Rusticana" the problem is compounded by a matrix of standard Tuscan language in which Sicilian dialect is embedded. Blessed with an ear for subtle variations in both Italian and spoken English, Professor Weisstein tests four translations, including one by D. H. Lawrence (who does not do very well), and deftly separates the successful renderings from clumsy approximations.

The problem of translation introduced in Professor Weisstein's paper is broadened to bridge not only two languages, but two cultures with very different concepts of the generation of literary texts in Jean Y. Toyama's paper "Intertextuality and the Problem of Translation: a Study of Two Translations of Verlaine's 'Chanson d'Automne.'" Professor Toyama examines translations of this poem by two Japanese writers, Horiguchi Daigaku and Ueda Bin, and points out that conventional images and phrases in Japanese clustered around the theme of "autumn" shape the reading of the poem for Japanese readers in ways that are not completely congruent with the original text.

Nobuko Miyama Ochner deals with a similar problem in "Robert Louis Stevenson through a Japanese Eye: The Silkworm Image in *Light, Wind, and Dreams."* Nakajima Atsushi's fictional biography (*rekishi shōsetsu*) of Robert Louis Stevenson, based on Stevenson's letters, diaries, and tales from the South Seas, uses the image of the silkworm spinning its cocoon and its transformation into a butterfly to describe Stevenson's struggle to complete his work before his death. Although the image is not taken from Stevenson's own work, it shifts his biography into a context that is meaningful for the Japanese.

Introduction

Mis-translations are always a source of innocent merriment to those who discover them in someone else's work; to the translator, as Professor Weisstein writes, they are a nightmare. To the dispassionate historian, they are facts that determine the course of literary, cultural, or political history. Svetlana Boym, in "Politics of Mis-translation: The Aragon Affair," traces Louis Aragon's attempts to combine Soviet orthodox ideology and poetic language, by imitating Mayakovsky's "poetry in the revolutionary march." Aragon insisted on subordinating the medium, poetic structure, to the message. As Professor Boym shows, the result, Aragon's poem, "Front Rouge," was a celebration of what was to become Stalinist repression and brutality, a poem which an older and presumably wiser Aragon later rejected.

Arnold Edelstein's paper, "The Lessons of Misreading," makes it clear that only Harold Bloom, the advocate of "creative misprision," could possibly teach American literature successfully in China. Professor Edelstein's account of his experience as a teacher in China reaches the same sad conclusion to which I alluded above: East and West do not meet, they do not collide; they pass each other with, at best, a friendly wave, proceeding in different directions. My own modest contribution, "Lafcadio Hearn's Translations and the Origins of Imagist Aesthetics," is a brief footnote to literary history that corrects the now canonical dogma that Ezra Pound's genius enabled him to grasp the essence of Japanese poetics without knowing a word of the language.

There is a subtle shift in these papers from specific problems of translation and intertextuality to the broader question of foreign literary influence and its effect on form and style. Evelyn Ellerman gives us a persuasive introduction to the problem in her paper, "Intertextuality in the Fiction of Camus and Wendt." Although it would be difficult to think of any more disparate topics than the world of the French existentialist hero and the traditional culture of Samoa, Professor Ellerman skillfully demonstrates Albert Wendt's use of the night/day opposition that runs through Camus's novels. Joseph Chadwick boldly goes to the heart of the matter in "Allegories of the Novel in Albert Wendt's *Pouliuli*," arguing that the novel, as a literary form, is itself a paradigm or model of the destructive power of the printed work of art in a culture based on oral or face-to-face communication. Chadwick expands Ellerman's thesis to show how the bourgeois or individual hero, with all his existential internal conflicts (as opposed to the traditional mythic or epic hero), makes his appearance in a totally alien society, creating contradictions which threaten its survival.

In contrast, cross-cultural literary influence between literate societies can be a means of restoring vigor and freedom to a tradition bound by convention, as Lucy Lower points out in her presentation of a significant chapter in the history of modern Japanese poetry, "*Poetorii* and New-Style Poetry in the *Shintaishishō*." Using Western models and translations, three junior members of the Japanese academic establishment, influenced by Darwinian concepts of evolution and progress, introduced new longer poetic forms. Kathy Phillips, writing on "Salman Rushdie's *Midnight's Children*: Models for Storytelling,

East and West," traces the patterns of reflexive irony through an implied dialogue between storyteller and listener within the story itself back to Hindu and Arabic sources, but, more directly, to Sterne's *Tristram Shandy*. Rushdie uses the self-deprecatory revelations of his hero to satirize the absurdities of life in post-colonial India.

Mark Heberle argues that cultural prejudice against the East has been part of the mainstream of Western literature at least since the Roman conquest of the Eastern Mediterranean and clearly since the Crusades and the rise of epics chronicling heroic deeds in the war against Islam. In "Pagans and Saracens in Spenser's *The Faerie Queen*," he shows that Spenser invariably places his Moslems and "pagans," who, for him, were synonymous, on the side of evil. But Spenser's "demonology," as Professor Heberle terms it, was not, I suggest, merely a matter of literary inheritance. In Spenser's lifetime the victory of the West at the battle of Lepanto (1571) changed the course of history and Spenser was certainly aware of it.

This exasperating intricacy of cross-cultural relations, which, for the historian, is not clarified by either defense or condemnation, is doubled in Herbert Knust's "East-West Encounters in Brecht's Szechwan Play." Professor Knust give us a review of sources, East and West, and then demonstrates the affinity of *The Good Person of Szechwan* with Strindberg's *A Dream Play*, an affinity of opposites, as Brecht opposes a pragmatic human approach to Strindberg's metaphysical musings. Perhaps Brecht's attitude, as Professor Knust describes it, is best summed up by the practical comment of Confucius, which, literally translated, reads: "Not know life, how know death?"

Marilyn Randall's paper, "The Context of Decolonialization and the Poetics of Plagiarism," gives us a fascinating account of how the pressures of a dominant culture on minority writers can produce a literature of *resentment*, characterized by strategies of literary sabotage, such as plagiarism. As a prospector who has picked up German nuggets in Coleridge's cunningly salted English mother-lode, I am grateful to Randall for throwing new light on plagiarism as a romantic reaction to the convention of originality.

As the feminist papers in this collection demonstrate, literary history can—and should—be rewritten to include the tradition of women's literature. When meticulous scholarship and sensitive criticism support theory, its importance and its validity cannot be ignored. Reopening the historical canon also reopens the critical canon. Judith L. Kellogg's paper, "Christine de Pizan and Boccaccio: Rewriting Classic Mythic Tradition," restores Christine de Pizan to her full stature as the creator of a new feminine mythography rather than a mere respondent to Boccaccio's traditional masculine image of women in *Concerning Famous Women*. Susan L. Wing traces the history of the character of Emilia from Boccaccio's *Teseida* through Chaucer's "The Knight's Tale" and Anne de Graville's fifteenth-century version to Shakespeare and Fletcher's adaptation of "The Knight's Tale" in *Two Noble Kinsman*. Professor Wing writes an objective and convincing historical portrait of a woman who is always the object (and prize) of masculine desire, never, not even for Shakespeare and Fletcher, the subject of her own desire.

Two papers complement each other, focusing on the relation between mother and daughter in East and West and reminding us that the most dangerous of all liaisons are family liaisons. Both place *sous rature* the quadrilateral Freudian family structure formed by cross-gender diagonals in order to emphasize the direct genealogy of mother and daughter. In "The Mold of Force: Maternal Transformations of Submission into Aggression in Modern Japanese Women's Literature," Victoria Vernon shows how Japanese women writers escape from the rigid constraints demanded by their culture, as recorded in their autobiographies, into fantasies of sado-masochistic punishment of daughters by mothers, a feminine parallel to Joyce's *Counterparts*, a story of a drunken father who beats his innocent son because he cannot strike back at those who are more powerful than he is. Marie-Regina Kecht discusses two German novels, both more or less autobiographical, which develop the same theme in "The Victim as Oppressor: Mirror Structures in Mother-Daughter Relations in Recent German Women's Fiction." One difference between the two cultures is immediately apparent: while physical violence as part of the discipline of childrearing appears in the German novels, the influence of the mother in the Japanese examples is more a matter of attitude and language, of cold rejection rather than brutal repression. Even where the Japanese mother dreams of torturing her child, it is only a fantasy to be made real by the child's future husband.

Feminist theory moves from historical and thematic studies to critical reading in Deborah Weiner's "'Difference that Kills' / Difference that Heals: Representing Latin America in the Poetry of Elizabeth Bishop and Margaret Atwood." Taking the reactions to Latin America expressed in their poems as a touchstone, Weiner contrasts Bishop's sharp distinctions, creating binary oppositions, to Atwood's more inclusive method, seeing both similarity and difference simultaneously.

Finally, in a different category, a paper on temporal structures in biographies, Anna Makolkina's "Temporality as a Fictional Device in Biography: Some Pushkin and Byron Biographies," examines the temporal patterns of narration adopted by biographers to impose the unity of a fictional work on what is basically a simple chronicle of events.

My task, in writing this foreword, has been to blend the multiple voices of a Bakhtinian carnival into a choral harmony. At times, it has been necessary to interpolate a Mephistophelean bass to protest, "O Freunde, nicht diese Töne!" I hope that the writers (and readers) of these papers will forgive me if I have misrepresented anyone's views. Since our culture, unlike Eastern cultures, equates advanced age with senility rather than wisdom, perhaps they will merely shake their heads sadly and dismiss me with a tolerant sigh.

I. CRITICAL THEORY

THE CONCEPT OF WORLD LITERATURE

Walter Cohen, Cornell University

If you depart from New York in the East and travel westward, you might eventually reach California in the West. If you then continue in a somewhat westerly direction from California, you could in due course come to Hawaii in the mid-Pacific. This second trip does not produce a shock, but neither does it have the semantic satisfaction of the first. We might begin to feel a certain disquietude about the terminology. For if we continue west from Hawaii, we will get to Asia in the East. We go west, and we arrive in the East. I am belaboring an obvious point: on a plane surface geographical directions are absolute; on a spherical surface such as the Earth—which after all is the only place these directions have any meaning—they are relational. At best, directions very approximately indicate the shortest route between two points. One can get from New York to California by traveling either east or west, but the easterly option is likely to take a good deal longer. On the other hand it is easy to be puzzled by the East-West Center here, from which one gets to the West by traveling east and to the East by traveling west. Scientifically we know that the world is round; ideologically—in Althusser's sense—we experience it as flat.[1]

But why brand as ideology a piece of common sense that, though inaccurate, is perfectly serviceable on most occasions? If you were to invert a map of North and South America or rather South and North America, you would notice that the designations South and North have the same relative validity as the use of East and West for New York and California. That is, it makes sense in terms of distance to go north if you are traveling from South America to North America. But, as such a map would reveal, the problem lies elsewhere, in our unexamined assumption that the North is on top. We might ask ourselves how long it would take us to get used to an inverted globe, for example, or how we would visualize South and North in photographs taken from space. In other words, this is one of those invidious binary oppositions concealing an unjustifiable hierarchy to which Derrida in particular has called attention.[2]

It is the same with East and West. This is a Europocentric distinction, in which the West has usually denoted some, often rather small, part of Europe, and the East has meant Asia, the Middle East, and quite frequently most of Europe.[3] For at least 500 years it has been apparent which the better half is—where "half" means the far smaller section not even of the globe but of that very limited portion of it known as the Eurasian land mass. For 40 years these geographical markers have carried a powerful, overt ideological charge, so that, for example, we now locate in the East the home of that distinguished Asiatic writer, Goethe, half of that renowned Oriental city, Berlin, and the birthplace of that traditional Eastern religion, Protestantism. In the continental United States this Western

European ideology is reinforced by the glad realization that we after all inhabit the *Western* Hemisphere.

An inverted map of that hemisphere would suggest one possible solution to the problem: the reversal of the hierarchy, the privileging of East over West. Like Derrida, however, Althusser has argued that this is only a partial solution, that it still leaves you in a hierarchical relationship and a binary opposition.[4] In addition, this move precludes recognition not only of other relationships, such as, most obviously, the one between North and South, but also of the differences internal to each marker—differentiation within the East, West, North, or South, for example. I will try to avoid these difficulties by invoking the totalizing category of world literature. But I want to emphasize not only that totalizing categories have their own problems, in this instance exacerbated by the unavailability of any other world except a prior version of our own with which to compare this one. More important, the invocation of world literature does not cause the ideology of East and West to disappear. The concept of world literature is in a certain sense the East-West dyad writ large, bound up as it, too, is with the adventures of Europe. Moreover, the bipolar terminology reviewed above indicates, however distortedly, a fundamental historical reality that it is the purpose of the notion of world literature not to obliterate but to bring into clearer view.

In what follows, then, I will first present a genealogical sketch both of the concept of world literature and of the closely related category—also highly relevant to this conference—of comparative literature. This account will provide the basis for a historical summary of the changing geographical locus of literary innovation, dominance, and especially prestige in the European languages, with special attention to the crucial shifts that occurred in the late eighteenth century and again after World War Two. And I will conclude by briefly surveying the obstacles to an adequate understanding of world literature today.

The practice of comparative literary criticism and theory is extremely venerable, dating back in the region that later became Europe at least to ancient Roman discussions of the relationship between Greek and Latin writers. But the concept of world literature does not emerge for two millennia, until the late writings of Goethe, where it seems to refer to the international intercourse among *European* literatures and is promoted on the grounds that contact with foreign literatures brings vitality to one's national literature while fostering international understanding and toleration.[5] Behind Goethe's formulations and those of the early, systematic comparatists in France, Germany, and England during the half century beginning in 1820, lies the pioneering work in comparative philology and in the study of individual national literatures.[6] But the latter in particular depends on the prior consolidation of nation-states, and especially on the generalized emergence of nationalism in Europe in the wake of the French Revolution and on the roughly contemporaneous establishment of the modern category of literature.[7] Comparative literature presupposes the existence both of something called literature and of at least two national instances of it that can form the basis for comparison. It is a symptom of differentiation and specialization—of the constitution of ostensibly coherent discursive and political entities—that at the same time represents a partial effort to establish or re-establish larger units of meaning.

How might this be accomplished? One answer that arises in this period—in my opinion the correct one—is offered by Marx and Engels in *The Communist Manifesto*. "The bourgeoisie has through its exploitation of the world-market given a cosmopolitan character to production and consumption in every country . . . . And as in material, so also in intellectual production . . . from the numerous national and local literatures, there arises a world literature."[8] Like much of their writing, this claim has a predictive quality, in the sense that it is truer today than it was 140 years ago. But it also suggests an approach to the new theories of comparative literature that emerge as early as the latter part of the nineteenth century, a period dominated by a positivist, nationalist, scientific, evolutionary method inspired by Darwin. One finds these motifs in Ferdinand Brunetière, for example.[9] But in two American critics, Charles Chauncy Shackford and Charles Mills Gayley, such a stance is combined with a more global perspective, with the commitment to, in Shackford's words, the "classification" of all literature under "universal laws of mental, social and moral development."[10] This is the era after the national consolidation effected by the Union victory in the Civil War. In international terms, however, it also witnessed perhaps the greatest land grab in human history, as the European powers—and the United States—formally or informally established colonial control over most of the rest of the planet. The condition for theorization of literature on a global scale was, then, the establishment not of a global community but of a global empire. It does not follow from this that all talk of world literature is necessarily imperialist in character. There are moments even in Shackford and Gayley where the planetary perspective seems to imply the equality of all literatures and cultures. Nonetheless, it *does* follow that any work on world literature begins from and is inflected by the fundamental asymmetry in power recognized by Marx and Engels.

I want now to skip forward to the post-World War Two years, the period when comparative literature established itself as a significant presence in universities in this country and also the period of American imperial hegemony. The rising internationalism of literary study here has surely been responsive to the global projection of power by the United States. One way of registering this connection is to note that the ostensible anti-provincialism of comparative literature studies has in fact meant an emphasis on Western European literature—an elite provincialism and ethnocentrism, in other words. Finally, it is just barely possible that the sudden surge of interest in "Third World" literature—the phrase is in quotation marks—during the last few years indicates a belated recognition of the relative decline of American power and of the consequent necessity of taking the rest of the world seriously. But even if this is the case, any resulting optimism must be tempered by the counter-awareness that the weakening of the U.S.'s international military and economic position has not been accompanied by a corresponding loss of cultural influence. Quite the opposite. The spread of the English language—in no small part a legacy of the British Empire—and of American culture—from movies and television to the instructions that accompany high tech commodities—continues into remote and formerly resistant regions. It is partly in this sense that we are entering the age of world literature.

A related pattern is discernible in the history of European literary influence. Beginning no later than AD 800 and continuing for just under a millennium, literary dominance coincided with economic or military/political dominance, or both. A simplified sequence would run as follows: the Latin of Carolingian France (9th century) and Ottonian Germany (10th century), feudal France (11th-13th century), the city-states of Italy (14th-16th century), Habsburg Spain (16th-17th century), absolutist France (17th century), and post-revolutionary England (18th century).[11] Since roughly 1775, however, the center has moved to the periphery. Much of the most innovative and influential writing has come from the fringes of European civilization. One thinks of Germany (late 18th-early 19th century), New England (mid-19th century), Russia (19th century), Scandinavia (late 19th century), Ireland (early 20th century), and the American South (interwar years). In the postwar period this trend has intensified to the point where the fringes of European civilization have come to mean the rest of the world. Putting the internal chronology of the last 40 years aside, one might stress literature from Eastern Europe, Latin America, Africa, India, Japan, perhaps the Middle East, and certainly the various ethnic minorities of the United States and elsewhere.

How are these shifts to be understood? In the last two centuries writers on the periphery have regularly synthesized or at least juxtaposed the most avant-garde aesthetic trends of the metropolitan countries with the generally more traditional cultures of their own societies.[12] The result has often been what, from a Bakhtinian perspective, might be called a powerful dialogical effect.[13] Especially since World War Two we may also be witnessing a relative exhaustion of European literary culture, perhaps owing in part to the difficulty of internally generating that effect. Certainly foreigners have dominated British intellectual and literary life throughout most of this century. The same holds to some extent for the theoretical innovations of the last generation in France, that is, for structuralism and its aftermath.[14] The current prominence of Afro-American writers, and especially of Afro-American women writers, in the United States may be a similar phenomenon.

On the other hand, probably the dominant vehicle of expression in the newly prominent peripheral literatures has been the novel, a distinctively European product whose appearance in these literatures often seems connected with the rise of nationalism.[15] Furthermore, much of that literature is composed in the languages of Western Europe, especially but not exclusively Spanish and English. This generalization holds true not only for the settler colonies that blanket the Americas, Australia, and New Zealand, but also to a considerable extent for Africa, Polynesia, and even the Philippines, and to a lesser extent for India. In areas where the literary language is not understood by the majority of the population, the traditional problem of the relationship between literature and literacy is exacerbated. But even when that is not the case, the question remains of the degree to which European languages and literary forms compromise the cultural interests of people on other continents.

For a number of reasons this does not seem like an inherently fatal limitation. First, the phenomenon is best understood not as derivative imitation but as creative appropriation. In no two countries is English the same language. More specifically, in novels like Chinua Achebe's *Things Fall Apart* and Albert Wendt's *Pouliuli*, a relatively recognizable literary idiom is modified by the inclusion of a variety of terms from the native language. In Peter Abraham's *Mine Boy* and, to shift languages and forms for a moment, in the poems of Aimé Césaire, the distinctively local vocabulary of an originally European language figures prominently in the overall effect. At the generic level the best-known works of Gabriel García Márquez, *One Hundred Years of Solitude* and *The Autumn of the Patriarch*, aim to convert the novel, which we tend to think of as a monument to bourgeois individualism, into a collective form. A similar enterprise informs Louise Erdrich's *Love Medicine*. And Achebe's and Wendt's novels powerfully evoke a pre-individualistic individual consciousness, in the crisis of its dissolution. These transformations may be understood as specific instances of the interaction between European and indigenous cultures mentioned above.

Second, the ambiguity surrounding appropriation from the colonialists is most intense in anticolonial struggles. There can be no doubt that anti-imperialism has been an important literary inspiration and remains so today, even though all but a few countries have won formal independence. The successor and more informal system of neocolonialism partially justifies Fredric Jameson's reading of "third-world texts . . . [as] *national allegories*."[16] Even in Anita Desai's *In Custody*, a novel that seems firmly rooted in the shabbiness of an overwhelmingly indigenous present, the tragedy of national division is rendered through the hopeless love of the professor of Hindi literature for Urdu poetry. But the justification remains only partial. Even if discussion is confined to political categories, a theory of national allegory privileges the metropole-colony relationship at the expense of other, arguably more internal issues: class, gender, ethnicity, and religion, for example.[17] The centrality of gender, for example, is obvious in Alice Walker's *The Color Purple*, Toni Morrison's *Sula*, or Maxine Hong Kingston's *The Woman Warrior*. These texts are all by writers belonging to ethnic minorities of the United States and so may represent a special case. But it is equally hard to detect the national allegory in R. K. Narayan's *A Tiger for Malgudi*, despite the characteristic combination of native tradition and European avant-garde—in this case, an unabashed mysticism of ideology and urbane modernity of narrative.

And finally, the question of influence is inevitably a two-way street. This has been true since the first period of European maritime expansion in the Renaissance, most obviously in those works like More's *Utopia* that make the discovery of a New World the occasion for profoundly rethinking their own, but perhaps also and less attractively in the constitution, partly through literature, of a distinctively European self, defined by its, or rather his, absolute alterity from a native other. One might mention as well the impact on Europe of the traditional literatures of the Middle East and Asia, an impact that of course begins long before, say, Columbus's voyages. Although other examples could be added, the most interesting phenomenon is the recent importance in Europe and North America of literature from elsewhere on the planet that itself was significantly shaped by Europe. One thinks of John Barth's admiration for Jorge Luis Borges.[18] As suggested earlier, in a broadly linguistic and cultural context this dialectical relationship remains decidedly unequal. When it comes to the more specialized matter of the novel, however, the outlook may be more promising, in part because questions of international influence sometimes now bypass Europe and North America entirely. If this is the case, then the concept of world literature might in time take on less hierarchical or oppressive connotations.

I have been trying to trace a dialectical movement in history through which European literature creates and dominates world literature, only to have the larger category develop a relatively autonomous logic, subsume the smaller category, and thereby reduce it to something like its rightful proportions. The purpose of such an account is to contribute, however modestly, to a non-ethnocentric understanding of contemporary literature and indeed of literature in general. (I should mention in passing that I lack the knowledge of non-European languages necessary for adequate work in this area.) But the movement toward a genuinely unhierarchical global literature is at best far from complete, and in any case only confusion can result from ignoring the specifically European imperial origins of that movement. How then might the current situation of world literature be theorized?

No answer is possible here beyond the briefest indication of the weaknesses of current models. The notion of three worlds, and especially of the Third World, has always been imprecise at best and tendentious at worst. Today, moreover, the rapidly increasing differentiation of the countries collectively designated the Third World threatens to render the category useless.[19] World-systems theory, developed by Immanuel Wallerstein, overcomes this problem by dividing the planet up into a core, semiperiphery, and periphery—all part of a single capitalist system.[20] One may doubt, however, whether that system is truly global, whether the model takes sufficient cognizance of the variety of social forms in existence, and whether a so single-mindedly economic interpretation can possibly avoid reductiveness. It is hard to imagine an approach to the contemporary literature of Communist countries that fails to emphasize the ruling Party and behind that organization, in many instances, the Soviet Union. In Christa Wolf's *The Quest for Christa T.*, for example, impressionistic female subjectivity constitutes a protest against the at least premature ideological insistence on collective harmony. More generally, both theories—and all others currently available as well—seem inadequate to the complexity of the modern world.

Clearly I am assuming that an *adequate* understanding of world literature is connected with an adequate understanding of the world. I am of course assuming even more: that an appropriate conceptualization of world literature would give prominent, though not necessarily central, place to former and present relations of imperial exploitation and domination. But I prefer to conclude by stressing the other side of the dialectical connectedness of literature and society. Perhaps one of the limitations of Marxist social theory has been insufficient attention to culture. If this is so, then systematic analysis of an increasingly global culture, including that part of it I have been calling world literature, should have something useful to tell us.

NOTES

1 Louis Althusser, "Ideology and Ideological State Apparatuses (Notes towards an Investigation)," in *Lenin and Philosophy and Other Essays*, trans. Ben Brewster (New York: Monthly Review Press, 1971) 127-86.
2 Jacques Derrida, *Positions*, trans. Alan Bass (Chicago: Univ. of Chicago Press, 1981) 41-42.
3 For recent discussion see Edward Said, *The World, the Text, and the Critic* (Cambridge, Mass.: Harvard UP, 1983) 248-89.
4 Althusser, "Contradiction and Over-determination," in *For Marx*, trans. Ben Brewster (London: NLB, 1977) 89-94.
5 Johann Wolfgang von Goethe, "Some Passages Pertaining to the Concept of World Literature" (from *Weltliteratur*, 1827 ff.), in *Comparative Literature: The Early Years*, ed. H. J. Schulz and P. H. Rhein (Chapel Hill: Univ. of North Carolina Press, 1973) 1-11.
6 Ulrich Weisstein, *Comparative Literature and Literary Theory: Survey and Introduction*, trans. William Riggen and Weisstein (Bloomington: Univ. of Indiana Press, 1973) 170, 186. See in general his "Appendix I: History," 167-252.
7 On the history of the term "literature," see Raymond Williams, *Marxism and Literature* (Oxford: Oxford UP, 1977) 45-54.
8 Karl Marx and Friedrich Engels, *Manifesto of the Communist Party* (1848), in *The Marx-Engels Reader*, ed. Robert C. Tucker, 2nd ed. (New York: Norton, 1978) 476-77.
9 Ferdinand Brunetière, "European Literature" (from *La Littérature européenne*, 1900), in *Comparative Literature: The Early Years* 153-82.
10 Charles Chauncy Shackford, "Comparative Literature" (1876; first delivered as a lecture at Cornell University in 1871), in *Comparative Literature: The Early Years* 39-51. The quoted passage appears on p. 43. See also Charles Mills Gayley, "A Society of Comparative Literature" (1894) and "What Is Comparative Literature?" (1903), in *Comparative Literature: The Early Years* 79-103.
11 For a similar chronology, see Brunetière 168-72.
12 For a similar argument, though limited to Russia and Scandinavia and to the question of realism, see Georg Lukács, "Tolstoy and the Development of Realism," in *Studies in European Realism* (New York: Grosset & Dunlap, 1964) 131-40.

13 M. M. Bakhtin, *The Dialogic Imagination: Four Essays*, ed. Michael Holquist, trans. Caryl Emerson and Holquist (Austin: Univ. of Texas Press, 1981).
14 On England, see Perry Anderson, "Components of the National Culture," *New Left Review* 50 (1968): 3-57, and Terry Eagleton, *Exiles and Émigrés: Studies in Modern Literature* (New York: Schocken, 1970). For France, I am thinking of Althusser and Derrida, from Algeria, and of Todorov and Kristeva, from Eastern Europe—hardly an exhaustive list.
15 Benedict Anderson, *Imagined Communities: Reflections on the Origin and Spread of Nationalism* (London: Verso, 1983) chs. 1-2.
16 Fredric Jameson, "Third-World Literature in the Era of Multinational Capital," *Social Text* 15 (1986): 69. See also Abdul JanMohammed, *Manichean Aesthetics: The Politics of Literature in Colonial Africa* (Amherst: Univ. of Massachusetts Press, 1983).
17 See Aijaz Ahmad, "Jameson's Rhetoric of Otherness and the 'National Allegory,'" *Social Text* 17 (1987): 3-25.
18 John Barth, "The Literature of Exhaustion," *Atlantic* August 1967: 29-34.
19 See the different views of this problem in the essays by Jameson and Ahmad cited in notes 17 and 18 above, and also Jameson's reply to Ahmad, "A Brief Response," *Social Text* 17 (1987): 26-27.
20 Immanuel Wallerstein, *The Modern World-System: Capitalist Agriculture and the Origins of the European World-Economy in the Sixteenth Century* (New York: Academic Press, 1974). The theory developed in this volume feels very much like an anachronistic backwards projection from the twentieth century, for which it has considerably greater plausibility.

POLAR PARADIGMS IN POETICS: CHINESE AND WESTERN LITERARY PREMISES

Eugene Eoyang, Indiana University

In the burgeoning field of East-West comparative literature, little consideration has been given to questions of methodology and to the logic of comparison. Tantalizing and presumably interesting questions like "Is there a Chinese tragedy?" "Why is there no epic in Chinese?" pique interest, but produce no real illumination. Of course, one fails to notice the bias in these questions. The obverse questions are rarely, if ever, asked. Why are there no dynastic histories in the West? Why has the West produced no counterpart to the *Shih ching*? Are their equivalents to the *lü-shih* and *tsa-chü* forms in the West? If these challenges to lacunae in the West strike one as slightly absurd, then we must consider the possibility that the original questions might be equally absurd.

The speculations are ultimately futile and meaningless because they fail to address the fundamental confusions of premise and methodology implicit in the unreflected—one might say the un-*self*-reflected—posing of these questions. Large issues are involved in their very formulation, and any answers they might occasion are compromised by an inherent confusion which can only render chimerical or meaningless any "insights" produced. In colloquial parlance, it is an "apples and oranges" problem: how does one judge an orange in terms of an apple, an apple in terms of an orange. We see clearly the methodological absurdity of trying to explain why one is an inadequate form of the other because we are ourselves neither apples nor oranges and we are, generically, neutral to fruit. However, that neutrality does not obtain when, in our culturally bound perspective, we inadvertently and unconsciously assume a point of reference of the West (say, apples) or East (say, oranges). We are judging from a premise which is itself an object of study, not an absolute point of reference.[1]

It is the realm of "pseudo-universals" that I would like to explore in this paper, to establish not so much a neutral point of reference (which, in any event, would be impossible) but a multiple perspective, from which biases and distortions can be effectively reduced, if not eliminated altogether.

I envision these points of reference as "polar" rather than categorical opposites, to emphasize that they are not mutually exclusive, fixed conceptual boxes which require a binary "either/or" logic. This also permits a guard against over-simplification, the mistake of the mythically monolithic. We are talking about cultural complexes which, despite their aggregate differences, contain within them worlds of difference and varieties of perspectives, so that any discussion of large-scale referents—whether "Western" or "Chinese"—must be provisional and contingent; it will provide only a rough order of approximation. Individual instances will inevitably depart from the norm, and there will be exceptions that prove the rule. The intellectual exercise is not to create

Draconian contrasts, but to see meaningful discriminations, so that the characteristics of each tradition might emerge more clearly by the comparison.

The "polar paradigms" that I wish to examine fall into four groups:[2] modal; conceptual; generic; and philosophical.

Modal Paradigms

Let us turn to modals, which highlight instrumentality, the effect of the tools on what is produced. In the West, since the introduction of papyrus, writing has involved a sharp edged, beveled instrument, which scratches the hard surface of the bark to make an impression. The lines it draws are incised, with only limited latitude in the width of the stroke. In China, however, the instrument from at least the Shang Dynasty has been the brush,[3] and the "tablet" on which writing takes place is not a smooth surface, like bark or papyri, but textured and absorbent, as in rice paper, or silk cloth. The lines of the brush are flexible, and the action of the writing instrument is flowing and requires little pressure. Where the pen requires force and pressure to make an impression and to make a mark, the action of the brush is quite the opposite: the slightest contact with the surface leaves a mark. The modulations of the line are much more varied with a brush than with a pen, and the rhythms of a brush stroke are much more expansive: they admit of more stylization than is possible with a pen. In the West, the emphasis is on clarity of form, on *penmanship*; in China, the emphasis is on calligraphy, the aesthetic and expressive representation of graphic symbols: there is no word for penmanship apart from the sense of calligraphy. Indeed, for some, like Li Meng-yang (1472-1529) "composing literature is like calligraphy."[4]

These technical details have far-reaching manifestations and account for very different aesthetic considerations in China and in the West. Whereas in the West, the arts of literature and of painting are separate, in China, Korea, and Japan, they are one. The adept at painting was equally—and naturally—adept at literature, because the same instrument, the brush, was being used.[5] The intellectual difficulties of the systematic and meaningful study of the relationship between literature and the other arts, which has occasioned such controversy and such irresolutions in the West, and the "avant-garde" attempts to integrate seemingly disparate arts within one new art form (whether "concrete poetry" or "word-pictures") would seem odd to the Chinese aesthetician, who is not surprised to see a poem inscribed in a painting; indeed, he would consider a painting without an inscription unfinished.

Another fundamental modal difference between Western and Chinese poetics relates to the "instrument" of feeling and the "instrument" of thinking, the seat of the emotions and the faculty of reason, generally regarded in the West as conventionally separable between the organ of the heart and the entity known as the mind. In the West, it is axiomatic to believe that the mind thinks, and the heart feels. Subject to the test of ordinary language, the obverses of these formulations seem awkward, far-fetched, if not meaningless: "the heart thinks," "the mind feels." In this premise, there are two possibly factitious assumptions:

1) that emotion and mentation are separate or separable; and 2) that each can be assigned to either the head or the heart. This dichotomy is so strong that common parlance enshrines the difference, when, for example, one is warned about "thinking with one's emotions," or when one is being asked, rhetorically, "Is that your head or your heart talking?"—as if to suggest that the "heart talking" is a supererogation of authority. These distinctions are left meaningfully vague in Chinese, which regards *"hsin"*[a] as the seat both of emotion and of thought. The very earliest dicta on Chinese poetry—*shih yen chih*[b]—will be affected by this disjunction between Western and Chinese notions of what might be "psychological physiology," for this phrase can be tenably translated either as: "Poetry expresses intention" (which is its usual rendering) or "Poetry expresses emotions." The word *"chih"*[c] is comprised of the ideographs for "scholar or soldier,"*shih*,[d] and the ideograph for "heart-mind," *hsin*. But neither alternative really does justice to the original, for poetry in Chinese can express both thought, unalloyed with emotion, as well as emotion devoid of thought. Most commonly, however, and there is in this an implicit value judgment, good poetry expresses a fusion of both feeling and thinking.

There is, in Chinese aesthetics as well as in Chinese ethical teaching, a distrust of both pure mentation and pure emotion. In Western terms, the heart is a check to the coldness of the mind; the mind is a check to the fervency of the heart. But, even in this formulation there is a bias, for it assumes that two prior entities must somehow be brought together in a symbiosis, when in the Chinese view, the situation is quite the opposite. The two faculties are not two, but one, and it is their separation, either in abstract or concrete terms, that violates the wholeness of things and creates distortions that disrupt the natural order.[6] We need not pause to consider which view of things is correct: indeed, there are adherents for both points of view, and it may turn out that they are not contradictory.[7]

To cite but one striking example, if we accept Ruskin's notion of "pathetic fallacy," which he characterizes as "a falseness in all our impressions of external things,"[8]—a morbidity that attributes life to the lifeless, and feeling to the unfeeling, then we would have to dismiss some of the most famous lines in Chinese literature as "pathetically fallacious." For Tu Fu attributes a feeling of sorrow to flowers in his "Spring Prospect":

> Country ruined, mountains and rivers remain;
> City in spring, grass and trees are thick.
> Moved by the times, flowers spill tears;
> Hate being apart, birds startle the heart.

To "attribute" human emotion to inanimate objects of nature is, far from being fallacious, merely a restitution of the sources of feeling, a return of semantic capital to the resources of meaning. In Tu Fu's poem, of course, it is all the more powerful, because the contrast of human dishevelment with the steadfastness of nature is superseded by the confluence and congruence of change and stability in the word "tears." The sense of the poem is precisely that human culture has strayed too far from nature, which is why the one atrophies and the other abides.

Conceptual Paradigms
The verse from Tu Fu's "Spring Prospect" brings out a disjunction in what I call "conceptual paradigms," which point to the "privileged" terms of reification in any discourse. Is the first line—"The country ruined, but the mountains and hills remain"—metaphor or anti-metaphor? There is contrast here, but there is no "figure of speech in which a name or a descriptive term is transferred to an object to which it is not properly applicable."[9] Yet, the line does unmistakably embody a homology, even if implicitly. Consider other contrasts where no implied metaphor is posited: "Human beings suffer, but life goes on" or "The world of man is everywhere in turmoil, yet Nature is serene." These contrasts, poignant as they may be, do not strike the reader as poetic: they do not engage one's emotions as directly as "Country ruined, mountains and hills remain." For the conjunction of two opposite phenomena within the same line implies what the situation should be: that human affairs should be consonant with Nature. That there is a contrast, rather than a parallel, constitutes the entire moral force of the poem. There is also another sense: "mountains and hills remain" suggests a haven from, as well as a recrimination against, the chaos of human history. But this line, which cannot be characterized as a metaphor, is a prime instance of what, in Chinese, is labeled *pi*,[e] which, although customarily translated as "metaphor," means, strictly speaking, "a comparison."

The complexities raised by this instance are not just caused by inaccurate equivalents: they are occasioned by a fundamental difference in premise and paradigm. To compare human affairs with nature in a willful act of imagination or fancy—i.e., to deliberately impute characteristics to an object which do not properly belong to it—is to assume the separateness and autonomy of each object, and the originality of the relationship posited. But, what if human affairs and Nature are conceived of as emanating from one and the same source? What if the world is conceived of as a unified whole which includes both the world of man and the world which surrounds him? Then there can be no false attribution of human qualities to non-human objects, for what is human is derived from Nature: the terms of human discourse, the vocabulary of human feeling, derive *from* Nature. Wordsworth's verse

> One impulse from a vernal wood
> Can teach you more of man.
> Of moral evil and of good
> Than all the sages can.

can then be taken not as romantic philosophy, not as subjunctive metaphor, but as both ontological and etymological fact.

In sum, one questions whether the basic terms with which one studies language are not themselves culturally bound. Are certain non-Western languages, like Chinese and Japanese, *deficient* because they do not have morphemic distinctions for number and tense, or are Western languages *excessive and arbitrary* in imposing categories where none are warranted. A simple illustration demonstrates the point succinctly: when one says "It is raining," no one questions the grammatical correctness of the sentence—there is a subject and a predicate. But, logically, one can ask what is the antecedent of the pronoun "it," since every pronoun, we have been taught, must refer to a previous noun. The lack of such a noun in all but the most mythological contexts for this phrase does not deter anyone from using this locution or anyone else from understanding it.[10]

There is a tendency to assume the universal validity of analytical terms of discourse, and to question the validity of intuitive descriptors that do not yield easily to precise definition.[11] Nowhere is this a greater problem than in East-West comparison. Many years ago, I heard an American scholar of Chinese literature publicly complain that Chinese writers (one can hardly call them theorists) were not systematic in their discussions of literature. As if it were Liu Hsieh's fault for not writing (or thinking) like Aristotle! Or that somehow it was unhelpful of the traditional Chinese literati to ramble on without conceiving of the advantages to later students (particularly to Western students!) of clearly articulating their arguments along logical lines. It is true that Chinese literary criticism, with its self-admitted informality, its tendency to emanate from the *pi-chi* tradition, which sees its insights as "literary jottings" rather than as full-fledged comprehensive analyses of theoretical subjects, lacks the breathtaking categoricalness of an Aristotle or a Kant: there are no self-declared "Summas" in the Chinese literary tradition, for it would be inconceivable folly, displaying an appalling lack of wisdom (to say nothing of bad form), for a Chinese literatus to present himself as the repository of all knowledge, even if he does approach omniscience in his erudition.[12] It is not a matter merely of cultural style, but a reflection of fundamentally different attitudes toward knowing and knowledge— that the Chinese have traditionally admired those who know and profess they do not, and that Westerners have been impressed by those who do not know but profess they do (the essence of speculative philosophy), whose knowledge evolves out of suasive certainties based on certain epistemological premises.

Generic Paradigms

Our discussion of disjunctions between Chinese and Western concepts of grammatical categories—whether person, number, or tense—affects the comparison of Western and Chinese literary genres. The triumvirate of classes of literature so familiar in the West today—lyric, narrative, and dramatic—may not serve every important or significant work in the West,[13] but the division is normative and useful enough in the West (especially in the United States) to have gained widespread currency. Yet, if we look at the traditional analyses (to say nothing of the defenses) of these three classes of literature, we find them neatly corresponding to three "radicals of presentation" (in Frye's terminology): the first, the lyric, is the first-person genre, where the poet is speaking to himself and—in Mill's telling insight—is overheard by the reader; the second, the narrative, involves a second-person dynamic with a storyteller addressing a present audience; the third, the dramatic, is narration at one remove: there is an author/narrator and there is an audience, but the third parties, the actors, enact what the author-narrator wants to convey to the audience. The persuasiveness of this paradigm lies partly in the convenient correspondence between the dialectics of each genre and the conventional grammatical divisions with respect to first-, second-, and third-person discourse. But, if, as we have suggested above, the divisions of the "three-person'd God" of grammatical personae are not sacrosanct, and far from universal, then these "radicals of presentation" are not likely to prove as convincing or as serviceable with literatures whose languages are not based on the three-personed paradigm.

Chinese poetry does not fit easily or conclusively into the "lyric" paradigm of the West: the ballads of the *Shih ching* share with the Western lyric its incantatory character; the *Nine Songs*, in particular, with its summons to the soul, and its supplications to the gods and to the spirits, bear a striking similarity to the tradition in the West that is hallowed by poems that begin with an invocation to the Muses. But neither the ballads in the *Shih ching* nor the songs in the *Songs of the South (Ch'u Tz'u)* are personal except in an allegorical way: there is nothing individualized or eccentric about these writings, as there is in the Western lyric. There is no specific biographical Beatrice addressed, no historical personage directly mentioned. This diffuseness in reference does not, of course, prevent personal meanings from being projected into the poem by countless generations of scholars and readers. I am making a distinction between the personal force of these poems as experiences for the reader, and the individual expressiveness of the historical composer of these poems. The *Shih ching* folk poems were formulaic compositions that spoke to personal longing in communal terms; the *Ch'u Tz'u* poems, on the other hand, even when written by and reflecting the personal recriminations and complaints of the historical Ch'ü Yüan, as in the *Li Sao,* hypostasize subjective feeling into objective imagery that is accessible beyond the personal biography of the poet. The *Li Sao* may be the most personal poem in Chinese, yet even that intensely subjective work has none of the "egotistical sublime" that one associates with the romantic lyric.

On the other hand, the *shih* poems of the T'ang poets are strikingly intimate expressions, and intensely personal in their sense of privacy and in their allusiveness: autobiographical inscriptions reinforce the sense of each poem's rootedness in historical time and in a specific biographical life. Yet, reading these poems, one doesn't have the feeling which one expects from reading a lyric, that one is "overhearing" a first-person speaking to himself. The poet is addressing another poet, not unlike himself, often identified in the inscription; as readers, we are assuming the role of a contemporary sharing the experience, the contextual reality that gave birth to the poem. Far from "overhearing" the poem, the reader is asked to engage in the dialectic of the poem, to supply the allusion, to recall the circumstances enshrined in the poem, to respond with his (or her) reactions (often in the form of an "answering" poem), and his recollections of the event, which now subsumes the poem before us. The division of author and reader, of poet and reader of poetry, is not as endemic to traditional Chinese literature as it has become in the study of literature in the West. There is an aspect of dialogue in traditional Chinese poetry which is overlooked if one conceives of the poem as a "lyric" to be overheard. The consequences of this distinction are by no means negligible: in the "lyric" to be overheard, certain confessional tendencies will be forgiven that would embarrass in direct address; conversely, the Chinese poem will seem to Western readers insufficiently daring, too occasional in its rhetoric, too ordinary and conventional in its discourse. Yet, Chinese poetry is, in the best if somewhat confounding sense of the word, occasional: it captures the moment, professes no great intentions beyond the moment, aspires to no universality of truth or insight beyond the desire to capture the "this-ness," the immanence, what might be called—borrowing Buddhist terminology—"the Tathagata of the moment." To put it no doubt oversimplistically, Chinese poetry tends toward the incidental and the commonplace; Western poetry aspires to the transcendental and the extraordinary. For most Western philosophers, universals are supernal; for most Chinese, universals are subordinate and sublunary. It is not a question of which is the "greater" or "lesser"[14] but a question of the adjustments one must make shifting from one ground of reference to another.

Of course, the generic distinctions that are serviceable with one tradition of literature should not be expected to be equally applicable to other traditions. Western theater is heavily involved in religious ritual, with a "tragic sense of life," embodying a sense of unity, whether in the form of the "three unities," as in the Neo-Classic period, or in the Wagnerian notion of *Gesamtskunstwerke*. The main thread of the Western dramatic tradition centers on the plot or *mythos* of the action: there is a strong sense of the implied audience being invited to identify with the action in order to achieve a catharsis in the "virtual" action (defined by Susanne Langer as being both life-like, yet clearly not life).[15] Traditional Chinese theater is a theater of spectacle and does not court the projected sympathies of the audience by inviting their identification with the tragic character. Chinese theater is occupied with stories that are furthest removed from reality, "distanced" from everyday life, where fancy rather than imagination is developed, and spectacle rather than "a purgation" through "pity and terror" is dominant. Instead of unity, Chinese theater provides variety and heterogeneity: acting, singing, dancing, acrobatics, and costume. The form of theater introduced by the Mongols in the Yüan Dynasty is *tsa-chü*, literally, "miscellaneous theater." There is more carnival than catharsis in Chinese theater.

Fair-minded cross-cultural comparisons cannot afford to prejudge Chinese theater as incoherent or Western theater as monolithic: there are two different strategies involved. One is to engage, the other is to impress. The "alienation effect" that Brecht so admired in Chinese theater eschews any attempt at imitating life, or of deluding the audience to imagine that what is being seen on the stage is life: quite the contrary, the action in Chinese theater is larger than life.

Philosophical Paradigms

World-views, *Weltanschauungen*, which determine the scope of one's exploratory vision and scope, are "philosophical paradigms." In the West, the dominance of corresponding abstract-concrete pairs, whether Ideal-Real, or abstract-concrete, or noumenon-phenomenon reflect a conception of validation posited on separable categorical worlds, whose very plausibility depends on their being autonomous realms of existence. Conflations of the ideal with the real, the abstract with the concrete, the noumenal with the phenomenal are difficult, if not impossible, to grasp. In any event, they would erode the clarity, hence the usefulness, of these concepts if their very conceptual purity were sullied. Furthermore, the logic of validation (and of epistemology) stresses the persuasiveness of correspondence as a factor in truth functions. One is more inclined to accept the validity of something when there is a correspondence than when there isn't a correspondence, although no prior proof has been given as to the role of correspondence as a warrant of validity. It may be that correspondence is a heuristic, rather than a validating factor, i.e., that it inspires the human brain with confidence because it is easier to understand (because it reinforces prior knowledge) than because it is inherently valid. Departures from correspondence schemes are viewed with suspicion, are seen *as* deviations, rather than as data in their own right. The character of knowledge gained by positing a correspondence between an other-worldly and a this-worldly realm is powerfully familiar, of course, through the Platonic vision of the cosmos, where the immutable realm of Ideas exist concurrently with the mutable realm of diurnal reality. This notion of the separateness of the permanent and the impermanent, of the universal and the particular, the perdurable and the ephemeral, pervades much Western philosophy and poetics.

The tendency in some Chinese texts to derive mysteries from actual experience may be contrasted with the Platonic practice of imagining an abstract realm that corresponds to concrete experience, or of Aristotle analyzing concrete particulars to discover abstract universals. For a number of significant Chinese philosophers, the division of the abstract and the concrete is untenable: truths derive from the actuality of experience, not in spite of it. An example from Liu Hsieh's *Wen-hsin tiao-lung* ("The Literary Mind") will illustrate the point:

> Natural excellence may be compared to the splendors of flowers in the woods; their vivid beauty is like the silk-dyed vermilion and green. Silks dyed vermilion and green are deep, rich and vibrant; the blossoms and the sun-drenched trees, blaze forth in glory. Brilliant writing radiates in the garden of literature in much the same way.[16]

It would be a serious misreading of this text to see Liu Hsieh as merely intending a metaphor between "the blossoms of nature" and the "flowers of literature," though the translation does easily accommodate such an interpretation. The aptness of the comparison lies in no correspondence between the characteristics of nature and of literature: the force lies in the similarity of experience in one's reaction to nature on the one hand and literature on the other. One accepts the validity of the comparison—which is not a metaphor (where two disparate entities are likened to each other)—only when one identifies the response to nature and to literature as one and the same. The homology borders on identity: "Brilliant writing radiates in the garden of literature in much the same way."

One could posit, by way of contrast, a poetics of correspondence (which one finds in Plato) alongside a poetics of resonance (which might be found in, among others, Wang Shih-chen [1634-1711]). In the first case, poetry establishes a truth through the sometimes allegorical, sometimes symbolic, sometimes metaphoric description of concrete details: the experience described and preserved in the poem always points to something else—whether moral truth, or aesthetic beauty, or romantic sentiment. The Western reader of Chinese poetry often searches in vain for the "point"—especially if he is reading in translation—because the poem is not mimesis either in the Platonic or the Aristotelian sense, i.e., it is not an imitation of ideal reality twice removed, nor is it the creation of the imagination. It is both the recording and the reenactment of an indicative moment, its realization in words.

For Chinese philosophers, truths are always contingent: one's knowledge is always compromised. There is little or no desire to extrapolate human truths beyond human experiences, even if the cosmic experiences are explained in terms of familiar human realities. We might posit on the one hand the truth of life, and on the other hand, the Tao of existence, and we might see a model of mimesis contrasted with a model of immanence. In the first instance, the model of mimesis, the unknown is conceived of as corresponding to the known, and is real and valid the more that correspondence can be established and reiterated. In the second instance, the model of immanence, the only reality is whatever is immanent, whatever is, at the moment, now, thus. In the first instance, the Truth is adducible and achievable, if elusive; in the second instance, the Tao is ever-present and yet not adducible. The Truth is replicable, accessible, and powerful: "Know the Truth and it will set you free." But the Tao is inimitable and unreproducible: "The Tao that can be said is not the universal Tao."

Our survey of polar paradigms has, if we have succeeded, made no invidious comparisons. The purpose in positing such polarities is to extend the basis for discussion, not from one vantage point or another, but from both. Our "horizon of expectations" must include more than one perspective, see from more than one reference point. The result will not be, as some indolent intellects too readily assume, a relativity of values, but a more rigorous, indeed, a more open recognition of values with due acknowledgement of tacit premises. Each set of premises, what Stephen Pepper calls "world hypotheses," highlights another aspect of reality. As heirs to the traditions in both East and West, we are the beneficiaries of a multiple perspective, but along with the panoptic perspective is the challenge to check our own myopia. The bigot with perfect eyesight should not be preferred to the blind man with perfect "vision."

The virtues and the limitations of both traditions should become more apparent in any comparison. Our task is not to disown our own heritage, but rather in its comparison with another heritage, to truly discover it, to see it in relief against the background of a different context. Too often what is accepted as universal is only that which is customary and commonplace. But commonplaces are not the same everywhere, and what is common to one may be uncommon to another. We can continue to pursue the mysteries, and we may even call our speculations the truth. What we discover may, in fact, be true with the facts on which we have based our theories. But, in the construction of any lasting theory, in the development of any durable understanding, analysis and intuition must proceed as one: the paradigms of correspondence must be melded with the paradigms of resonance.

The study of comparative literature relating to East and West solves a problem in heuristic epistemology. If physicists and journalists now routinely acknowledge that the objectivity so vaunted by eighteenth-century rationalists and nineteenth-century logical positivists is no longer possible, that all discourse is influenced by the speaker and distorted by the receiver, that all knowledge reflects as much on the knower as on what is known, then how can one achieve the dispassionate and disinterested state required of any disciplined pursuit of knowledge? The answer is, certainly from the perspective of the human sciences, to adopt a pluralistic perspective. We can become objective only to the extent that we can recognize that we are subjective, and measure meaningfully the degree to which each of us is subjective. And we can begin to transcend this subjectivity only as we adopt the subjective vision of the other as our own. Our objectivity then becomes not a denial of our individual point of view, but an understanding of many points of view. By an act of analytical intuition, we must adopt both a synoptic and a panoptic perspective. We must see ourselves as we are, and by viewing and understanding the other, see ourselves as we are not.

NOTES

1 There is an important distinction between the inescapable tendency to use one's own experience as a reference, as a point of departure, and the epistemological error of regarding that point of reference as universal and absolute, for any inquiry, by any inquirer.
2 I have no reason to believe that there are necessarily only four groups, but each of these seems to me to represent enough instances to warrant separate consideration.
3 18th-12th centuries B.C. See T. H. Tsien, *Written on Bamboo and Silk* (Chicago: Univ. of Chicago Press, 1962) 116, 158-160.
4 Cf. James J. Y. Liu, *Chinese Theories of Literature* (Chicago: Univ. of Chicago Press, 1975) 91.

5   Michelangelo and Blake, geniuses in both the written word and in the visual arts, are more the exception than the rule.
6   Two passages in the *Mencius*, fairly close to each other, illustrate the latitude of the word *hsin*. Book II, A, Chapter 2, Verse 1 refers to the "unperturbed mind." When asked if his mind were perturbed or not, Mencius replies: "No. At forty, my mind was unperturbed." Yet, several verses later (2A:6), Mencius says: "All men have a mind which cannot bear to see the sufferings of others."
7   Recent developments in Western medicine have revived previously discarded notions of mind-body influences, although "holistic medicine" is still greeted with skepticism from the majority of doctors trained in Western medicine; see Daniel Goleman, "The Mind over the Body," *The New York Times Magazine* 27 September 1987: 36ff.
8   *The Literary Criticism of John Ruskin* (New York: Anchor Books, 1965) 63.
9   Definition of "metaphor" in the *Oxford Universal Dictionary* (Oxford, 1955).
10 This field of ordinary language analysis has been brilliantly explored, of course, by Gilbert Ryle and J. L. Austin.
11 Linguistics itself has begun to question both the universality and the precision of its terminology, its taxonomy of language characteristics: see David Crystal, *Linguistics* (Harmondsworth: Penguin Books, 1971) 57-76.
12 For example, the most erudite of modern Chinese scholars, Ch'ien Chung-shu, calls his four-volume magnum opus *Kuan chui pien*, which means, disarmingly, "Pipe-Awl Chapters."
13 The triumvirate leaves out essays, autobiographies (except as narrative), diaries, proverbs and aphorisms, etc.
14 The notion of "greatness" embodies its own evaluative bias and betrays what I have called a "bias of scale," a notion I developed in an unpublished paper delivered before the American Comparative Literature Association at Ann Arbor, Michigan, on March 22, 1986, entitled, "Changing the Canon: The Challenge of Non-Western Literatures."
15 *Feeling and Form: A Theory of Art* (New York: Charles Scribner's Sons, 1953) especially chapters 5, 6, 11, and 15.
16 *Wen-hsin tiao-lung* (Hong Kong: Shang-wu yih-shu kuan, 1960) 633; Vincent Yu-chung Shih, *The Literary Mind and the Carving of Dragons* (Taipei: Chunghua, 1970) 305.

a 心

b 詩 言 志

c 志

d 心

e 比

THE TRANSFORMATION PROBLEM AND CULTURAL THEORY

Carl Freedman, Louisiana State University

It is at least sometimes observable that, in a fully rigorous field of discourse, the most highly technical questions are (or ought to be) inseparable from the most conceptually profound. In what follows I have to discuss a fairly arcane matter of Marxist economic theory, namely, the problem of how surplus-value is transformed into profit and—what in the end amounts to the same thing—how profit is transformed into average profit. This issue has been of intense interest to professional economists, perhaps more often to those concerned to undermine than to uphold the essential Marxian paradigm; so far as I am aware, it has hardly ever proved of interest to anyone else. My own aims, however, are rather those of the cultural theorist than of the economist—a claim I make with both apology and affirmation. On the one hand, as academic disciplines go, those which concentrate on the study of culture neither possess nor merit a particularly distinguished reputation for intellectual substance or integrity. On the other hand, it may nonetheless be the case that cultural studies has a unique potential for dismantling the prevailing disciplinary reification and for reconstituting intellectual labor on a more genuinely comparative and concrete foundation.[1] While making no excuses for the economic illiteracy that generally obtains among humanists, I do insist that economics is too important to be left to the economists.

From the point of view of volume 1 of *Capital*—that is, from the point of view of the *production of capital,* which is by no means to be identified with the capitalist system as a whole—the problem of value is the problem of the production of value as such production is manifest within the individual capitalist firm; and surplus-value and profit are, at this moment of the argument, indeed essentially equivalent products. Over the course of a certain period of time—say a year—the firm produces a certain total amount of value: and since this amount is typically greater than the value of the capital which the capitalist has advanced during the year in order to purchase labor-power and the other necessities of doing business, a differential called surplus-value remains. This differential is equivalent to the capitalist's profit, though in order to become profit in the stronger sense it must be realized; in other words, it must be translated from the commodity form of value to the money form by being sold on the capitalist market. Because a lucky or canny capitalist may, in any given case, manage to sell his commodities for more money than they are actually worth—and because, on the other hand, an unlucky or inept capitalist may have to accept a sale price below actual value—it is in fact possible for profit to vary either upwards or downwards from surplus-value. But such variation is strictly atypical of capitalism, one of the governing assumptions of which is—as Marx always insists—that commodities are bought and sold at their true values.

If surplus-value and profit vary only inessentially, however, there is a far more significant distinction—still remaining within the "productionist" perspective of volume 1—between *rate* of profit and *rate* of surplus-value. This distinction may first of all be expressed in purely mathematical terms, though its implications are far wider. Rate of profit is calculated on the basis of the ratio of surplus-value to the total capital advanced, while rate of surplus-value depends on the ratio of surplus-value only to the variable capital advanced (the latter defined as the capital laid out in the form of wages in order to purchase the labor-power of living workers). It is arithmetically evident that rate of surplus-value must always be greater than rate of profit (assuming the constant—that is, non-labor-power-purchasing—capital expended by the firm to have a value greater than zero), but the distinction is really as much political as arithmetical in significance. Rate of surplus-value is of great interest from the workers' point of view, for it registers the rate at which their labor is being exploited, or, in other words, the proportion of their labor which goes unpaid (even while their labor-*power* is of course typically paid for in full). To the capitalist, on the other hand, only rate of profit is significant: he is presumably not psychologically inclined to dwell on the exploitation of workers' labor, and, in any case, his books reflect no ultimately important difference between a unit of value expended to purchase labor-power and an equal unit expended to purchase buildings, machinery, fuel, raw materials, or any other of the elements of constant capital.

There is, of course, another and rather different sort of distinction between rate of profit and rate of surplus-value. The former is, for the reasons just suggested, an eminently "practical" reality of capitalist balance-sheets and holds an esteemed place in a society which exalts unindicted Ivan Boeskys and which has metaphorized the term *bottom line* into a synonym for absolute importance. The latter is "merely" a construction of Marxist economic theory, and the coherence of Marx's theory of value and its relation to the observable realities of the capitalist system have been favored areas by many of those wishing to attack the basis of Marx's critique of political economy.[2] Indeed, the apparent difficulties raised by the transformation problem seem to follow directly from Marx's own presentation of the matter. Though there are many factors which can lead to different rates of surplus-value in different firms or different branches of industry—the length of the working day, the intensity of the labor process, the value of labor-power—there are two notable factors which can lead to different *profit* rates even given the *same* rate of surplus-value. One, which is named in volume 1, we have already discussed: this is the organic composition of capital, that is, the relative proportions of variable and constant capital in the total capital advanced. A firm which expends a relatively high proportion of its capital in variable capital (in recent jargon, a "labor-intensive" firm) will show a relatively high profit rate, as the profit rate will approximate more nearly to the rate of surplus-value than in a firm which expends a higher proportion on constant capital. A second factor which can yield different profit rates from the same rate of surplus-value is the turnover time of capital. Introduced in volume 2 of *Capital,* which adds a "circulationist" perspective to the "productionist" one of the earlier volume, turnover time is partly determined by factors not directly dependent on industrial production—for instance, the development of the banking system and the speed of communications—and yet directly affects profitability: the turnover of variable capital in a comparatively short period of time amounts to a practical "multiplication" of the variable capital advanced and hence, insofar as the profit rate is concerned, has much the same impact as a rise in the proportion of variable capital within the organic composition of the capital as a whole.[3]

Yet this mathematically lucid point results in severe difficulties. The variations in organic composition of capital and in turnover time ought to yield far greater variations in profit rates among different branches of industry than do (or even in principle could) exist. Since profit rate (not—recall—rate of surplus-value) is all that interests the capitalist, and since investment capital thus inevitably seeks those branches of industry that offer the highest return, the variations in profit rate which Marxist value theory evidently promises would result in whole branches of industry being starved of capital while a very few highly profitable firms would attract all the capital investment available within the capitalist system; and the system would accordingly collapse in less than six months. What precludes such a catastrophe is a certain mechanism which operates not at the level of the individual capitalist firm or even the individual branch of industry but at the level of the capitalist system as a whole. This mechanism produces an *average* profit rate throughout the system to which the profitability of each of the major branches of industry conforms—not perfectly, of course, but nearly enough to prevent the absurdly huge variations that we might otherwise be forced to expect. The transformation of theoretical surplus-value into actual profit is only completed when the latter becomes average profit: and, at this stage of the argument, there is indeed real variation not only between profit rate and rate of surplus-value but between profit and surplus-value considered as actual magnitudes. And yet what is the mechanism of this final stage of the transformation? It must seem as if, with the concept of average profit, we have in fact *detached* profit from surplus-value and thus called into question the coherence of the latter and indeed of value theory itself.

Marx faces the problem squarely in volume 3 of *Capital,*[4] but few have felt that he resolves it in a completely clear and satisfactory manner. My own reading of the matter is admittedly somewhat symptomatic (in the Althusserian sense),[5] but the essential clues we need are I think provided when Marx describes the plan of *Capital* as a whole in the subtitles of the several volumes. Many readers have doubtless been somewhat confused by the subtitle of volume 3, "the process of capitalist production as a whole." What could this mean apart from "the process of production of capital" (volume 1), at least as the latter is supplemented by "the process of circulation of capital" (volume 2)? What, precisely, is the force of the apparently simple phrase *as a whole*? It is here that the transformation problem is crucial to the understanding of the plan of *Capital* and indeed to the understanding of Marxist epistemology in general.

Marx makes quite clear that competition among capitals is the mechanism which yields average profit out of profit and thus (indirectly) out of surplus-value—a solution that might be inferred from the hypothetical (though impossible) situation which we have already considered, namely, that in which variations in turnover time and organic composition of capital do lead to the variations in profitability which the value theory of volume 1 and volume 2 would predict. For if—to take the ultimate case—*all* the investment capital within a given capitalist system were to flow into the single most profitable firm in the system, the firm would of course promptly cease to show a profit: instead, the firm would experience massive overproduction leading to a crippling realization crisis. Competition, then, evens out actual profit rates, resulting in an average profit throughout the system. So much is fairly clear. What is less clear is how this average profit can be squared with the productionist value theory of volume 1, and my suggestion is that not only can it *not* be thus squared but that it is not meant to be. In other words, value theory itself is transformed—though, I admit, never quite explicitly—in volume 3, where the perspective shifts to that of "the process of capitalist production as a whole." Marx had good reason to begin his delineation of value theory with the productionism of volume 1: production is primary because without it no other sort of activity (economic or otherwise) is conceivable, and, politically, the primacy of production corresponds to the privileged position of the industrial proletariat in the Marxist theory of socialist revolution. But primacy is here a relative, not a metaphysical, term. Productionism, however crucial, is nonetheless incomplete. When, in volume 3, we consider not merely the production of capital within the industrial workplace but the capitalist system as a whole, we must understand value as created only primarily through industrial production but ultimately through the *total* capitalist system: which is to say that strictly unproductive labor (such as is, for example, prominent in the competition among investment capitals) does after all play a part not only in the exchange, circulation, and distribution of value, but in the actual creation of value itself. The apparent incommensurability between average profit and surplus-value remains a problem only so long as we unwarrantably assume that the creation of the latter *ends* where it in fact only begins, that is, within the sphere of industrial production. If we instead accept that value-creation is an ongoing process throughout capitalism, and that it is value as yielded up by the system *in toto* that results in the final mathematical expressions of value, then the transformation problem is essentially solved. The evident threat to the integrity of the Marxian paradigm—that value may be incoherent with profit and average profit—remains potent only so long as the productionism of volume 1 of *Capital* is illegitimately projected onto the more totalizing perspective of volume 3. The dogmatic "orthodoxy" of productionism in fact enables the "revisionism" of the attack on value theory; but neither is really viable, and they fall to the ground together.[6]

The matter is, however, more usefully put in positive terms. What Marx achieves in the discussion of transformation in volume 3—though he achieves it somewhat between the lines of the manifest text—is nothing less than the invention of the properly Marxist concept of totality. It is not a concept well understood today, and certainly not in the terrain of cultural studies, where thinking about totality is frequently polarized in a highly reductive fashion. On the one hand, there are those who conceive of totality as an ultimately continuous unity in which some underlying essence monocausally expresses itself throughout all the (superficially) various levels of the socio-cultural field. This mode of thought may have its origin in religion (that is, in the notion that the entire cosmos expresses the divine essence which is the singular motivating force of the former), but, in the realm of the critique of political economy, it corresponds to a misreading of *Capital* which we have already briefly considered: namely, to the dogmatic productionism that illicitly generalizes from volume 1. In this view, the production of value as it takes place within the factory constitutes the invariable essence of value, and the social totality consists merely of the infinite replaying of this productionist essence, to be sure with appropriate (and non-fundamental) variation. On the other hand, we have also today to deal with the reactive dismissal of totality altogether, and the concomitant intellectual defeatism which abjures all but micrological analysis of culture and society: the result is of course an empiricism finally subversive of conceptual thought itself and indirectly (at least) supportive of the status quo. This view may also possess a religious origin—in the metaphysical disappointments of nominalism and negative theology—but my point here is that it too corresponds to a certain misreading of *Capital,* that is, to the absolute severance of surplus-value from average profit and to the resulting skepticism toward value as a concept. Totality proves strictly unthinkable for this point of view, and we are thrown back on the empiricism of the actually existing capitalist enterprise. There is perhaps no middle ground between these two diametrically opposed views of totality, but there is a third alternative, which corresponds to the resolution of the transformation problem that, I have argued, may be found in volume 3. Totality as Marx thinks it is radically *nonidentical:* it is by no means without structure, and yet is never quite fully at one with itself, for its structuring principle is fundamentally discontinuous with other determinants, themselves discontinuous with one another. Capitalism as an economic totality is indeed structured on the primacy of the production of value as industrial capital, but production is never an omnipotent indwelling essence from which all the adventures of value can be deduced. The totality is, as Althusser would say, overdetermined.

It is, of course, Althusser's school which has in our time done most to recall and enforce the Marxist concept of totality. But the achievements of his school, though impressive in many ways, do not necessarily exhaust the potential of Marx's breakthrough, and Althusser himself, ironically enough, somewhat understates the degree to which the Marxist totality is thought in the value theory of *Capital.* The possible applications of the concept in the realm of cultural studies are so numerous that I need not dwell on them at length here. One need only think of how many fairly sterile debates have moved between essentialism and skepticism to see the importance of the Marxist totality. How often, for instance, have critics of Romanticism attempted to define that phenomenon in terms of some monocausal essence (return to feeling, return to nature, movement from history to consciousness, among many other candidates)—and how unsurprising that others have begun to doubt whether any governing principle actually structures what generally goes under the term. A properly Marxist theorization of Romanticism would, in any case, resolve that dilemma. In conclusion, however, I want to pick up an earlier hint of mine and consider the matter from the other way around: not, that is, from the point of view of what the Marxist totality has to offer to cultural theory, but rather why cultural theory may be able to enforce the Marxist totality. What I propose is a certain special application of the law of combined and uneven development. The lack of rigor—and especially technical rigor—from which the study of culture has suffered has as its more promising obverse the disinclination to reduce theory to technique. This is a temptation from which academic economics—not excluding the Marxist variety—has too often suffered: the overwhelming technical mastery of *Capital* may practically occlude for many readers the more fundamental conceptual breakthroughs. Indeed, the transformation problem itself has proved popular among economists less for the issues of totality at stake than because it provides a way of connecting abstract Marxian categories to the comparative (but technically rich) banalities of capitalist balance-sheets. Cultural theory has no balance-sheets, so to speak, and this particular blindness can yield its corresponding insight. Never completely penetrated by the prevailing positivism, the study of culture may retain a perhaps unique ability to see its object whole: if so, it may, in fundamental ways, prove capable of solving the transformation problem again and again.

NOTES

1 Cf. the interesting suggestions to this effect in Fredric Jameson, *Marxism and Form* (Princeton: Princeton UP, 1971) 415-416.
2 The most celebrated recent such attack is probably Ian Steedman, *Marx After Sraffa* (London: Verso, 1981). Though this is hardly the place to engage Steedman in full-scale debate, it may be pointed out that his use of Piero Sraffa's *Production of Commodities by Means of Commodities* to undermine Marx finds no warrant in Sraffa himself, who (as Steedman candidly acknowledges) makes no criticisms of *Capital;* whether Steedman has in fact illegitimately generalized from Sraffa's quite specific if powerful work ought to be a matter of lively theoretical debate. Some debate occasioned by Steedman's intervention, most of it not as lively as one might wish, may be found in Ian Steedman *et alia, The Value Controversy* (London: Verso, 1981); the volume contains contributions by Paul Sweezy, Erik Olin Wright, G. A. Cohen, and others.
3 See Karl Marx, *Capital,* volume 2, trans. David Fernbach (Middlesex: Penguin Books, 1978) 233-424, especially 369-393.

4 "We have shown, therefore, that in different branches of industry unequal profit rates prevail, corresponding to the different organic composition of capitals, and, within the indicated limits, corresponding also to their different turnover times. . . . The above argument is true on the same basis as our whole investigation so far: that commodities are sold at their values. There is no doubt, however, that in actual fact, ignoring inessential, accidental circumstances that cancel each other out, no such variation in the average rate of profit exists between different branches of industry, and it could not exist without abolishing the entire system of capitalist production. The theory of value thus appears incompatible with the actual movement, incompatible with the actual phenomena of production, and it might seem that we must abandon all hope of understanding these phenomena" (Karl Marx, *Capital,* volume 3, trans. David Fernbach [Middlesex: Penguin Books, 1981] 252).

5 See Louis Althusser and Etienne Balibar, *Reading Capital,* trans. Ben Brewster (London: Verso, 1979) 13-69.

6 I must acknowledge how much my understanding of *Capital* has gained from conversations with Professor Richard D. Wolff of the Department of Economics of the University of Massachusetts at Amherst. I need hardly add that Professor Wolff is not to be held responsible for any of my own formulations.

II. WEST COMES EAST

LAFCADIO HEARN'S TRANSLATIONS AND THE ORIGINS OF IMAGIST AESTHETICS

Daniel Stempel, University of Hawaii

Lafcadio Hearn is a minor figure in American literary history, a transplanted exotic who flourished in the hothouse atmosphere of late nineteenth century aesthetic impressionism. But literary history, like political history or economic history, too often ignores what lies outside its self-defined limits. It constructs what it imagines is a temporal narrative of authors and works when it is, in fact, deciding in advance just which texts can be admitted into the canon of so-called "literary" documents. It ignores those which may lie in the border regions of journalism and travel literature, for example. There are times when literary historians must be reminded that there is a broader history outside their discipline and that it cannot be isolated from that history without becoming a victim of its own myopic methods. Poets do not spend their lives reading only poetry, novelists do not read only the novels of their predecessors. Literature, like every other human activity, interacts with society, past and present.

As a specific example, we search in vain for any mention of Lafcadio Hearn in the histories of the Imagist movement of the first two decades of this century. The Imagists claimed to have derived their principles of economy of diction and sharp visual focus from the poetry and art of Japan, among other sources, but the literary historians seem to be unaware of the contribution of the Japanese poems and songs which Hearn collected, translated, and explicated in the articles and books which he published between 1894 and 1904.

Yet there is ample evidence that anyone interested in Japan at that time would have turned to Hearn as the most popular and most readable expert on Japan. Richard Aldington, who was in the movement from the time that it was named and founded by Ezra Pound in 1912 in a Kensington tea-shop to its gradual demise a decade later, wrote that he had read Lafcadio Hearn when he was a schoolboy, in the aftermath of the Russo-Japanese war of 1904-5.[1] We do not know when Pound himself read Hearn, but in 1916 and 1917 he urged James Joyce to read George Gould's 1908 biography of Hearn. Gould was a Philadelphia ophthalmologist who had treated Hearn for failing vision with some degree of success. It is significant, I think, that Pound did not have to explain to Joyce who Hearn was.[2] John Gould Fletcher recalled that he had read Hearn's translations of Japanese poetry, among others, when he was associated with the Imagists.[3] In 1915 Amy Lowell delivered a lecture on "The New Manner in Modern Poetry" and illustrated it by reading poems by Ezra Pound, Richard Aldington, H.D., and translations of Japanese poems by Lafcadio Hearn.[4]

But perhaps more important was the fact that two influential men of letters in America and England, Ferris Greenslet, Hearn's editor at Houghton Mifflin, and Edward Thomas, critic and poet, were actively campaigning for recognition of the value of Hearn's writings. Greenslet contributed an article on John Gould Fletcher to the special issue on Imagism of *The Egoist* (May 1915) and published a collection of some of Hearn's translations in the same year. His prefatory Publisher's Note observes: "In their limitation of a poem to the presentation of a single impression and in their ability to present that impression with the utmost vividness and with the sternest economy of words, these Japanese poets are strangely akin to the Imagists, the youngest of the modern schools."[5] Edward Thomas, already respected and admired by poets like the young Robert Frost, published a short biography of Hearn in 1912, at about the same time that the Imagist movement officially began. Rather than asking if any Imagists had read Hearn's translations, perhaps we should ask if there were any who had not.

J. B. Harmer's history of Imagism and the Imagists, *Victory in Limbo: Imagism 1908-17* (1975), is the latest and most thoroughly researched of the three standard histories. Harmer devotes ten pages to the Japanese influence on the Imagists without once mentioning Hearn's work. Why not? I suspect that the answer lies in the unfortunate practice of writing literary history by relying on other literary histories rather than by checking the original texts. Harmer's major source is Earl Miner's *The Japanese Tradition in British and American Literature*, published in 1958 and based on his 1955 doctoral dissertation. Miner recognizes Hearn's "enormous popular appeal"[6] and attempts to distinguish between what was mere romantic journalism and what was of lasting literary value in Hearn's work, but he has very little to say about Hearn's translations of Japanese poetry and what little there is, is incorrect.

Miner notes that Hearn "recognized himself that he had no poetic genius." But he goes on to make questionable literary judgments: "He did have a talent approaching genius for that rhythmical prose which is frequently and mistakenly called poetic, but it is easy to see that concentrated and brief poems like the Japanese forms cannot be adequately translated by a writer of periodic prose.... Hearn did adapt the translations of his acquaintances, but only to flavor his prose or for short chapters on special subjects such as poems about insects or folk songs, and with no aim to set himself up as a translator. All of his translations of Japanese poetry, culled from here and there, have made up only one small, posthumous volume."[7] This is a reference to Greenslet's collection which does *not* contain all of Hearn's translations of Japanese poetry. It is, in fact, composed almost entirely of translations into prose, but much of his work was in verse, not prose.

Miner is forced to confess at one point that Hearn's translations had some influence on American poets. Conrad Aiken wrote him: "Of course [Japanese poetry] was all in the air—at Harvard [and everyone] around the Harvard Advocate was already aware of Hearn's hokku, and we all had shots at them. So when Fletcher and I dived into Japanese and Chinese poetry and art [in the years between 1915 and 1917] it was already old stuff for me."[8] Miner seems to be taken aback by this statement: "The intermingling of talk about Hearn and haiku makes more sense than it at first seems to, because the section indebted to Hearn [in Aiken's *The House of Dust*] offers examples of Pound's super-pository technique which recur in Aiken's work of this period . . . ."⁹

Miner refuses to accept his own evidence that Aiken could have learned "Pound's super-pository technique" from Hearn's translations, which he had read at Harvard before Basil Hall Chamberlain's *Japanese Poetry* (1911) appeared and certainly before Pound began to devise his program for the Imagists. Perhaps Miner was too quick in dismissing the influence of Hearn's translations on modern poetry.

Let us take a look at the translations which Miner excludes from consideration. Anyone who has read Hearn's essays and his correspondence soon realizes that he had thought deeply about the problems of translation and that he would never have dashed off a sloppy rendering of an original merely to supply some romantic atmosphere for his travel sketches. The fact that he did not think of himself as a poet was a point in his favor as a translator. Instead of Pound's "creative misprision," to use contemporary critical jargon, he sought accuracy in translation. Translation, Hearn believed, begins with total fidelity to the original, although the best translations—which are very rare—do not halt there.

Hearn was not a novice in the art of translation when he came to Japan in 1890. In 1882 he published a book of translations of Théophile Gautier's short stories, a task which he had begun when he went to New Orleans in 1877 to work as a journalist. He had no illusions about his work, remarking wryly, "Verily the path of the translator is hard."¹⁰ Perhaps even more rare in translators, he had a generous appreciation of the work of his rivals. In a letter to Jerome A. Hart of San Francisco, commenting on Hart's review of his book, Hearn corrected a rather free rendering of a line from Gautier's epitaph for Clarimonde (in the story of that name) which Hart had offered as a substitute for Hearn's original rendering. He added apologetically, "But I think your second line is a masterpiece of faithfulness; and, as you justly remark, my hobby is literalism."¹¹ He carried this hobby to its logical extreme in his first translations from Japanese, which tried to capture for Western readers the peculiarities of Japanese syntax. These translations of prose, not poetry, follow exactly the form of the interlinear translations in Chamberlain's *A Handbook of Colloquial Japanese* (1888). Chamberlain was trying to convey in English the levels of honorific usage in Japanese:

Otottsan wa, dō de gozaimasu?
Honourable-father-Mr. as-for, how is?
Or, more politely
Go shimpu wa, ikaga de irasshaimasu?
August real-father as-for, how deigns-to-be?¹²

When Hearn tried to capture the language of an innkeeper chasing away the curious villagers from his foreign guests, he used the same technique: "Now august-to-eat-time-is; to-look-at *evil* matter is. *Honorable-returning-time-in*-to-look-at-as-for-is-good."¹³

For his translations of Japanese poetry Hearn used a variety of methods, ranging from literal word by word renderings to paraphrases in English metrical forms. For the purposes of this paper, however, the most interesting translations are those for which Hearn chose an unrhymed couplet, either metrical or in free verse. He often used the couplet form for different Japanese verse forms, without regard for the number of lines in the originals, which might vary from three for the haiku to four for the *dodoitsu*, a folk song form, and five for the tanka. One of his most successful efforts is this translation of a *dodoitsu*, a street song:

Kamiyo konokata
Kawaranu mono wa
Midzu no nagare to
   Koi no michi.

Things never changed since the Time of the Gods:
The flowing of water, the Way of Love.[14]

Although Hearn had to shift the word order to fit English patterns, he did not add anything which was not in the original. Moreover he succeeded in reproducing the effect of the short five-syllable final line. This was rarely possible, Hearn believed, without confusing the Western reader who lacked the background to understand the elliptical references of Japanese verse. "So the term 'ittakkiri'—meaning 'all gone,' or 'entirely vanished' is contemptuously applied to verses in which the versemaker has uttered his whole thought;—praise being reserved for compositions that leave in the mind the thrilling of a something unsaid." He warned, "The impossibility of preserving the inner quality of such poems in a literal rendering will now be obvious. Whatever I attempt in this direction must of necessity be ittakkiri; for the unspoken has to be expressed; and what the Japanese poet is able to say in seventeen or twenty-one syllables may need in English more than double that number of words."[15] So, for example, Hearn translates a haiku on the *higurashi*, a species of cicada, whose name signifies that its cry heralds the coming of twilight:

Already, O Higurashi, your call announces the evening! Alas, for the passing day, with its duties left undone![16]

The first line of his couplet expands and explains the meaning of the simple apostrophe "Higurashi ya!" which is the first line of the haiku. The second and third lines "Kyō no ketai wo / Omou toki", literally translated, mean simply: "Time to think of today's unfinished work."

This juxtaposition of an explanatory or descriptive line and a line containing a personal image or impression can be found throughout Hearn's translations. In one instance he even supplied an explanatory line which is not found in the original:

> However fickle I seem, my heart is never unfaithful: Out of the slime itself, spotless the lotus grows.[17]

The original, the song of a prostitute, is simply: "In muddy water / Though it is raised / With roots growing here and there / The lotus blossoms / As a beautiful flower." Hearn's couplet pairs the image in the second line, which needs no explanation for a Japanese audience, with a preceding line that gives its significance for the Western reader.

These are not isolated examples, although someone acquainted only with Greenslet's collection might think so. Of course, he also translated many haiku into prose, but there is one characteristic of his translations, prose or poetry, which one does not find in Chamberlain's essay on "Bashō and the Poetical Epigram," which first appeared in the *Transactions of the Asiatic Society of Japan* in 1902 and was reprinted in *Japanese Poetry* (1911).[18] Hearn sensed the division between thematic statement and specific impression and arranged his translations to mirror that contrast. Chamberlain used shorter couplets with run-on lines that compress the haiku into a single English sentence that ignores the dual structure.

This brings us back to Miner's discussion of Pound's "super-pository technique." Describing his efforts to crystallize in as short a form as possible the experience of seeing beautiful faces as he got out of a train in the Paris métro, Pound writes:

> The 'one image' poem is a form of super-position, that is to say, it is one idea set on top of another. I found it useful in getting out of the impasse in which I had been left by my métro emotion. I wrote a thirty-line poem, and destroyed it because it was what we call work 'of second intensity.' Six months later I made a poem half that length; a year later I made the following *hokku*-like sentence:
>
> The apparition of these faces in the crowd: Petals, on a wet black bough.
>
> I dare say it is meaningless unless one has drifted into a certain vein of thought. In a poem of this sort one is trying to record the precise instant when a thing outward and objective transforms itself, or darts into a thing inward and subjective.[19]

Miner describes this poem, "In a Station of the Métro," as a "*discordia concors*," a combination of a line which is "a relatively straightforward, unmetaphorical statement" and a line which is a "sharply defined metaphorical image. . . ." He praises Pound for being the first to discover and define this technique: "The discovery of this technique in a poetic form written in a language he did not know is one of the insights of Pound's genius."[20] Miner then goes on to trace its use throughout Pound's writings, including the *Cantos*.

As I have shown in a few examples, one of Hearn's techniques of translation was to provide an explanatory line combined with the image in the Japanese original and this is exactly what Pound did in his "In a Station of the Métro." It is not a haiku—only the thematic subject simply named or announced, as in Japanese, combined with the image or impression can create a true haiku. Perhaps if Pound had written "Métro Station— / Petals on a wet black bough" that would have been a haiku. As it is, he imitated Hearn's practice of going beyond the limits of the literal in order to guide the Western reader to the proper interpretation, thinking that this was a Japanese technique. So Pound's "superpository method" turns out to be based on the translations of that minor exotic, Lafcadio Hearn.

Miner pokes fun at the popular conception of Hearn as the romanticizer of all things Japanese: "It is this view of Japan replacing Loti's harsher one, which probably helped give currency to the stage and fictional types of the refined and intrepid Japanese, which makes dowagers gush and gruff men sigh, and which the mature reader can only feel is an impairment of the spirit called Lafcadio Hearnia."[21] That view of both Hearn and Japan has long since disappeared and we no longer romanticize either. Unfortunately, one cannot say the same about the critical adulation of Ezra Pound which (uncritically) credits him with something between papal infallibility and divine omniscience. I think it is time that we began to ask for another view of Ezra Pound—one that goes beyond the ideal image of Pound as the only begetter of all that is new in modern poetry to an understanding of his faults as well as his virtues. For Pound, who spent a long life playing the *enfant terrible* in a world he never understood, was human, all-too-human. I am merely asking for a Pound of flesh.

NOTES

1 Alister Kershaw and Frédéric-Jacques Temple, eds., *Richard Aldington: An Intimate Portrait* (Carbondale and Edwardsville: Southern Illinois UP, 1965) 74.
2 Forrest Reid, ed., *Pound/Joyce* (New York: New Directions, 1967) 85, 96, 97.
3 Earl Miner, *The Japanese Tradition in British and American Literature* (Princeton: Princeton UP, 1958) 91.
4 S. Foster Damon, *Amy Lowell* (Boston: Houghton Mifflin, 1935) 301.
5 Lafcadio Hearn, trans., *Japanese Lyrics* (Boston: Houghton Mifflin, 1915) n.p.
6 Miner 62-63.
7 Miner 90-91.
8 Miner 183.
9 Miner 183-184.
10 Elizabeth Bisland, *The Life and Letters of Lafcadio Hearn,* vol. 1 (Boston: Houghton Mifflin, 1906) 250.
11 Bisland 244.
12 Basil Hall Chamberlain, *A Handbook of Colloquial Japanese* (London: Trubner, 1888) 4.
13 Lafcadio Hearn, *Glimpses of Unfamiliar Japan*, vol. 5 of *The Writings of Lafcadio Hearn*, Koizumi edition (Boston and New York: Houghton Mifflin, 1923) 263.

14 Lafcadio Hearn, *Gleanings in Buddha-Fields*, vol. 8 of *The Writings of Lafcadio Hearn* 24-27.
15 Lafcadio Hearn, *In Ghostly Japan*, vol. 9 of *The Writings of Lafcadio Hearn* 313-316.
16 Lafcadio Hearn, *Shadowings*, vol. 10 of *The Writings of Lafcadio Hearn* 55.
17 The original, which Hearn does not supply, is: "Doro mizu ni / Sodaterarete mo / Ne wa shosho ni / Saite kirena / Hasu no hana." See John F. Embree, *Japanese Peasant Songs. Memoirs of the American Folklore Society* 38 (Philadelphia: American Folklore Society, 1943) 28.
18 In a note appended to this essay, Chamberlain writes, "Since the present essay was completed, the writer's attention has been drawn to Mr. Hearn's two latest works, 'Shadowings,' pp. 69-100 (1901), and 'A Japanese Miscellany,' pp. 92-118 (1901), containing respectively collections of epigrams on the curious subjects of cicadae and dragon-flies,—no less than 107 in all, or more, if those are counted of which not the original text, but only the translation is given. Some of the renderings are in the metre of the elegiac distich, which, owing to the far larger number of syllables of that form of verse, necessitates more or less expansion of the originals. Others, rendered literally, though less attractive as English—or Anglicized—poems, possess superior value for the scientific inquirer. All well exhibit the endless dexterity with which the Japanese epigrammatist can modulate the trilling of his tiny pipe" ("Bashō and the Japanese Poetical Epigram," *Transactions of the Asiatic Society of Japan*, vol. XXX [Tokyo: Rikkyo Gakuin Press, 1902] 362).
19 Ezra Pound, "Vorticism," *Fortnightly Review* 96 (1914): 467.
20 Miner 115.
21 Miner 61-62.

THE LESSONS OF MISREADING

Arnold Edelstein, University of Hawaii

For three years I taught English and American literature in the People's Republic of China—first in Tianjin as a Foreign Expert employed by the Chinese, and then, after three years back in Hawaii, in Jinan as a Fulbright lecturer. I was not an anthropologist or a China scholar, consciously studying a culture different from my own but in which I had a professional interest; rather, I was an Americanist teaching my own speciality in my own language but to Chinese students in their own country. I emphasize the distinction because it transformed my classroom into a cross-cultural laboratory, which, at times, was a "third place" situated between the two cultures. More often, however, it was a theater, where the teacher and the students performed their native culture as if it were pure spectacle, or a battle zone, where the teacher and the students fought for a form of cultural sovereignty.

Much of my mental energy of the last eighteen months has been directed towards taking the anecdotal experience of those three years and trying to transform it into some kind of knowledge. I will limit myself to two or three of those anecdotes that relate to a single subject and to the very tentative conclusions that I have begun to draw from them. I will focus on the problem of how attitudes towards revenge interfere with the interpretation of two specific literary works. I will try to use the idea of interference in the same sense that E.S.L. teachers use it, but one way of defining my experience questions the authority of a received interpretation, upon which the concept of interference itself depends. But, first, there are the stories.

I was teaching Hawthorne's *The Scarlet Letter*. Several obvious cultural facts prepared me for the ease with which my students seemed to understand Hawthorne's ambivalence towards Hester Prynne's hard-won freedom. First, in spite of radical politics and in spite of a strong anarchist tradition, the Chinese have at least since the triumph of Confucianism, officially and in practice, valued the group over the individual. Second, at least between Liberation and the early eighties, the Chinese have been puritanical in sexual matters. Given these two facts, my Chinese students were somewhat better prepared, emotionally, to deal with Hawthorne than students of the same age in the United States. On the day when my illumination began, my students were discussing the difficulty of choosing between the tyranny of the majority, which they had experienced during the Cultural Revolution and which they identified with the elders in Hawthorne's text, and the potential wrong-headedness of bourgeois individualism, to which they were continually alerted by their Friday afternoon political sessions and which they identified with Hester.

My surprise came when we began talking about Roger Chillingworth. An argument that had gone on between two factions of Chinese with the American teacher serving as mediator instantly changed into a clash between Chinese and foreigner. My students simply couldn't understand what they considered my hostility to Chillingworth—and I couldn't understand their misunderstanding. We agreed easily enough that Dimmesdale was a weakling who had cuckolded Chillingworth almost in spite of himself. But my students argued that Chillingworth wasn't a monster at all, in spite of having violated the "sanctity of the human heart"; he was only a husband entitled to his revenge, if he could get away with it. When I pointed out all the Satanic imagery that Hawthorne used to describe Chillingworth and argued that their "reading" made it very difficult to understand the final scaffold scene, they only became confused. Following a visible moment of enlightenment, one of the more demonstrative students leaped to his feet: "Do you mean that Christians believe in forgiveness?" he asked me. "Yes, they do," I answered. Mr. Zhao, always willing to make cultural generalizations, remained on his feet in order to make the statement that would end the discussion. "Chinese don't," he said.

Only a week later we were reading Edgar Allan Poe. Very few Western critics of "The Cask of Amontillado" believe that Montresor has taken his revenge on Fortunato with impunity. Although there is great disagreement over Montresor's *motives* for his revenge, there is general agreement that he has been haunted for fifty years by his act and is finally unburdening himself to his confessor, perhaps on his deathbed. Some argue that Montresor's desire for revenge has been frustrated because Fortunato—true to his name—has died too quickly, without knowing *why* he has been victimized. A few, seeing Montresor as a kind of Iago, talk about motiveless perversity. Michael Bakhtin hears the echo of an ancient, non-Christian affirmation of life behind the death rattle of Poe's story but finally dismisses the carnival imagery as degraded and his brief comments finally conform to the received reading. Not so my Chinese students. One of them, for example, included the following in her answer to a midterm question on the story, blending her misunderstanding of what she'd learned about Western religion with a traditional Chinese acceptance of revenge:

> "The Cask of Amontillado tells about how Montressor revenges a greedy villain who makes use of his job to take advantage of people and benefit himself. When at last Mr. F. was trapped he asked M to be merciful. "Yes, let us begone," answered M who wanted to end all this. F begged M to spare his life for he was also loved by God and should not be kill so cruelly. Yes, M answered, it was because for the love of God (here means "I love God") he would end the sins of F. The dialogue indicates the different attitudes towards life. One is selfish, and the other wanted to do justice for the sake of God.

Her response was the most subtle because she created clear motives for Montresor's revenge out of Poe's uncertainty—motives, of course, that justified her enjoyment of Montresor's revenge. Most of the other students seemed to enjoy the story as a straightforward celebration of revenge and, once again, found my questions about guilt and confession confusing rather than helpful.

The Chinese government, at least, is not confused. It considers the widespread acceptance of personal revenge as one of the vestiges of feudalism. We saw a two-hour soap opera on Chinese television that showed a young man being swindled. But rather than becoming a political comment on the rather volatile entrepreneurial situation in a China where the reformers are trying to reconcile free market techniques with a controlled economy, the program turned out to be a lesson in culture and law. Once he knew that he'd been swindled, the young man and a group of his friends found the culprit and beat him up, as they would have done in Song or Ming times, and as my students would have done, they told me when I discussed the drama in class the next day. But modern Chinese law had the young man arrested for assault, not the swindler for fraud. The final "message" of the piece was that we all had to march forward into the future without feudal ideas of revenge. Let the State deal with the culprit. My students, who approved of both Chillingworth and Montresor, disagreed with the action of the court, at least in the relative safety of my classroom.

This television drama makes it clear that the issue of revenge is only part of a much larger cultural issue: the Law. Another of my Jinan students came to my office one afternoon with a confused look on his face and a copy of Thomas Pynchon's *Slow Learner* in his hands. As luck would have it, his first questions concerned "Entropy." Always willing to talk about Pynchon, I plunged in and began talking about how the story was divided between Callisto's speculations in the apartment upstairs and the lease-breaking party Meatball Mulligan is throwing downstairs. When it became clear that the first confusing item was the concept of "lease-breaking party," something that also confuses my Hawaii students, I launched into what I considered a perfectly lucid explanation. Nevertheless, the look of confusion remained on his face. Unlike my Hawaii students, neither his personal experience nor Chinese law had prepared him for the concept of "lease." Housing is provided in China, either by the family or the work unit, which has taken over many of the functions of the traditional extended Chinese family. If he could stretch his imagination to the point where he could understand renting an apartment from a stranger, he could not understand why that relationship could not be terminated when it was no longer convenient for one of the parties. When I tried to explain, the student began to giggle, a sure sign that I had crossed a cultural border into never-never land. If I had acted according to my experience, I would have treated that nervous laughter as an exit line and moved on to something simple, like explaining the concept of entropy and tracing it into Pynchon's later work. Instead, I tackled the next logical problem: the concept of law itself. Within only minutes, my Socratic method broke down completely and we were close to shouting at one another.

All classrooms resemble my Chinese classroom in that the students and the teacher create together a set of common values that guide our readings of specific texts. True "interpretive communities" are rarely achieved because the students too often are interested in "wiring the teacher" and the teacher is just as frequently unaware of how his or her interpretation may be constrained by culture, class, and gender. My Chinese students were not interested in arguing with what I said, either because they respected my authority, at least when in its presence, or because they were eager to please a teacher who might be able to aid their passage into an American doctoral program. When their disagreement did emerge, as in the incidents I've described here, that emergence was almost involuntary and resulted from powerful cultural assumptions that we did not share. I wasn't wrong to think Chillingworth a monster; I was crazy.

The *concept* of revenge is similar in both cultures but the signals evoke different emotions depending upon the larger cultural context. In other words, in order to understand the materials I was teaching, my students tried to learn how to read the text *as if they were Americans*, but their creative mimicry failed when the imaginative leap from culture to culture was too great. Their attitudes towards nature, death, courtship, or the family structure tended to interfere just as clearly and in the same way as their attitudes towards revenge.

All encounters with literary texts can be seen as cross-cultural experiences. A New Yorker reads Faulkner across a geographical barrier; a Chicagoan of the nineteen-eighties reads *Sister Carrie* across a temporal barrier; an Anglo reading New Mexico hispanic fiction, a European American teaching in Hawaii, and a generalized American teaching in China all function on a scale of cultural alienation. There is no cultural purity, no total isolation, no complete difference between readers (as there is no complete sameness). Reading my assignments in their dorm rooms, my Chinese students were no different from students anywhere else, trying to make sense of the text by parlaying their personal experience and their understanding of what their teachers—including their foreign teachers—expected. While they were in my classroom, their "working culture" had to expand to include American expectations; but expansion can occur only under a great deal of pressure.

The classroom itself becomes a place that can exist out of space and out of time, a place where alternatives are explored and ideas are tested—a place, in my Chinese experience, belonging to neither culture, sometimes almost becoming a third culture. Personally, I found living in this synthetic third culture exciting and preferred it to the alternatives—which seemed to be either pretending that I was Chinese or becoming an aggressive representative of what the Chinese considered my native culture. Such a classroom, however, is a fragile and temporary construct and breaks down easily under the stress of cultural difference, as the discussion of Pynchon's "Entropy" indicates. My students continued to speak to one another in Chinese, no matter how I insisted on English as the language of the classroom, and there is no evidence that whatever understanding of cultural difference they acquired in that third place carried over into their Chinese classrooms—or that such understanding would be rewarded by the system to which they would be returned once they completed their graduate programs. It would come in very handy, however, if they made it to the U.S. for a doctoral program.

Finally, such a third place is completely artificial. Although in the course of play both students and teachers recognize the existence of multiple points of view, they can adopt only one at a time and the last one tends to be the first one they brought with them into the game. One of my more reflective students in Tianjin once asked me if, in fact, adopting a point of view that would allow her to understand a story the way an American understood it also meant becoming American. Heavy then into the expatriate's ideal of freedom and self-control, I answered, "No." Her question assumed that the received interpretation of a story, although it changes over time, always has cultural, if not textual, authority; my answer was dependent on a more anarchistic idea of the self and a relativistic reader-response theory based on it. The position I took seems to imply a criticism that must constantly define its own parameters; the position my student took implies a historically and culturally based criticism far more interested in the conditions that make meaning possible than in interpretations of individual works. I was the post-modernist, my student a practitioner of the new literary history.

It seems to me now that I was also the sentimentalist, looking for some international community that transcended America and China and transformed all literary studies into comparative literature. Although I again feel nostalgic for the excitement that such a community offers, I no longer believe that either American or Chinese literature exists there, although discrete texts obviously do. Teaching literature is teaching culture, and that job becomes more difficult as cultural difference increases, particularly because teaching culture can never be a politically neutral act—remember the confusion over Meatball Mulligan's lease-breaking party. Similarly, the practice of comparative literature can also never be politically neutral. And in the country of the blind the one-eyed American lit teacher is an alien, not a king.

INTERTEXTUALITY IN THE FICTION OF CAMUS AND WENDT

Evelyn Ellerman, University of Alberta

In *Leaves of the Banyan Tree*, Albert Wendt performs the unusual conjuring trick of producing a new and powerful character near the end of the narrative. Galupo, an allegorical figure of reconciliation, rides into town at high noon like the marshall come to clean up Dodge City: his trusty steed—the Apia to Sapepe bus; his weapons—a suitcase full of books. Galupo's selection is a revealing one:

> He kept the Bible he had stolen from the Protestant church, Camus' *Myth of Sisyphus* and *The Plague*, a paperback copy of Frazer's *Golden Bough*, Dostoevsky's *Idiot* and *Crime and Punishment*, an unexpurgated edition of *Lady Chatterley's Lover*, a collection of pornographic Japanese prints, Dreiser's *American Tragedy*, Norman Mailer's *The Naked and the Dead*, V. S. Naipaul's *A House for Mr. Biswas*, Luis Borge's *Ficciones*, and ten volumes of the Encyclopedia Britannica.[1]

As rich and suggestive as the contents of Galupo's suitcase may be for interpretation, I would like to focus here on Wendt's relations with Albert Camus. For this is not the first overt reference in Wendt's fiction to the formative influence played on his characters by Camus' works. In *Sons for the Return Home*, the Samoan gives as a present to his white girlfriend, a book of Camus' essays. And, on the level of plot, the close resemblance between Pepe's trial in *Leaves* and that of Meursault in *The Stranger* has not only been noticed by such critics as Helen Tiffin and John Beston, but was confirmed as intentional by Wendt in a 1977 interview with Beston.[2]

I would like to suggest in this paper that there is an even closer relationship between the work of these two authors. And, in order to demonstrate my point, I should like to focus on their mutual quest for balance. This quest is best illustrated by the struggle of their major characters to move from chaos to harmony, and, more specifically, by a struggle to balance both night and day. My purpose, however, is not to present a simple display of influence or affinity, but to indicate the rewards of intertextual studies between new literatures and old. We are all aware, in Comparative Literature, of the reassessment of the importance of influence studies which has taken place over the last few decades. Dissatisfied with the static and unidirectional implications of the term "influence," we have in turn tried on the new shoes of such terms as "tradition and development," "affinity," and most recently, "intertextuality"—all in an effort to recognize and demonstrate the complex set of interrelations that can exist among literary texts, and the process of literary creation itself.

As difficult as this process of redefinition and redirection can be, it becomes even more complicated when we come to examine post-colonial literature or, for that matter, any literature which Western literary criticism considers marginal. In this situation, the term "influenced" often acquires the connotation "derivative" or "second-class," in much the same way the term "Third World Literature" can connote "third class." This is a political and economic fact of literary life which denies the thriving, multi-directional commerce that now exists among world literatures. It is a fact of literary life which explains, in part, the scarcity of intertextual studies between post-colonial literatures and the literatures of Europe. Nevertheless, as comparatists we do ourselves and world literature a disservice if we do not conduct such studies. The most recently coined term, "intertextuality," may help us out of our difficulty. It implies a dynamic network of relations that "influence" does not. It allows us to move from a later text back to a re-reading of an earlier text. And it allows us more freedom to look at poetic creation in new authors. Both of these processes are possible when we examine the relations between the work of Wendt and Camus.

Albert Wendt's concern with balance and harmony has been noted by a number of critics. W. D. Ashcroft claims the swing in narration between past and present in *Sons for the Return Home* is meant to display a consciousness torn between two cultures.[3] Harmony is achieved in the end when the Samoan is suspended in the airplane between earth and sky, between New Zealand and Samoa. Subramani has described *Leaves* as a novel where balance is achieved between the mimetic and allegorical. He says the novel ultimately becomes a "half-historical and half-mythological diagnosis of the spiritual malaise of a culture,"[4] and that, "ideologically what Galupo exemplifies is the possibility of synthesis of individual freedom and corporate responsibility."[5] A strong functional correlation between inner states of chaos and harmony in major characters and the natural imagery around them in Wendt's fiction has been posited by Roger Robinson. Robinson writes that the Samoan environment becomes a "correlative to the moral or mental state of his characters."[6]

The same tendency towards establishing balance has been noted by critics of Camus. H. M. Block claims that all of Camus' work shows a quest for primal self. In a godless universe, the individual must assume total responsibility for his own existence. This quest is intimately associated with a sense of oneness with nature and precedes the possibility of the individual to act in communion with others.[7] Tom Bishop states that the absence or excess of one element or another in nature can be destructive. In Camus' fiction, real happiness is associated with a balance of the elements.[8]

Not only is the notion of balance a key element in Camus' work, the connection between balance in man and balance in nature is a clear one. Anna Balakian has shown a strong correlation between the internal states of Camus' characters and the natural imagery.[9] However, where Balakian's work differs markedly from that of others is in its functional approach. Her analysis does not assign static correspondences for sun, sea, wind, and desert which must be altered from work to work. Rather, she sees the natural imagery as an indicator of internal events, a kind of barometer of the emotions. Viewed in this way, Camus' North African fiction, in particular, can be studied as a whole, the natural imagery functioning consistently throughout.

While all the elements play a part in this pattern in both authors, the imagery of night (or dark, moon, black) and day (or light, sun, white) predominates. For each of these authors, the inquiring individual, the individual who is closest to his inner self, is the one who most readily inhabits the night. The individual who is most alienated from self is the one who inhabits the day. And in both Wendt and Camus, night and day assume the equivalence of internal and external existence which must be brought to balance. In the end, the potential for success in these characters lies in a willingness to embrace night. They are willing to engage in self-examination: for them the night represents wholeness, the natural, the healing, the sensual, and the individual. It is at night that the full play of the senses is possible, as the eyes can no longer dominate perception. It is at night that the individual can retreat into healing silence to know himself and his past.

The characters who are unwilling to embrace the night have a different understanding of its qualities and possibilities: for them, the night represents the unknown, the unpleasant, the sinful, and the dangerous. Daylight, for a "night" person, can be just as unpleasant and frightening; if he is resisting the inner quest, consciously, or unconsciously, daylight can represent the artificial and the destructive, the disorienting, the communal. When these characters are out of balance, they are often blinded, made sleepy or dizzy by the daylight: they become lost in the labyrinth of social exigency, unhappily controlled by or controlling others, or pursued by a sense of betrayal. On the other hand, the "day" people are content to accept society's values: they become powerful and self-assured in daylight. When these characters can no longer function within those values, they, too, become threatened by daylight, losing their orientation. Often, in order to make these values clear, the authors make use of allegory. Minor characters frequently represent the ideal "day" or "night" people. Night people are those who are in touch with their true selves: in Wendt, these are always Samoans, like Lupe and Fanua in *Leaves,* who have not accepted *papalagi* ("European") ways and who are still in contact with the land; in Camus, these are characters, like Rieux's mother in *The Plague,* who live contentedly in the shadows and alleviate human suffering.

Day people are interested in the exercise of power, or in the maintenance of the dominant social order; they refuse introspection, are divorced from nature and cling solely to the values of society. In Wendt, these characters are most often Samoans who have opted for *papalagi* life, like Malaga in *Pouliuli,* or the white man himself—the lawyer Ashton in *Leaves,* for example; in Camus, day people represent the values of society as does the examining magistrate in *The Stranger,* or Dr. Richard in *The Plague.*

Of course, few characters in the novels are so clearly allegorical. Both authors make use of the duality of nature to maintain tension within the personalities of their main characters and within the plots themselves. The main characters all have predispositions towards night or day, but because of the imbalance in their own world, are often shown to be suffering in that world, or struggling feebly in its diurnal opposite, drowning in the air, unable or unwilling to find a balance. Only the arrival at internal balance makes both night and day habitable for the successful characters.

Discovering such a pervasive pattern in one text, and then reading backward or forward to an influencing or influenced text, can radically alter our perceptions of each. For instance, Wendt's investigations into the standard metaphor for European culture (sun, light, white) and for traditional Samoan culture (moon, dark, black) adds a new dimension to the society/self polarities explored by Camus. Wendt's novels reverse the Western concept of the Oriental "other." In his fiction, the "Arab" on the sands speaks; he even becomes the protagonist. Night has arrived as an active force rivalling the sun in intensity, commanding reader interest in a way it cannot and does not in *The Stranger* and *The Plague*.

After looking at Wendt's fiction, the reader is sensitized to night and not so easily beguiled by the prevailing sun imagery in the first half of *The Stranger*, for example. The neat division of the novel into two reflecting halves becomes more visible: the preliminary part, where the sun dominates (that is, the struggle of the protagonist with his half-hearted attempts to adopt society's values) balances with the second part, where night dominates (that is, the inner struggle of the protagonist to establish his own values). Clear, too, from the novel's inception, is the steady increase in the power of the night, which eventually meets and balances with the waning strength of the sun. Meursault had banished night when he sent his mother to the Home. Unlike Dr. Rieux in *The Plague*, whose night-person mother proved such a positive influence on those around her, Meursault was uncomfortable with the woman who just sat and watched him from the shadows. But, with her death, night is forcibly reintroduced into his life in a way he cannot banish. At his mother's wake sits an Arab nurse; around the coffin sit living corpses. Meursault feels surrounded and threatened. Here is the first mention of Arab as night. Andre Elbaz points this out when he writes that Camus' North African fiction treats the Arab as the "other."[10] Indeed, when we examine the movement from chaos to harmony in this novel, we can see that, in the first half, "Arab" *is* the personification of chaos in the night. When Meursault is confused and resisting self-examination, the night has two legs and a black face. However, when he tries to convince himself the struggle is over, that all is harmonious, as when he returns home to Marie after dutifully attending his mother's funeral, the night appears as itself and benign. He leaves his window open and writes, "it was pleasant to feel the cool night air flowing over our sunburned bodies."[11] But even after trying to kill night on the beach at high noon, Meursault discovers it is still there. Shadows pursue him in the courthouse. And who does he encounter in the visiting room of the jail, but an affectionate mother and son—Arabs. He has not destroyed (indeed, cannot destroy) the night, but must learn to accept it.

This is, in fact, a turning point of the novel. It is the last time he sees Marie, or the Arabs, and it is the beginning of a process of introspection which leads to his acceptance of the night. From dreading the heat of the courtroom and fearing the deathly black of his cell, he eventually moves to the more balanced position of considering a reprieve for twelve hours and no reprieve for the other twelve. He starts to sleep during the day and stay awake at night, inhabiting the night for the first time in the narrative. The final coincidence of internal and external harmony is indicated in the novel's closing lines:

> Sounds of the countryside came faintly in, and the cool night air, veined with smells of earth and salt, fanned my cheeks. The marvelous peace of the sleepbound summer night flooded through me like a tide.[12]

This brief and inadequate examination of the role played by night in *The Stranger* is meant to indicate some areas for investigation in Camus' work which suggested themselves to me after I had read Albert Wendt. The prospects for the analysis of the function of the natural elements in this novel and in Camus' other desert pieces, as well as for the analysis of the enigmatic Meursault, are interesting indeed. Intertextuality, however, is at least a two-way street. There are numerous facets of Wendt's work which display Camus' influence, but perhaps we can focus on one aspect of his creative development. The Pepe character of *Leaves of a Banyon Tree* is built around the 1963 story "Tagata, the Man Who Search for the Freedom Tree,"[13] where there is minimal use of natural imagery. However, by the time the collection *Flying Fox in a Freedom Tree*[14] was published, in 1974, Wendt had been experimenting with the functional pattern of imagery I have described above, especially in his 1973 novel *Sons for the Return Home*.[15] As a result, these patterns were introduced into the "Flying Fox" story. And they were later expanded in *Leaves*, where they complement the myth he was constructing for that novel.

Tauilopepe, for example, is not only the Samoan who opts for the white man's ways, but a sun-god, or sun-king, a powerful creative/destructive force against which must be balanced an equally powerful force of darkness. Pepe becomes, for the people of his village, the re-incarnation of Pepesa, a half-god who will one day return to unite the people. With this strong introduction of myth, Wendt reshapes the tool he has borrowed. Now, the elements not only indicate chaos or harmony within the character on-stage, as it were, but of characters off-stage as well. For instance, Pepe wakes up one morning to oppressive heat, but finds out only later that his father is in a rage. Thus, the addition of myth to the elemental pattern already established allows Wendt to transmute the action of the novel to the cataclysmic battles that take place in the creation myths and legends of any culture.

Like *The Stranger*, the Pepe story is the autobiography of a condemned man; but, unlike Meursault, Pepe does not find harmony. He is a child of darkness: while still a young boy in Sapepe he frequently finds refuge in the night from his father Tauilopepe, a sun figure. As Tauilo moves steadily toward the acquisition of the white man's wealth and power, a decision which eventually destroys every member of his family, his son Pepe recedes into the shadows.

This is Pepe's undoing. All his life, he re-acts, rather than acts, playing against his father's wishes until the end.

Pepe's story begins and ends in fire. He has decided to write a death-bed autobiography as he gazes out the window at the hospital crematorium. The hot sun burns towards his bed. He sees a fly, "hitting against the wire screen all the time, killing the self slowly,"[16] just as Pepe himself has been doing for years. He insists that he has no regrets, but wakes up in a sweat remembering the old men stoking the urn with "white parcels . . . guts, bits and pieces of people from the surgery department."[17] The heat buzzes in his ears as he prepares to record his life.

It is Tauilo who first takes Pepe to the Vaipe ("Dead-Water"), the Apia slum where Samoan villagers live when they move from country to town. Father and son leave their village as the sun is rising. It is hot in the bus and Pepe sleeps most of the way: this is Tauilo's dream for the future, not Pepe's. The Vaipe is truly the Land of the Shades for the boy. The stream which flows past his new home brings only death and decay; the Vaipe is a living hell for Pepe where the "fale ["houses"] look like old men who are waiting to die."[18] Across the stream is a prison. Tauilopepe has pulled Pepe away from the land and the night and left him in limbo with the other condemned men.

During his school years in the Vaipe, Pepe boards with his fat uncle, Tautala, the Samoan civil servant whom Tauilo intends as a model for Pepe. Tauilo wears white tropical gear and imitates white ways as closely as he can, living in a neat pink house where all is bright and shiny. Yet, alone among the Samoans, Tautala is especially oppressed by the heat: he sweats profusely and pants as though he is drowning; he rushes back and forth to the toilet, commenting, "Hot, is it not?" His wife blames his continual sleepiness at home to overwork.

In the Vaipe, Pepe has been neutralized as a counteractive force to his father. Before the awesome power of Tauilo, all that is natural and Samoan seems to wither and die. Yet there are two occasions when Pepe challenges his father. He robs Tauilo's store at midnight with some friends, and feels powerful and invisible in the dark. But he is pursued by flashlights, street lights, headlights, and fire; he is found out and jailed. One other time, he argues with his father over his sister Niu's proposed marriage to an old man. For one brief afternoon, Pepe does not feel the heat, although it is a hot day. But his brief feeling of power over Tauilo does not last, and his final day finds him once more oppressed by the sun and heat and the knowledge that, to his dying moments, he has refused to reconcile with his father.

Pepe is caught between two cultures just as he is caught between night and day. He can neither accept the white man's ways as his father has, nor the tradition of old Samoa kept alive by the village wiseman, Toasa. By refusing to learn and believe in the old ways, Pepe knows he has lost the night forever. Guilt at his neglect of Toasa wells up as "the heat presses in on [his] head" at Toasa's funeral.[19] The guilt manifests also as fire. He walks into the fale toward the bier, his "body burning inside like the stones under [his] feet . . ."[20] Pepe feels dead, a "shell that will walk the earth like the shadowless noon."[21]

In the end, Pepe cannot answer his friend Simi's question, "You have no regrets about how you spent your life? About what you chose?"[22] Pepe looks away, and after Simi leaves, he awakens to find the night forever invaded by light and fire, and beside him

> only the night nurse in her white uniform without a smile on her face. From the window comes the smell of the fire and the burning flesh. Through the windows I watch the mountains disappear, like Simi, into the night-time.[23]

This brief example of the function of the night/day imagery in Wendt provides not only an approach to the analysis of character in Wendt, but an indication of how Camus' existential concerns were adopted and modified to fit the needs of another writer, in another place, at another time. Both this example, and that of Meursault in *The Stranger*, demonstrate the fertile ground which await the scholar who investigates the complex set of relations which exist between post-colonial literatures and those of Europe.

NOTES

1. Albert Wendt, *Leaves of the Banyan Tree* (Harmondsworth, England: Penguin, 1981) 366.
2. John Beston, "An Interview with Albert Wendt," *World Literature Written in English* 16.1 (1977): 157; Helen Tiffin, "'You Can't Go Home Again': The Colonial Dilemma in the Work of Albert Wendt," *Meanjin* 37.1 (1978): 119-26.
3. W. D. Ashcroft, "The Place of the Spirit: Albert Wendt's *Sons for the Return Home*," *The New Literatures Review* 9 (1981): 24-33.
4. Subramani, *South Pacific Literature: From Myth to Fabulation* (Suva, Fiji: University of the South Pacific, 1985) 137.
5. Subramani 142.
6. Roger Robinson, "Albert Wendt: An Assessment," *Landfall* 34.3 (1980): 280.
7. H. M. Block, "Spiritual Regeneration in the Work of Camus," in W. T. Zyla and M. Aycock, eds., *Albert Camus' Literary Milieu: Arid Lands. Proceedings of the Comparative Literature Symposium. 22-24 Jan. 1975* (Lubbock, Texas: Texas Tech University, 1976) 81
8. Tom Bishop, "Camus and Beckett: Variations on an Absurd Landscape," *Albert Camus' Literary Milieu* 65.
9. Anna Balakian, "Alienation and Aridity: The Climactic Correlative in Camus' Writings," *Albert Camus' Literary Milieu* 37-52.
10. André E. Elbaz, "Albert Camus et la littérature algérienne d'expression française," *Proceedings of the Eighth Congress of the International Comparative Literature Association, vol. 2.* (1976) 237-244.
11. Albert Camus, *The Plague*, trans. Stuart Gilbert (London: Hamish Hamilton, 1973) 44.
12. Camus 153.

13 Albert Wendt, "Tagata, the Man Who Search for the Freedom Tree," *New Zealand Universities Arts Festival Yearbook* (1963): 24-29.
14 Albert Wendt, *Flying-Fox in a Freedom Tree* (Auckland: Longman Paul, 1982).
15 Albert Wendt, *Sons for the Return Home* (Auckland: Longman Paul, 1973).
16 Wendt, *Leaves* 157.
17 Wendt, *Leaves* 157.
18 Wendt, *Leaves* 162.
19 Wendt, *Leaves* 203.
20 Wendt, *Leaves* 204.
21 Wendt, *Leaves* 203.
22 Wendt, *Leaves* 186.
23 Wendt, *Leaves* 186.

STYLE AND SUBSTANCE: TWO INSTANCES OF CROSS-CULTURAL HERMENEUTICS

P. Joseph Cahill, University of Alberta

Introduction

From among the varied research possibilities offered by the incursion of Matteo Ricci into sixteenth-century Peking, I wish to confine myself to the components operative in this classic cross-cultural hermeneutic. To recover the theme latent in one dramatic meeting of east and west, some personal and historical observations are first necessary.

An earlier study of this event suggested style and substance to be the controlling and hence informative categories in what was and is a sophisticated and elusive interchange. Though the superintendatory value of these categories has diminished, their heuristic value moved to concepts of encounter, dialectic, and conversion. For, while Ricci and the Chinese furnish a classical encounter of styles and substance, the participants experience through dialectic a conversion, a change of horizons. This cross-cultural hermeneutics embraces, therefore, a number of discrete and, at times, reasonably tractable phenomena.

I

Matteo Ricci (Li Ma-tou in Chinese) followed Francis Xavier to China. Whereas the charismatic Xavier, animated by a vision and a dream, simply reached China in 1552, Ricci penetrated both geographically and spiritually to the very center of China.

Born on October 6, 1552 at Mascerata, the Italian Jesuit priest arrived in Kwangtung province in 1582 where he and his companion, Ruggieri, immersed themselves in the study of the Chinese language and culture. In 1589, Ricci adopted the dress, the idiom, the style of the Chinese literati. This was not what would later be called acculturation but part of a deliberate strategy and desire. Conventional missionary wisdom was yielding to a course soon to be misinterpreted by curial authorities as clandestine corruption or perversion of doctrinal integrity. In 1595 Ricci moved to Nan-ch'ang, in 1597 to Nanking; and in 1601 he entered Peking where he spent the remaining nine years of his life.

Part of Ricci's intellectual capital was the scriptural proposition that God wills the salvation of *all*. (One may readily adduce texts: I Timothy 2:3-6; II Timothy 1:14, or invoke the literary design of the Christian Bible. So too may one refer to the universal mission delineated in the Jesuit constitutions.) This efficacious will transcended cultural styles. Precisely how this equipoise might be explained and maintained had not yet come up for conscious discussion.

The *Proemium* of the constitutions of the Jesuit Order clearly indicates that it was not external constitutions or rules which were to guide this new Order but rather the *"interna caritatis et amoris illius lex quam Sanctus Spiritus scribere et in cordibus imprimere solet. . . ."*[1] How to view the universal salvific will, even within an institutional Church tending to preserve old ways and to identify nation and religion, was now vulnerable to imaginative interpretations when the ultimate norm was as lithe as the afflatus of the Holy Spirit.

Such a flexible hermeneutic principle might well be expected in an Order which had in its rules the obligation to move around, to live in any place where the work of God and the good of souls might be achieved. *"Nostrae vocationis est diversa loca peragrare et vitam agere in quavis mundi plaga ubi maius Dei obsequium et animarum auxilium speratur."*[2] This mandate was congruent with the larger dimensions of the new religious Order. The Order had no distinctive garb, no prescribed time or form of prayer, no choral recitation of the Divine Office, no vow of stability, no prescribed physical isolation from the world. Such breaches of tradition would furnish even jejune minds with a very flexible hermeneutic indeed. The cited texts indicate clearly that the principles of interpretation are resident within the interpreter. This interpreter is to "lead his life" any place in the world. "Leading one's life" here involves a context in which one's life is appropriate to any new and foreign culture. Within the interpreter arises a double dialectic: first, an encounter with what *is* foreign; secondly, a dialogue with what *was* foreign. In the latter stage Ricci the interpreter moved to such a point where he could present the substance of his religion in the light of the classical Chinese texts: the *Analects*, the *Book of Mencius, Doctrine of the Mean,* and the *Great Learning*. It would appear that Ricci began to find a shared subject matter in two constitutive bodies of writings.

The first literary result was his book, *The True Meaning of the Lord of Heaven*. Though not the first book written by missionaries to China, it was the first book by a foreigner to begin with Chinese presuppositions, the Chinese traditional wisdom, and Chinese vehicles of religious and cultural mediation. Ricci's equation of Christianity with "Celestial Wisdom," his conviction that history teaches by analogy and not maxims, his intense and sincere accommodation and adoption of the Chinese lifestyle, terminology, rites, and ethics—all of this constituted a gigantic imaginative leap from the Latin form of Christianity in which Ricci had been reared. In terms of hermeneutics, Ricci charted unknown territory. This is not to affirm that Ricci was so naive as to identify one religion with another or to assume that cultural variations due to religious beliefs were simply irrelevant deferences to circumstance or temperament. But Ricci's behavior intimated that interpretation must transcend the hitherto accepted confrontation of styles.[3]

II

"A style . . . may be said to be a way of achieving definiteness and effectiveness in human relations by choosing or evolving one line of procedure out of several possible ones, and sticking to it."⁴ It is "a system of coherent ways or patterns of doing certain things."⁵ Style is part of a common sense method of dealing with the routine affairs of everyday life, both individual and communal. It may rise to higher levels befitting elevated ceremonials. Styles give definition to cultures, to institutions within the cultures, and to individuals, particularly if they play significant roles in a society.

While styles tend to be virtually irreversible, there are instances of reconstitution when a particular style has lost its creative energy and seems to be moribund.⁶ Styles and codes, as we know from many sources, are closely enough allied to perform the same functions. But that is a topic for investigation elsewhere.⁷

It would seem that Ricci's horizon included the notion that diverse styles might conceal similar substances, even though on second glance the substances might not be that similar. Here one must recall that the notion of historicity, so much a part of our intellectual landscape, had not yet been thematized. In China virtually nothing was known about other cultures. The question of diverse styles and their possible relations to similar substances would not be an issue because the Chinese never thought anything of value could be present in the west. "The Chinese Empire was unquestionably the greatest in the world."⁸

Ricci first indicated that there was another culture and civilization besides that of the Chinese. Secondly, Ricci persuaded the wise men of the East it was in their self-interest to profit from this culture and civilization. Thirdly, this antiphonal relationship could lead to accepting Christianity, though not in any crudely fundamentalistic fashion. So true was this aspiration that Church authorities found it difficult to ascertain who was converting whom and to what. Evidence of ecclesiastical malaise was apparent in the 1645 condemnation by Rome of the rites and rituals honoring Confucius and one's ancestors—rites and rituals Ricci had incorporated into Catholic practice. In terms of Roman Catholic interpretative theory, the fear was not, therefore, without foundation.

While Ricci was examining the Chinese classics and attempting to explain the Christian tradition to the Chinese, he himself sensed that styles concealed a similar subject matter and as such were something like the "accidents" of the Aristotelian classifications of being. It is possible that this subsidiary awareness arose from the new religious style created by the founding of the Jesuits. And it may be that his stance was occasioned or augmented by the pertinacious Biblical strand that God is always creating something new. What we can affirm with certainty is that both the Bible and the Constitutions of the Jesuits teach the possibility and necessity of newness, renovation, renewal, restoration, reconstitution. One can here only pause to mention the intriguing hermeneutic at work between the authors of the documents, the documents themselves, and one gifted with prophetic impulse.[9] Moreover, the encounter with the Chinese culture raised the serious and as yet unanswered question of the truth claims inherent in classic religious bodies of literature. How exactly is one to read seriously heterogeneous religious texts?[10] Ricci did not formulate an answer. But he and his followers did begin a pragmatic balance between the best that could be achieved in the light of the best that could be imagined.

This leads us to reflection on the interior rearrangement that we shall call conversion.

III

Though one does not see much written about conversion either as a state or activity connected with reading or much less with hermeneutics, there assuredly can be a relation between the world created by texts and what is generally called conversion. Clearly texts such as those of Marx and Engels generated "a change of direction,"[11] which is an acceptable description of conversion. While conversion is a mode of self-transcendence and self-transformation, it likewise transforms the world in which the subject dwells. Everything becomes different than it once was. When we have the gradual transformation of two subjects about a common subject matter, we have a rare tensive occurrence somewhat parallel to the procedure of dialogue in the well-known sense described by Josiah Royce. In any case, the incipient differentiations of consciousness in both partners in the encounter are the constitutive elements of conversion. Lonergan speaks of three kinds of conversion: intellectual, moral and religious, not necessarily occurring in sequence.[12] Ramsey MacMullen examined the Question at length in his study, *Christianizing the Roman Empire*.[13] The book, incidently, bred a symposium.[14] Ramsey's concern was with the third type of conversion: religious. How deep were the early Christian conversions of which we read? Must conversion be a profound transformation to deserve the name? MacMullen's conclusion is that religious conversions were not so profound as we once may have thought. One or two respondents to MacMullen in the subsequent symposium distinguish between philosophic and Christian conversion. Some also speak of psychic conversion. Though Northrop Frye speaks primarily of imaginative vision, he does indicate that the union of professed belief and practiced faith is a state at which one arrives.[15] If actions do not conform to belief, one is in need of conversion or the imaginative vision to which Frye so often refers.

Intellectual, moral, and religious conversions are, as mentioned, epigenetic differentiations of consciousness. Intellectual conversion is, with Lonergan, a change in our cognitional structure which convinces us that knowledge is not simply seeing but a compound of experiencing, understanding, judging, and believing.[16] It is, therefore, a *fundamental* transformation affecting all intellectual procedures. Moral conversion is the differentiation of consciousness when we decide on and do *the good*. Religious conversion occurs when one is seized or grasped on all levels by ultimate concern and when one's behavior is correspondingly modified by the internal transformation.[17]

But what does this have to do with the cross-cultural hermeneutic at work with Ricci and the Chinese?

IV

Ricci seems to have undergone a religious conversion accompanied by a degree of intellectual and moral conversion congruent with the religious conversion. Where one begins and the other takes up is probably a question for psychoanalysis or pure guess work. Ricci's thesis to the Chinese that self-cultivation, the primary task in life for a good Chinese, could be attained by worshiping the Lord of Heaven was not a sophist ploy buttressed by quotations from the Chinese classics. Ricci grasped that reputable Christian theology could easily have located self-cultivation as incumbent on all creatures either in Biblical or Patristic sources. But this did not occupy center stage as in Chinese thought. What seems more credible is that Ricci experienced a transformation from the more generally accepted Latin dogmas and practices to what the Chinese considered primary. There began a merging of horizons. Technically, this may be called a dialectic which occurs in encounter.[18]

Dialectic, which Lonergan calls a functional specialty, "adds to the interpretation that understands a further interpretation that appreciates."[19] Obviously this dialectic occurs primarily in encounter and takes place only in the converted. The unconverted will attempt disguised forms of confrontation and forms of dominion. It is not to our point to distinguish the levels of encounter exemplified through the meeting of people or the reading of texts or both. But we may assert, "Encounter is more. It is meeting persons, appreciating the values they represent, criticizing their defects, and allowing one's living to be challenged at its very roots by their words and by their deeds."[20]

Reciprocally, Ricci's Chinese audience saw in Ricci's use of scholastic philosophy the possibility of complementing Confucian thought. To a grasp of meaning had been added appreciation. Thus the merging of horizons was mutual. When we turn more specifically to a consideration of religion and the confrontation of cultures which gave form to the religions, an interesting and modern phenomenon appears. Both parties seem to have grasped that religion is not a series of isolated propositions lifted out of and supported by religious classics and then mediated by certain cultural forms. Nor is religion an idiosyncratic matter of internal personal choice with consequences only for the interior and private life of the individual. Rather, "Because of religion, culture, social organization form a single cogent system in country after country."[21] Religion is belief in some transcendent reality, open to rational scrutiny, with accompanying personal and social behavioral characteristics. In fact, religion creates the style of culture. So could one have a profitable dialectic and genuine encounter.

These are the contours of religion modifying the manner in which Ricci would view religious texts and, correspondingly, the texts establishing and directing his Jesuit Order. Classic religious texts express the religious convictions of their authors and prescribe forms of behavior which should inform the person and subsequently the community. Religion was intrinsically connected with action, with doing. Activities in certain areas produce culture. So the encounter between Ricci and the Chinese was based on comprehending revelatory texts and the actions prescribed by these texts. One thinks immediately of the true and the good. And there are the reminders of Micah 6:8:

> He has showed you, O man,
>   what is good;
>   and what does the Lord require of you
>   but to do justice and to love kindness
>   and to walk humbly with your God.

We have attempted a schematic presentation of a cross-cultural hermeneutic. Literature as such has been in the background. Hopefully we have not ignored the fact that religious texts postulate an encounter and religious literatures and their cultural embodiments offer rich opportunities for dialectic. One such occurrence has occupied our attention. It is unique and at the same time exemplary.

NOTES

1. *Societatis Iesu Constitutiones et Epitome Instituti* (Romae [Rome]: Apud Curiam Praepositi Generalis, 1949) n. 134.
2. *Thesaurus Spiritualis Societatis Iesu* (Romae: Typis Polyglottis Vaticanis, 1948) 417, n. 3.
3. This is very similar to a systems-integration approach.
4. A. L. Kroeber, *Anthropology: Culture Patterns and Processes* (New York: Harcourt, Brace, & World, Inc., 1963) 137.
5. John Edward Sullivan, *Prophets of the West* (New York: Holt, Rinehart and Winston Inc., 1970) 228, quoting Kroeber.
6. What Kroeber has called a "superstyle" is the perceptible pattern of styles within a culture, the whole configuration or constellation of styles. It is not a style which replaces a prior style.
7. Cf. Wolfgang Roth, "Scriptural Coding in the Fourth Gospel," *Biblical Research* 23 (1987): 6-29. Also, Northrop Frye, *The Great Code: The Bible and Literature* (New York: Harcourt Brace Jovanovich, 1982).
8. Jonathan Spence, *To Change China: Western Advisers in China 1620-1960* (Boston: Little, Brown and Company, 1969) 4.
9. The Lord spoke through Isaiah, saying "new things I do" (Isaiah 42:9). He urged the people to "Sing unto the Lord a new song," (Isaiah 42:10). Yahweh promised to create "new heavens, and a new earth," (Isaiah 65:17). Jeremiah echoed similar sentiments (Jeremiah 31:22; 31:31) and said there would be a new gate (Jeremiah 36:10). Ezekiel spoke of a "new heart and a new spirit"

(Ezekiel 18:31), Paul of a "new creature" (Galatians 6:15), "a new man" (Ephesians 4:24). The last book of the Bible is a monument to ocular, imaginative, and cosmic newness.
10 Cf. P. J. Cahill, "Interpreting Religions," *Religious Studies and Theology* 5.1 (1985): 39-43.
11 Bernard J. F. Lonergan, S.J., *Method in Theology* (New York: Herder and Herder, 1972) 238-246.
12 Lonergan, *Method* 238-246.
13 Ramsey MacMullen, *Christianizing the Roman Empire* (New Haven: Yale UP, 1984).
14 *The Second Century: A Journal of Early Christian Studies* (5/2 Summer 1985/86).
15 Frye 229.
16 Lonergan, *Method* 238; and Bernard J. F. Lonergan, S.J., *Insight: A Study of Human Understanding* (New York: Longmans, Green and Co., 1957).
17 Here I draw on material sent to me by my friend and colleague, Jacob Neusner. Neusner notes that Religious Studies has two enemies: a theology which confines religion to the internal forum with no behavioral consequences and virtually no external visible shape of any consequence; and a secularism which confines the study of religion to the periphery of the great universities, i.e., to divinity schools. Neusner might have added a third category, including administrators who pay reluctant lip service to the study of religions but who do not at all grasp the nature of the enterprise and hence allocate only survival resources.
18 Lonergan, *Method* 247. The category of encounter, used so very casually, had been thematized by Ebner. It was given new meaning by Rudolf Bultmann who wrote of the three primary encounters: with God, with the neighbor, and with the self.
19 Lonergan, *Method* 246.
20 Lonergan, *Method* 246.
21 Jacob Neusner, "Theological Enemies of Religious Studies," unpublished manuscript 003.

ROBERT LOUIS STEVENSON THROUGH A JAPANESE EYE: THE SILKWORM IMAGE IN *LIGHT, WIND, AND DREAMS*

Nobuko Miyama Ochner, University of Hawaii

Hikari to kaze to yume ("Light, Wind, and Dreams"), which was first published in the May 1942 issue of the literary magazine *Bungakkai* ("Literary World"), is the longest narrative written by the modern Japanese writer Nakajima Atsushi (1909-1942).[1] It treats the last four years of the Scottish writer Robert Louis Stevenson's life in Samoa. Because of favorable critical reception, during the summer 1942 this work was considered for the Akutagawa Ryūnosuke Prize, the most prestigious literary prize awarded to a work of serious fiction by a new writer in Japan. However, for that round of competition, no prize was awarded to any work, a fact which was regretted by the writer Kawabata Yasunari, one of the judges who believed Nakajima's work worthy of the award.[2] Clearly, *Hikari to kaze to yume* is an important work. The narrative was originally titled *Tsushitara no shi* ("The Death of a *Tusitala*" [Samoan: "storyteller"]), but it was retitled at the editor's request when it was published.[3] The work is almost wholly a product of Nakajima's reading and imagination.

Nakajima derived a large part of *Hikari to kaze to yume* from Stevenson's *Vailima Letters* (1895). This collection of letters, which Stevenson wrote to his friend Sidney Colvin in London between November 1890 and October 1894 when he was living at Vailima, Samoa, describes the last few years of Stevenson's life and thought in great detail.[4] Nakajima also used material from Stevenson's other nonfictional writings about the Pacific region, such as *In the South Seas*,[5] a collection of literary sketches of the Marquesas, the Paumotus, and the Gilbert islands, and "A Footnote to History: Eight Years of Trouble in Samoa,"[6] which recounts the troubled colonial rule of Samoa by Germany, Britain, and the United States. Nakajima also used the 1937 biography of Stevenson by Janet Adam Smith,[7] as well as Stevenson's ideas expressed in several of his essays.[8] Nakajima read these works between September 1940 and June 1941. He selected parts of these materials, and then rearranged and blended them to depict a slightly fictionalized portrait of Stevenson. In twenty chapters, he used alternately the first-person narration in diary form and the third-person narration, to portray Stevenson both from the inside and from the outside. The narrative is, therefore, neither completely factual biography nor totally fiction, but rather what the Japanese call *rekishi shōsetsu* ("historical fiction"), which is narrative based on historical events or personages, containing varying degrees of fictionality.[9]

Hikari to kaze to yume is unusual among Japanese literary works of the early 1940s for several reasons. Unlike most contemporaneous narrative fiction, *Hikari to kaze to yume* is not a thinly veiled autobiographical story, but depicts the life of a Western writer in an exotic tropical setting. Nakajima's taste for the exotic may be attributed to his six years' stay in Korea during adolescence, from 1920 to 1926. *Hikari to kaze to yume* is also distinctive in its sympathetic treatment of a Western subject, particularly in the historical context of the time of its publication, May 1942. Japan had plunged into the war in the Pacific against the Allied Forces five months earlier. Naturally, with the exception of the Germans and the Italians, Westerners were regarded with antipathy by the general Japanese public. Yet, as far as the main figure, Stevenson, is concerned, there is little if any antipathy toward or rejection of Western people and ideas in Nakajima's narrative. In fact, the work displays a surprisingly high degree of sympathy for, and at times even empathy with, Stevenson. Any anti-Western sentiment expressed in this work concerns the specific ills of greed and injustice on the part of some colonial administrators in Samoa, and does not extend to a general condemnation of the Western presence there.

The narrative also expresses Nakajima's strong admiration for Stevenson's courage as a Western writer who, despite suffering recurrent lung hemorrhages from tuberculosis, tries his utmost to help the Samoans in their unsuccessful independence movement. Nakajima evidently saw in Stevenson significant similarities to himself. For instance, both had chronic respiratory illnesses. Nakajima had developed asthma at the age of seventeen, suffering recurrent attacks every winter; in 1934 he became critically ill from it; and eight years later he died of asthmatic heart failure at age thirty-three. Stevenson was a virtual invalid who was able to survive only in the tropical climate of Samoa; even Hawaii had been too cold for him. Thus, Nakajima discovered in Stevenson a man who, like himself, had an almost constant sense of living in proximity to death. Nakajima's reading of Stevenson also inspired him to go to a tropical climate to avoid asthma attacks; in 1941 he resigned from his teaching position and moved to Palau, Micronesia, one of the islands mandated to Japan by the League of Nations. He worked at the *Nan'yōchō* ("South Seas Government," the Japanese territorial administration in Palau) from July 1941 to March 1942 as a clerk in charge of Japanese language textbook compilation.

Nakajima admired the fact that Stevenson had not been hindered by his precarious health from active involvement with the people around him, especially the Samoans. In his efforts to bring about peace and fair government, Stevenson met with colonial administrators, leading white residents, and the two Samoan leaders—the nominal king, Laupepa, who was controlled by the colonists, and the contender, Mataafa, who truly enjoyed the support of his people. Stevenson wrote letters to newspapers abroad, such as the London *Times*, in order to expose the injustice and avarice of the colonists and to effect a change through public pressure.

Concurrently with his efforts as a man of action in helping the Samoans to achieve fair and equitable treatment, Stevenson assiduously pursued his literary career, partly to support his family and the growing number of hangers-on in his role as the "clan chief" at Vailima. During his stay in Samoa he produced several short stories, novels, travel sketches, poems, and other writings. Thus,

Stevenson's life was a model for Nakajima, who, burdened with poor health and having yearned since adolescence for a life devoted to writing, lacked the self-confidence to launch a literary career and needed to work as a teacher to support his family.

Nakajima also found another similarity between himself and Stevenson: the strong power of sympathetic imagination—an ability to put oneself in someone else's position. This quality enabled Stevenson to treat the Pacific islanders in a realistic and understanding manner, as is evidenced in literary sketches such as *In the South Seas* and short stories and novellas such as *The Beach of Falesá*.[10] Nakajima amply exhibits a similar ability in his treatment of Stevenson in *Hikari to kaze to yume*.

In giving an account of Stevenson's life, Nakajima was, on the whole, faithful to his sources; however, in descriptions of Stevenson's inner life Nakajima projected on to Stevenson's character much of his own thoughts and emotions, his self-doubt and desire to break away from an enervating spiritual paralysis. Throughout the narrative Stevenson is depicted as struggling with recurrent self-doubt regarding his achievement as a writer. This is emphasized particularly in connection with the writing of the novel *The Ebb-Tide*. Stevenson is described as being so dissatisfied with this work that he cannot bear to read it after it is completed. Admittedly, Stevenson in real life had difficulties with this novel, which he wrote in collaboration with his stepson Lloyd Osbourne, but his evaluation of the work was not so consistently negative as Nakajima would have us believe. Sometimes Stevenson called the novel "grim," "grimy," and "hateful," but after its completion he stated in a letter to Colvin, "I did not dream it was near as good; I am afraid I think it excellent."[11] Thus we see that Nakajima misrepresented Stevenson's opinion of *The Ebb-Tide* in order to portray an author whose ebb-tide of creative energy closely paralleled his waning health and the negative outcome of the Samoan civil war.

When the rebellious Samoan chiefs were imprisoned after their failed uprising, Stevenson expressed open support for them: making a formal visit to them in prison, sending a physician to treat them, posting bail, and so on. Upon their release, to express their gratitude, they voluntarily built a road for Stevenson. In the Samoa of those days, road construction was the most hated work. Therefore, the gesture exemplifies the affection and gratitude that the Samoans felt for their *tusitala* ("storyteller"). When Stevenson died suddenly from a cerebral hemorrhage, in accordance with his wishes, he was buried on the summit of a nearby mountain. The Samoans voluntarily cleared the mountain path and carried his coffin up the mountain. Nakajima's narrative recounts these events and ends with a quietly moving funeral scene, embellished from his imagination. An elderly Samoan chief, in tears, murmurs, "*Tofa, tusitala!*" ("Sleep, storyteller!").[12] Thus, as a man of action, Stevenson is depicted as having accomplished a significant task and forged meaning from his life.

Stevenson's life as a man of action, however, comprises only half of his life. The other, and probably more important, half is his life as a writer. Stevenson had an almost religious devotion to the vocation of writing, and could hardly pass a day without writing; even during serious illness, he would dictate from his bed. Nakajima compares this attitude in Stevenson to a wager against death: "Before the cold hand of death catches him, how much of this beautiful 'fabric of words and imagination' can he weave?"[13] Despite such single-minded dedication to his craft, toward the end of his life Stevenson began to suffer from a physical and emotional exhaustion, thinking that he had already lived too long. A decade earlier, he had fallen seriously ill in California, yet had persevered because he had wanted to live long enough to produce a masterpiece. But now, according to his biographer, Smith, Stevenson felt that he had "done all that he was able, and there was little more to live for."[14] Nakajima depicts Stevenson's exhaustion through the use of the silkworm image:

> Have I not lived too long? . . . . I have done all the work that I was able . . . . Ever since my illness made it impossible for me to desire action, life for me came to mean literature only. To create literature—it was neither pleasure nor pain, simply a thing unto itself; therefore, my life was neither happy nor unhappy. I was a silkworm. Just as a silkworm must weave its own cocoon, no matter whether it is happy or unhappy, I simply wove the cocoon of stories with my thread of words. Now, the poor sick silkworm has finally finished weaving its cocoon. There is no longer any purpose for its continuing survival.[15]

This image or metaphor of the writer as silkworm is absent in Stevenson's own writings; it is Nakajima's invention, a product of his Japanese sensibility. It functions as an important thematic device throughout Nakajima's text.

Although some critics have mentioned Nakajima's use of the silkworm image as a metaphor for the writer,[16] no critic has yet pointed out the subtle way in which Nakajima develops the silkworm theme not only as a metaphor for the writer's industriousness and devotion to his work but as a symbol of his spiritual transformation. Following the comparison of Stevenson to a silkworm, Nakajima suggests a way for Stevenson to end his predicament: "A friend of mine said, 'There is a purpose! The silkworm shall transform itself, become a moth, eat through the cocoon, and fly out!'"[17] Stevenson wonders if he has enough spiritual and physical strength left to "eat through the cocoon." Three chapters earlier, in his account of the aftermath of the Samoan civil war, Nakajima describes a Samoan folk belief concerning spirits:

> A kinswoman of someone killed in a war goes to the place of death and spreads a mat on the ground. A butterfly or some other insect comes and alights on the mat. She brushes it away. But it comes back. Again she brushes it away. When it returns for the third time, she regards it as the spirit of the one who died there. The woman then carefully catches the insect, takes it home, and offers it prayers.[18]

Although the folk belief is derived from Stevenson's description in the sketch *In the South Seas*, in the original version it is not "a butterfly or some other insect" but "any living thing" that comes three times which can be regarded as the spirit of the dead.[19] Nakajima's decision to use a butterfly as the embodiment of the spirit of the dead appears to have been motivated by a desire to link the Samoan belief with his silkworm theme through the biological similarities of moths and butterflies; the fact, for example, that both spin cocoons from which they later emerge transformed.[20] Later, when Stevenson's life is drawing to an end, Nakajima once again builds on the transformative aspect of his silkworm theme when he describes Stevenson as writing in his diary: "I mustn't be afraid. I am sure I have the courage. Without fear, I must greet the change that is happening to me. For the chrysalis to become a moth and fly, it must ruthlessly eat through the beautiful cocoon that it has woven up to now."[21]

In this context, the image of the butterfly at Stevenson's funeral, which comprises the final scene of *Hikari to kaze to yume*, acquires a symbolic significance. Again, the butterfly is Nakajima's invention; Smith's biography has no such reference. Nakajima describes the funeral scene as follows: "The congregation silently hung their heads in the hot air filled with an almost stiflingly strong scent of citrons. Upon the pure white petal of the lilies which covered the graveside, a large velvety black swallowtail was resting its wings and breathing . . . "[22] Clearly, the butterfly symbolizes Stevenson's spirit, which has achieved its symbolic transformation. Stevenson, the writer-silkworm, has woven a cocoon of stories with his thread of words, and then he has broken through the cocoon, which was encasing and limiting him. Nakajima describes this spiritual transformation as having occurred shortly before Stevenson's death: at gray dawn, Stevenson stands upon a hill, bracing himself against the strong wind and rain; he thinks, "I want to throw myself at something fierce, violent, and stormy. And by so doing, I want to smash the shell which is encasing and limiting me."[23] Then he sees the most colorful and glorious sunrise he has ever seen; this "miracle" of nature's transformation prompts him to feel that the "night" within him has fled at long last; he returns home triumphant. Having achieved such a transformation, his body, the physical husk of his spirit, falls in death. However, as in the Samoan belief, his spirit, in the form of a butterfly which has achieved its physical transformation, rests at his grave, the place of death. Moreover, the butterfly may be considered both a symbol and a manifestation of Stevenson's triumph, which ironically was achieved by his death.

The original title of this work, *Tsushitara no shi* ("The Death of a Tusitala"), is indeed significant in this sense. Stevenson, who had dedicated his life to literature, is thus poetically rewarded in death by Nakajima. The double triumph, as a writer and as a man of action, thus lends a bright, reassuring quality to this narrative. The silkworm image which Nakajima incorporated into *Hikari to kaze to yume* thus functions as an important thematic device which enhances the artistic unity of this Japanese portrait of Stevenson.

NOTES

1 I wish to thank the Research Relations Fund of the University of Hawaii for providing assistance that enabled me to conduct research for this article. Japanese names are given in the usual Japanese order, with surname preceding the given name. Page references to Nakajima's works follow the definitive edition, Nakamura Mitsuo et al., eds., *Nakajima Atsushi zenshū* [Collected Works of Nakajima Atsushi], 3 vols. (Tokyo: Chikuma Shobō, 1976), hereafter cited as *NAZ; Hikari to kaze to yume,* Nakajima's longest narrative, comprises 116 pages of the first volume of *NAZ.* The literary journal *Bungakkai* has been in existence since 1933, except for a hiatus (1944-1947) at the end of World War II; it was Japan's leading coterie journal at Nakajima's time. *Hikari to kaze to yume* has been translated into English by Miwa Akira, as *Light, Wind, and Dreams: An Interpretation of the Life and Mind of Robert Louis Stevenson* (Tokyo: The Hokuseidō Press, 1962). Miwa's translation is generally faithful to the original; however, it contains a number of relatively serious mistranslations: for instance, a transliterated foreign term "dēmon," which represents "daemon," a word of Latin origin meaning "divinity or spirit," is rendered by Miwa as Damien, the Catholic priest who sacrificed his life for the lepers of Hawaii (Miwa 104). The translation also contains some lapses in style and inappropriate choices of words. Therefore, unless otherwise noted, all translations of *Hikari to kaze to yume* and other Japanese sources in this study are my own.

2 Kawabata Yasunari stated that he could not believe that neither of the two works he considered the best, i.e., "Matsukaze" ("Wind among Pines") and *Hikari to kaze to yume,* received the Akutagawa Prize, even though he was aware of the precedent for no awards being given. See "Dai jūgokai Akutagawa shō sempyō" [Judges' Comments on the Fifteenth Akutagawa Prize Selection], reprinted in Nakamura Mitsuo et al, eds., *Nakajima Atsushi kenkyū* [Studies on Nakajima Atsushi] (Tokyo: Chikuma Shobō, 1978) 310; originally published in the magazine *Bungei shunjū* (Sept. 1942).

3 Ono Senzō, an editor of *Bungakkai,* wrote to Nakajima on April 8, 1942, asking him to change the title from *Tsushitara no shi* ("The Death of a Tusitala") to one that was more "abstract" and did not give away the content of the narrative; see *NAZ,* III, 747.

4 Robert Louis Stevenson, *Vailima Letters: Being Correspondence Addressed by Robert Louis Stevenson to Sidney Colvin, November 1890-October 1894* (London: Methuen, 1895).

5 Stevenson, *In the South Seas: Being an Account of Experiences and Observations in the Marquesas, Paumotus and Gilbert Islands in the Course of Two Cruises, on the Yacht 'Casco' (1888) and the Schooner 'Equator' (1889)* (London: Chatto & Windus, 1900).

6 Stevenson, "A Footnote to History: Eight Years of Trouble in Samoa," in *Vailima Papers and A Footnote to History* (New York: Scribner's, 1925); "Footnote" was originally published simultaneously by Scribner's and Cassell in July 1892.

7 Janet Adam Smith, *R. L. Stevenson* (London: The Camelot Press, 1937). A copy of Smith's biography remains in Nakajima's personal library, cf. Nihon Daigaku Hōgakubu Toshokan, comp., *Nakajima Atsushi Bunko mokuroku*

[Catalogue of the Holdings in the Nakajima Atsushi Library] (Tokyo: Nihon Daigaku Hōgakubu Toshokan, 1980) 16.

8 For example, Stevenson, *Virginibus Puerisque; Familiar Studies of Men and Books*, Everyman's Library (London: Dent, 1925), and *Memories and Portraits* (New York: Scribner's, 1900). Both titles are in Nakajima's personal library.

9 The term *rekishi shōsetsu* is used, for instance, by the critic Yamamoto Kenkichi in "Denki to rekishi shōsetsu," his discussion of *Hikari to Kaze to Yume*, collected in Nakamura Mitsuo et al., eds., *Nakajima Atsushi kenkyū* 104-115.

10 *The Beach of Falesá*, for instance, treats such subject matter as white men's exploitation of the natives of Samoa, both economically, as in the case of Chase who monopolizes trading on the island, and sexually, as in the case of Wiltshire who makes a Samoan girl his mistress through the use of forged marriage license. Stevenson's stance is realistic with no attempt at romanticizing or making excuses for the Europeans' conduct, even in the early published text, which is described as "mutilated and corrupted" to suit the Victorian sensibility, in Barry Menikoff, *Robert Louis Stevenson and 'The Beach of Falesá': A Study in Victorian Publishing* (Stanford: Stanford UP, 1984) 5.

11 Stevenson, *Vailima Letters* 274, 322.

12 *NAZ*, I, 288. The Samoan chief's farewell itself seems to have been derived from Sagara Jirō, *Sutiivunsun* [Stevenson] (Tokyo: Kenkyūsha, 1938) 162; this is pointed out by Tanabe Yukinobu in "*Hikari to Kaze to yume* ni okeru Sutiivunsun" [Stevenson in *Light, Wind, and Dreams*], Geijutsugaku 8 (1964): 18. Nevertheless, the other details of the funeral scene can be credited to Nakajima.

13 *NAZ*, I, 226.

14 Smith 136.

15 *NAZ*, I, 266-267.

16 Iwata Kazuo, "*Hikari to kaze to yume* ni tsuite" [On *Light, Wind, and Dreams*], *Kajii Motojirō; Nakajima Atsushi*, ed. by Nihon Bungaku Kenkyū Shiryō Kankōkai (Tokyo: Yūseidō, 1978) 226-234; Tanabe 2-25.

17 *NAZ*, I, 267.

18 *NAZ*, I, 249.

19 Stevenson, *In the South Seas* 197.

20 *Nihon kokugo daijiten* [Dictionary of the Japanese Language] (Tokyo: Shōgakukan, 1975), Vol. 18, for instance, lists the expressions "mayu no ga" ("a moth newly emerged from its cocoon") and "mayu no chō" ("a butterfly newly emerged from its cocoon") 439.

21 *NAZ*, I, 281.

22 *NAZ*, I, 288.

23 *NAZ*, I, 286.

INTERTEXTUALITY AND THE PROBLEM OF TRANSLATION: A STUDY OF TWO TRANSLATIONS OF PAUL VERLAINE'S "CHANSON D'AUTOMNE"

Jean Yamasaki Toyama, University of Hawaii

In their comparison of the styles of translation of Ueda Bin and Horiguchi Daigaku Japanese critics are apt to describe the strategy of the former as an effort to "naturalize" the text, whereas that of the latter, a desire to retain the flavor of the original. "Unlike Ueda Bin, who attempted to 'Japanize' the original poems by employing poetic conceptions already existing in Japanese literature, Horiguchi made the Japanese language fit the images in the original poems. For this reason, he produced simple and witty lines of poetry, employing the language of everyday speech, a language which had never before been considered poetic."[1]

In spite of claims of great difference between their strategies of translation, a cursory reading of their versions of Verlaine's "Chanson d'automne" seems to belie this assertion.[2] Both translations appear very classical, containing the conventions of a 900-year-old poetic tradition. Both use classical particles and suffixes, tend to nominalize verbs, and repeat the classical diction reserved for the thirty-one-syllable *tanka*. Is this an exception to the generalization? No. Even in their apparently similar approaches to "Chanson d'automne" their real difference is quantifiable. All texts, not only translations, must be rendered readable; that is, made to fit into the mosaic of already existing texts in order to correspond with the cultural discourse. Ueda's effort to Japanize or *tatamiser*, as the French would say, the text is a naturalization process that brings the text in relation to other texts within his own literary discourse.[3] One might say that Ueda Bin takes into account the intertextual nature of literature, unlike the translators of the first collection of Western verse in Japanese translation, *Shintaishishō* ("Selection of Poetry in the New Style"), an 1882 work which was criticized as "vulgar," "most strange," and "crude to the extreme."[4]

Japanese poetic tradition like all literary traditions depends on intertextuality but of a different variety.[5] In contrast to Western literary traditions that prize originality, Japanese poetics valorizes conformity to convention. This explains to some extent why the literary codes (which are essential parts of the intertext) practiced in the Heian era were the very ones exercised hundreds of years later in the Meiji era of Ueda Bin and the following Taishō era of Horiguchi Daigaku. Indeed, they are still today actively exploited by writers of *tanka*. These conventions allow only words of Japanese origin, a limited classical vocabulary, and the strict syllabic scheme of 5-7-5-7-7. There are other conventions that dictate the choice of images for certain seasons. Thus, autumn, one of the most common nature subjects, perforce evokes references to the flowering of chrysanthemums, the falling of maple leaves, the milky way, the moon, quail, dew, the seven flowers of autumn, etc. But the choice of images was limited; for example, to mention a flower which bloomed in the autumn but was not part of the traditional literary discourse for that season would seem odd indeed.

The classical use of intertextuality goes even further. While scholars of Western literature must first discover the intertexts of works and then convince their peers that they have found the "right" one,[6] Japanese intertexts or *lexie* (an actual line of recycled verse)[7] are easily recognizable because they are not hidden. A respected poetic practice called *honkadori*[8] involves the use of *lexie* of other poems as the initial line of a new poem. The poet's purpose is to breathe new life into a fragment of the existing poetic discourse.

The difference between the translation strategies of Ueda and Horiguchi lies in their varied uses of *lexie* and the general intertext. Ueda's style is guided by his understanding of French Symbolist poetry, which he explains as the attempt "to help create in the reader a mental state similar to that in the poet's mind. Symbols do not necessarily communicate the same meanings to everyone. . . . The essential thing is that a similar mental state be evoked."[9] The Symbolist endeavor to evoke feelings through symbols corresponds closely to Japanese poetic practice. Meaning in Japanese poetry is secondary; it is the power of the poem to provoke feelings that counts. A *tanka* functions as a means to organize subjectivity, a management of sensibility.[10] For example, it is said that "with the *Shin-Kokinshū* (1205) of the Kamakura period, we find that the emotional meaning of certain seasonal objects is so well understood that in successful *tanka* the object can stand alone, without explanatory remarks by the writer."[11] What better way to duplicate the feelings kindled by "Chanson d'automne" than to use lines of Japanese poetry that incite those very feelings.

By consulting the *Kokka taikan*, a compendium of *tanka* written between 905-1433, one can easily determine which lines of the translations are actually lines of previously composed verse.[12]

Since Horiguchi's objective in translation was to retain the language of the original, one would not expect many *lexie* in his version. In fact, he uses only one exact *lexie*, "aki kaze no" ("the autumn wind's") (Ll). However, this very line occurs 102 times in the *Kokka taikan*. Of all the *lexie* used in both translations this one dominates. Ueda's lexie for the same Verlaine line "de l'automne," "aki no hi no" ("the autumn day's") (Ll) appears in this form only five times. However, Ueda has recourse to exact *lexie* six more times than Horiguchi. These vary in number of appearances and variants. For example, "mi ni shimite" (L4), which closely resembles Verlaine's "blessent mon coeur," appears 13 times but also has hundreds of variants. This line also appears in conjunction with autumn and the wind. His "ura kanashii" ("sad to the core") (L6), appears only twice with 14 variants. Ueda's other lines in this category are "hitaburi ni" ("single-mindedly") (L5) 1 exact, 8 variants; "kane no oto ni" ("at the gong's sound") (L7) 13 exact, 24 variants; "iro kaete" ("color changed") (L9) 3 exact, 2 variants; and "ura burete" ("down-trodden") (L14) 7 exact.

Interlinear Translations

Chanson d'automne (Verlaine)
Autumn Song (Toyama)
Raku yō (Ueda)
Aki no uta (Horiguchi)

L1
Les sanglots longs
The long sobs
aki no hi no   (Ueda)
aki kaze no   (Horiguchi)

L2
Des violons
of the violins
vioron no
vioron no

L3
De l'automne
of autumn
tameiki no
fushi nagaki
  susurinaki

L4
Blessent mon coeur
Pierce my heart
mi ni shimite
monouki kanashimi ni

L5
D'une langueur
with a monotonous
hitaburu ni
waga tamashii o

L6
Monotone.
languor.
ura kanashi.
itamashimu.

L7
Tout suffocant
All suffocating
kane no oto ni
toki no kane

L8
Et bleme, quand
and pale, when
mune futagi
nari mo izureba

L9
Sonne l'heure
the hour sounds
iro kaete
setsunaku mo
  mune semari

L10
Je me souviens
I remember
namida gumu
omoi zo izuru

L11
Des jours anciens
days gone by
sugishi hi no
(waga) koshikata ni

L12
Et je pleure;
and I cry
omoideya.
namida wa waku.

L13
Et je m'en vais
And I leave
ge ni ware wa
ochiba narane

L14
Au vent mauvais
with the ill wind
uraburete
mi oba yaru

L15
Qui m'emporte
that blows me
koko kashiko
ware mo,

L16
Deça, delà
Here and there
Sadame naku
kanata konata

L17
Pareille à la
just like
tobichiro
fukimakure

L18
Feuille morte.
a dead leaf.
ochiba kana.
saka kaze yo.

It is clear, in this category at least, that Ueda purposefully exploited the intertext. In the category of uses of variations of *lexie* (by "variations" I mean lines of verse similar to *lexie* plus the variants of that *lexie*), Horiguchi has a slight edge with nine to Ueda's seven. Here again, the number of appearances differs sharply. For example, Ueda's "omoideya" ("remembering is") (L12) appears as "omoideyo" (8 times) and "omoidekana" (18 times) in the *Kokka taikan*. Both suffixes function like the exclamatory particle *ya*. Although the exact *lexie* is lacking, there are hundreds of variants on the theme of remembrance. His "koko kashiko" ("here to there") (L15) appears once with the concessive conjunction *tomo* added. On the other hand, Horiguchi's variation "namida wa waku" ("tears well up") (L12), like his single exact *lexie* "aki kaze no," has hundreds of variants, some of which are linked to autumn.

While Horiguchi might not use the greatest number of lexie, the ones that he does resort to dominate the poetic discourse. It may be for this reason that his translation still has the capacity to provoke classical, poetic feelings. Whether these choices represent a conscious effort to exploit the intertext is not known. It is interesting to note, however, that in Horiguchi's rewrite of his translation he changed the conventional five-syllable line of "aki kaze no" to "aki no," which, because it contains only three syllables, could never have been a line of a *tanka*. Was he trying to create distance between his translation and the classical intertext?

The other variations for Ueda are: L3, L10, L13, L16 and L17. For Horiguchi: L3, L4, L5, L10, L11, L13, L15, and L16. Based on the use of exact *lexie* and variations of *lexie*, one might arrive at a Japanizing quotient of 14 for Ueda (7 + 7) and 10 for Horiguchi (1 + 9). Up to this point the difference does not seem that great. However, subtracting the instances of the disuse of lexie from the instances of the use of lexie Ueda (14 - 4) would still have ten, while Horiguchi (10 - 8) would be left with only two.

Of the lines in which there exists neither lexie nor variant in the classical poetic discourse, the most unusual is "vioron no" (L2), which occurs in both translations. Because it refers to a Western musical instrument, it would not appear in a classical poem, even if by chance a violin had been imported and become familiar to the culture; foreign loan words are not tolerated in *tanka*. To the Japanese of today "vioron no" still elicits a certain exoticism because *baiorin*, which is derived from the English word for the instrument, is the normal Japanese rendering rather than "vioron," which comes from the French *violon*. Of Ueda's three other lines "mune futagi" ("the heart constrained") (L8) and "sugishi hi no" ("of days passed") (L11) both are in the classical non-active verbal form, while "ochiba kana" ("fallen leaf is") (L18) ends with a classical copula. Thus we see that Ueda's non-lexical lines still are part of the classical intertext, since they conform to the poetic code.

A few of Horiguchi's lines depart more from classical, literary diction: "toki no kane" ("time's gong") (L7) is more pedestrian than Ueda's "kane no oto ni," which is an exact *lexie*. Also, the descriptive words in "setsunaku mo mune semari" ("oppressive, suffocating, tightening heart") (L9) are not part of the classical vocabulary.

Thus, it is not necessary to manipulate numbers in order to assert that there is a marked difference in the translating strategies of the two. Moreover, consider another aspect of the intertext: the code of poetic form.

The most glaring difference between the translations lies in prosody. Needless to say, both are audacious in departing from the strict 5-7-5-7-7 scheme. However, the degree of their departure differs. Although Ueda's use of a succession of only five-syllable lines with one six-syllable substitution is daring, the five-syllable line and its substitute are completely within the authorized canon; it would not fall queerly on the Japanese ear. Horiguchi, however, uses only eight five-syllable lines with three six-syllable substitutions and three seven-syllable lines, the other accepted length. The rest are quite foreign. One could argue that the two ten-syllable lines could be halved and still remain orthodox; in fact, such a length is acceptable in Noh verse. However, the nine and three-syllable lines have no counterpart in Japanese poetry. All together, the very irregular combination of 3-5-6-7-9-10 syllable lines in and of itself is an unorthodox innovation. Since prosodic matters, being part of the poetic code, are very much an element of the intertext, such differences would greatly diminish Horiguchi's Japanizing quotient.

This is not to say that Ueda has completely Japanized Verlaine. His insertion of an obviously foreign element, "vioron no," between two classical lines "aki no hi no" ("the autumn day's") and "tameiki no" ("the sob's") must have seemed an intrepid, if not revolutionary, act to readers of 1905, the year of its publication. Then, too, the combination of so many familiar *lexie* in a succession of five-syllable lines must have revitalized a somewhat stagnant tradition, creating a new sensation with old feelings. However, he attenuated what could have been culture shock through a more active cultivation of the literary intertext. Twenty years later, in 1925, Horiguchi's version appeared. With the benefit of assimilation, Verlaine must not have seemed that strange in his hands. The reader had been prepared.

Because of the remarkable resemblances between the original poem and the Japanese classical poetic tradition, the intertextual strategies of both Ueda and Horiguchi do not seem to do any real violence to Verlaine. By capturing the sentimental simplicity of the autumnal images, both were able to fit their versions of his poem into their own literary discourse.[13] However, if, as Barthes says, literature is society's way to institutionalize subjectivity, does the Japanese intertext function as the French one does? In other words, does Verlaine's original affect the French reader in the same way as the translations affect the Japanese reader? Is the intertextual play of texts comparable?

As the study of the act of reading centers more and more on the interaction between the text and the reader and by extension other texts, the question of the possibility of "accurate" translation becomes more and more moot. If reading in fact is more what is brought *to* the text and not what is contained *in* the text, how much more complicated becomes the enterprise of translation!

NOTES

1. Watanabe Kazutami, translated and quoted by Donald Keene, *Dawn to the West*, vol. II (New York: Holt, Rinehart and Winston, 1984) 260. Watanabe's original article "Gekka no ichigun," appeared in *Hon no techō* 4.8 (Oct. 1964): 640-644.
2. A romanized version of the two translations along with Verlaine's original and a literal English version are provided on page 67 for easy comparison. The L(for *lexie*) and number refer to sections discussed in the text.
3. Jonathan Culler writes, "To naturalize a text is to bring it into relation with a type of discourse or model which is already, in some sense, natural and legible." *Structuralist Poetics* (New York: Cornell UP, 1975) 138.
4. Okazaki Yoshie, *Japanese Literature in the Meiji Era*, V. H. Viglielmo, trans. and adaptor (Japan: Obunsha, 1955) 318.
5. By "intertextuality" I mean "the relation of a particular text to other texts," *Structuralist Poetics* 139.
6. Consider Michael Riffaterre's efforts to ferret out the clichés embedded in the poems he explicates. *Semiotics of Poetry* (Bloomington & London: Indiana UP, 1978) 5.
7. I have adopted and adapted Roland Barthes' term as explained by Todorov and Ducrot: "Plutôt que la *phrase* ou le *mot*, unités linguistiques dont la pertinence discursive est incertaine, on s'orientera vers la *lexie*, unité de lecture qui, comme l'écrit R. Barthes, 'comprendra tantôt peu de mots, tantôt quelques phrases'; elle est définie comme 'le meilleur espace possible où l'on puisse observer les sens'. Les dimensions de la lexie seront donc fonction du type de lecture adoptée. L'analyse *lexique* s'apparente d'une part à celle de la *sonorité*, du *rythme*, des structures grammaticales ou stylistiques, dans la mesure où elle s'attache à l'aspect verbal du texte, aux formes linguistiques présentes; d'autre part, elle touche à l'analyse *narrative* et *thématique* puisqu'elle a trait au sens" in the *Dictionnaire encyclopédique des sciences du langage* (Paris: Editions du Seuil, 1972) 280.
8. I am grateful to Professor Robert Huey for indicating this convention to me. And also for his generous help.
9. Translated and quoted by Keene in *Dawn to the West* 228.
10. Roland Barthes explains the function of literature as society's effort to "institutionalize subjectivity." We are never the origin of our own subjectivity but reflect society's effort to define us as subjective beings. *Sur Racine* (Paris: Editions du Seuil, 1963).
11. Kenneth Yasuda, *The Japanese Haiku* (Rutland & Tokyo: Charles E. Tuttle Company, 1957) 147.
12. Matsushita Daizaburō and Watanabe Fumio, *Kokka taikan* (Tokyo: Kyōbunsha, 1903).
13. It is tempting to speculate about a previous intertextual encounter between France and Japan, but the records show that the first translation of Japanese poetry appeared in 1871 with Leon de Rosny's *Anthologie Japonaise*. Verlaine's "Chanson d'automne" dates from 1867. Although intriguing, there is no evidence that Japanese poetry influenced the symbolist movement in France. Leonard Schwartz, *The Imaginative Interpretation of the Far East in Modern French Literature 1800-1925* (Paris: Librairie Ancienne Honoré Champion, 1927).

III. EAST COMES WEST

EAST-WEST ENCOUNTERS IN BRECHT'S SZECHWAN PLAY

Herbert Knust, University of Illinois at Urbana-Champaign

In the last decade or so, critical studies of the works of Bertolt Brecht have increasingly contributed non-Western perspectives to trends of inquiry long dominated by Western approaches. To a large extent, this new critical attention reflects the expanding relevance of Brecht's theater in non-Western countries,[1] a development illustrated in spectacular form by a sequence of fascinating performances by Chinese, Japanese, Indian and Filipino companies during the last Congress of the International Brecht Society in Hong Kong.[2] To a considerable extent, however, new investigations were also prompted by the awareness that Brecht was not only a great playwright of international appeal, but also one of the most "Oriented" Occidental writers of his time, judging by the extent and variety of the Asian (especially Chinese) component in his work. Thus a number of scholars have taken Brecht's Sinophilia for more than mere exoticism or chinoiserie, and have thoroughly explored Brecht's interest in—and use of—Oriental philosophy, literature, and acting style.[3] Such cross-cultural studies are at their comparative best when they not only show that certain materials were taken over into an authentic work of art, but when they also reveal how intricately and to what purpose influences from different traditions were blended into the creative process. To illustrate this point, let me pursue a discussion on the interplay of Western and Eastern elements in *The Good Person of Szechwan* in the hope of taking the argument one step further.[4]

There is general agreement that, at first sight, the *Szechwan* play appears to be the most "Chinese" of Brecht's theater experiments. Setting and milieu, names, theatrical devices such as the characters' self-introduction, the use of song as commentary, pantomime, as well as quotations from Chinese poets and philosophers, would seem to contribute to this impression. On closer look, however, Brecht's characteristic mixing of elements becomes equally obvious. European and especially German sources have been located and stand side by side with the Chinese.[5] Even in the gradual genesis of the play this duality can be traced. One of the early plot lines is set in a German milieu, others in a Chinese milieu. One of the "Chinese" versions of the fable is given distinctly Biblical (i. e., Lutheran) expression. Some see in Brecht's first poem on a Chinese motif, "The Song from the Opium Den," the nucleus of the play; others point to the similarity and priority of Nietzsche's famous poem on the futility of life (likened to smoke) which Brecht adapted for his play. Another ambiguity surrounds the "Song of the Eighth Elephant," which, as a borrowing from Kipling, has been claimed as a European element although it develops an Oriental, if not strictly Chinese, motif. The proponents of socio-political topicality have deepened the bilateral argument. Some see significance in the fact that during the extended period of the play's origination, Brecht not only incorporated Chinese motifs from works familiar to him, but that he became quite interested, politically, in the Chinese revolution of the 1920s and in the transformation of the province of Szechwan into a battlefield of the Chinese-Japanese War in the 1930s. Others point to Brecht's intensified study of Marxism and his unceasing attention to the central European situation, i.e., the socio-political problems during Germany's Weimar Republic and the rise of fascism. German critics elaborated these historical references "behind" the plot, such as mass unemployment during inflation, the abuse of technology for capitalist exploitation, the crises of overproduction, the forced labor programs, and the general failure of a "golden legend" identified as the "golden twenties." Yet the spokesmen of the Eastern perspective, doubting that Brecht took China merely as a disguise for European problems but really meant China when he said China, pointed to the practical importance of old Chinese wisdom, which they found reconfirmed by Marxism and developments in Europe; an attitude of cunning passivity combining survival with resistance; the flow of things as dialectic movement; the difficulty of remaining good in a bad society—a problem reflected in Chinese rather than Christian ethics; the disruption of Chinese values of conduct by Western technology and methods of exploitation. Such evidence would certainly suggest that in this case Brecht must have meant China itself, and not just "Chima" as an estranging disguise for Europe.[6] Yet even the advocates of the disguise theory would admit that Brecht apparently wavered all along between the Chinese and the European variant.

But his apparent vacillation between the two options is more likely a skilful balancing act in an attempt to avoid giving priority to either side. After all, the play is Brecht's master parable. Both China and Chima (read "Germany") are "lands in the middle"—but so are the poetic meeting grounds of the parable. Brecht kept the parabolic texture and applicability open quite successfully, as is apparent from the variety of critical responses the play has generated. And it is precisely by taking the Chinese references seriously, by avoiding chinoiserie or mere disguise, that such a balance becomes credible. However, there is still another comparative tack that sheds light on the interaction of Eastern and Western elements in the play. It is a kind of intertextuality best explained by Brecht's major method of adaptation—or what might be more appropriately termed "confrontation." For whenever his interest and spirit of contradiction were sufficiently challenged by a significant work of world literature, he would take issue with it in a work of his own. This is quite obvious in his reworking of Sophocles' *Antigone,* Lenz's *Hofmeister,* Shakespeare's *Coriolanus,* Segher's story of the trial of Jeanne d'Arc at Rouen, Molière's *Don Juan,* and Farquhar's *The Recruiting Officer*—these adaptations form a separate volume in Brecht's collected oeuvre. But it is also apparent that plays such as *The Life of King Edward II, The Threepenny Opera, Saint Joan of the Stockyards, The Mother, Schweyk in World War II,* or *Turandot* are, to a liberal extent, critical confrontations with Marlowe, Gay, Schiller, Gorki, Hašek, and Gozzi (Busoni, Puccini), respectively. Additionally, there are texts, the titles of which do not immediately indicate a remodeling of works of others; nonetheless, Brecht's modernization uses, as he called it, the "material value"[7] of a given work by transposing it to a new setting, but by retaining parallels of structure, motifs, and various details similar to the technique in his more obvious reworking of older subjects. Thus it has been shown that already his early one-act play *The Catch* is a synthetic transformation of both a Homeric episode and a Biblical one;[8] that *Baal* is a vitalistic response to Johst's psychologizing expressionist play *The Solitary*;[9] that *Roundheads and Peakheads* is a class struggle variant of Shakespeare's *Measure for Measure*;[10] that *The Rifles of Señora Carrar* is modelled after Synge's *Riders to the Sea*;[11] that *Puntila and his Man Matti* may be read as a politicized variation of Zuckmayer's *The Merry Vineyard*;[12] that the film script *All Our Yesterdays* is an updated, modernized version of Shakespeare's *Macbeth*;[13] and that even *Life of Galileo*, while using much authentic biographical material, is, at the same time, cast into a secularized analogy to the life of Christ in the gospels.[14] The common denominator of Brecht's variable adaptations, reinterpretations, or creative "vandalism"[15] is, in his own formulation, the concept of "counterplay" (*Gegenentwurf*);[16] which, in a dialectical, progressive sense, aims to historicize, i.e., to "distance" past stages of development, in order to proclaim the changeability of history and of the human condition by bringing social issues critically up-to-date with a view to a better future.

The "counterplay" theory was applied also to the *Szechwan* play, but not with very satisfactory results. Those who point to the "Chinese" plays of Klabund and Wolf which Brecht saw performed in Berlin[17] may, of course, argue that Brecht disagreed with the portrayal of the central character in either of the plays and was challenged enough to give his own version of the abused good prostitute. But he did not need an Oriental introduction to prostitution, which, indeed, constitutes a major theme and metaphor throughout his work. Nor are there sufficient parallels of plot and structure to prove *The Good Person of Szechwan* a "counterplay" to the plays of Klabund and Wolf.

Those who see a "counterplay" to a Biblical scene point out the inversion of two questions:[18] What minimum number of good people must there be so that God will spare the cities of Sodom and Gomorrah? Will there be enough good people (or, at least, one good person) in Szechwan so that the world does not need to be changed? But again, this is just one motif and not a complex structure remodelled by Brecht. Besides, there are several other examples of gods visiting, testing, and judging mankind, both in Oriental and in Western legends,[19] that could more fully profile Brecht's inquisitive gods coming to Szechwan.

The most extensive "counterplay" argument sees in Brecht's Szechwan play an inversion and annulment of Calderon's *El gran teatro del mundo*.[20] As criticism of the whole paradigm of the world theater, orchestrated by God as theater director and as judge of the roles He assigned to human society on the world as stage, Brecht's contradiction points to the dilemma of a world that cannot justly exist by divine precepts but cries out to human judgment for social change. Although this anti-model would address general structure and some motifs,[21] the Calderonian prototype does not account for the more detailed elements in the texture of Brecht's play, and certainly not for its Oriental components.

But there is a play which does precisely that. It is neither a minor work nor a work distant in time or geography. It is a masterwork of world literature which Brecht had seen performed in Berlin and with which he took issue in his diaries. It is a play which in its own way had grappled with the Calderonian paradigm and in doing so had introduced Oriental philosophy and figures. It is the most noteworthy example of a new dream dramaturgy *and* of its author's experimentation with "epic technique." It is, of course, Strindberg's *Dream Play* which, for all the above reasons, drew Brecht's attention and became the most substantial target of his "counterplay" *The Good Person of Szechwan*.

Striking resemblances of plot, structure, and motifs cannot be ignored.[22] In an issue over the relationship between lofty gods and earthbound mankind, a good woman of Oriental appearance—Indra's daughter, child of heaven, and Shen Te, angel of the suburbs, both symbols of love[23]—become divine test objects of the human condition through their involvement in worldly affairs, only to be split apart by the impossibility of combining love with justice and happiness. Indeed, the greatest difficulty in this test of goodness, Strindberg said, is that one is forced to be bad to others if one also wants to live oneself.[24] This is the very problem that Brecht addresses;[25] but where Strindberg waxes metaphysical, Brecht secularizes, materializes, and politicizes the issue, while exposing the gods who in Strindberg still seem a potential source of help.

Brecht, who frequently used the dream motif throughout his work,[26] condemned the escapist drug-dream dramaturgy of emotional theater with its evocation of a false world sadly distorted by wishes and fears. Instead, he brought out the dialectic nature of dreams which reflect an unsatisfactory social reality and provoke an awakening of a rational impulse for change. Reinhardt's performance of Strindberg's *Dream Play* paralyzed Brecht through the smoothness of the dream scenes that were not estranging enough, were without "curve" (i.e., without digression for critical reflection), and hence not provocative enough to shake the viewers awake.[27] And to hear Strindberg say something like "an awakening reconciles the sufferer with reality. For no matter how agonizing real life may be, at this moment, compared with a tormenting dream, it is a pleasure,"[28] meant to Brecht that advanced dream dramaturgy was wasted on joyous, pain-embracing philosophy. So he responded with a dream technique of his own. He turned Strindberg's conclusion upside down and presented a harsh awakening from the "golden legend," one which was activated by the epilogue's call to wakefulness: an appeal not to the gods, but to the viewers as judges and helpers in the quest for answers to those questions left open.

The epilogue is of course not the only "epic" device. In contradistinction to Strindberg's superior narrator, in whose unifying consciousness "anything can happen; everything is possible and probable," without "incongruities, scruples or laws," and whose dreams therefore are an indiscriminate fusion of "reality, imagination . . . memories, experiences, unfettered fancies, absurdities and improvisations,"[29] Brecht projects the poor, abused water-carrier Wang as continuous narrator, whose dream sequence in five interludes, interrupting the action, functions as a progressively distancing commentary which questions and criticizes the gods' precepts as incompatible with the actual conditions of life. Through these dreams, and the parabolic dreams within the dreams, Wang's critical curiosity is heightened, and the play's problems are reflected in terms of social ethics. As Shen Te's affliction materializes and grows,[30] the battered and demoralized gods retreat and vanish. Thus Strindberg's dreams within a dreamplay which (in the dialogue's between the Poet and Indra's Daughter) are meant to signify a poetic transcendence of a reality of conflicts, are also answered by Brecht's rationalizing dream dramaturgy, which does not draw spiritual promise from the tortures of life but inverts this dialectic by a strategy of secular reasoning.

And here again the Chinese element becomes part of the counterplay. Among the focal points of the juxtaposition of dream scenes are the cave episodes. In Fingal's cavern, shaped in the form of Indra's ear, are channeled all human laments written in the poet's script but conveyed by heart through the dreamer's invocation to the Lord of Heaven. Characteristically, Brecht transforms this cavern of lament into a culvert of an underground canal from which Wang communicates his deep concerns to the gods above. This too is projected through a dream; not reading from the book in his lap but reciting by heart from an imaginary script. Within the parallel contexts, Strindberg's fusion of Christian and Hindu visions of redemption is countered by Brecht's use of a Chinese anti-spiritualist parable on "the penalty for usefulness,"[31] which, applied to Shen Te's dilemma, holds out self-preservation against complete surrender, thus disagreeing with the god's severe (and un-Chinese) dictum "Suffering purifies."[32]

Another case in point is Strindberg's leitmotif of the mysterious door behind which is sought the secret of existence. It finds its counterpart in Brecht's entry to the hidden compartment where Shen Te secretly changes into Shui Ta (and vice versa) to solve existential (i.e., economic) problems. In both cases the forced entry reveals nothing, and the indicted victims must answer the world riddle. But where the parable told by Indra's daughter explains the "nothing" in terms of illusion caused by the fall of the divine spirit Brahma to the seductive Earthmother Maya, Shen Te identifies the "nothing" (or, more accurately, the "kein Mensch"[33]) by her own terrible, "inhuman" fall from "wahre Liebe" to "Ware Liebe"[34] in a prostituted world that has been proven an illusion, a falsity of the gods, very much in need of deliverance. If Indra's Daughter embodies the seduction of Divinity by a problematic World, Shen Te embodies the seduction of the World by a problematic Divinity.

Accordingly, Strindberg's and Brecht's notions of deliverance represent opposites. Indra's Daughter can escape back to higher regions by dying to this illusory world, in which she played a human role as best she could. Here Christian and Hindu thought would seem to merge. Strindberg's funeral pyre, the burning castle, and the budding Chrysanthemum bring home the message of spirituality released from suffering. But Shen Te, who is a mortal, cannot simply fly away with the gods who have deserted an all-too-real world.[35] She is left in the nightmare. Brecht parodied the symbolism of the Chrysanthemum and the growing castle of imprisonment to highlight the meeting of capitalist souls scheming an expanding labor force in imprisoning factory barracks.[36] Deliverance remains a social task, not an individual quest for truth. If Brecht considered himself "too Asiatic to die on a funeral pyre of truth,"[37] he thought of the practical, anti-metaphysical conduct which he had studied in the teaching of Chinese philosophy and which he brought to bear on his most "Chinese" play, a play which is also a challenge to Strindberg's most "Oriental" play.[38] Whereas Strindberg conjoined Western and Eastern transcendental philosophy in a quest for spiritual liberation through suffering, Brecht blended Eastern and Western social wisdom in a plea for secular justice and happiness. The counter-play as meta-drama thus extends the bilateral argument into a multilateral discourse.

NOTES

1 See, for example, Antony Tatlow and Tak-Wai Wong, eds., *Brecht and East Asian Theatre* (Hong Kong UP, 1982).
2 For a summary of the proceedings, see *Communications from the International Brecht Society* 16.2 (1987): 18-56.
3 See, for example, Antony Tatlow, *The Mask of Evil* (Bern: Lang, 1977); Yun-Yeop Song, *Bertolt Brecht und die chinesische Philosophie* (Bonn: Bouvier, 1978); Renata Berg-Pan, *Bertolt Brecht and China* (Bonn: Bouvier, 1979); Han-Soon Yim, *Bertolt Brecht und sein Verhältnis zur chinesischen Philosophie* (Bonn: Institut für koreanische Kultur, 1984).
4 The main points of the East-West debate are summarized in Jan Knopf, *Brecht Handbuch. Theater* (Stuttgart: Metzler, 1980), 202-204; but see also Tatlow and Wong.
5 For a concise summary of sources, see Knopf 203-204; see also the collection of source materials and Brecht's notes in Jan Knopf, ed., *Brechts "Guter Mensch von Sezuan"* (Frankfurt a. M.: Suhrkamp, 1982) 29-130.
6 See especially Antony Tatlow, "China oder Chima?" *Brecht Heute—Brecht Today. Jahrbuch der internationalen Brecht-Gesellschaft* 1 (1971): 27-47.
7 Bertolt Brecht, *Gesammelte Werke in 20 Bänden*, vol. 15 (Frankfurt a. M.: Suhrkamp, 1967) 105.
8 Herbert Knust, "Brechts *Fischzug*," *Brecht Heute—Brecht Today. Jahrbuch der internationalen Brecht-Gesellschaft* 1 (1971): 98-109.
9 Dieter Schmidt, *"Baal" und der junge Brecht* (Stuttgart: Metzler, 1966) 27-30.
10 Bertolt Brecht, *Die Rundköpfe und die Spitzköpfe. Bühnenfassung, Einzelszenen, Varianten*, ed. Gisela Bahr (Frankfurt a. M.: Suhrkamp, 1979).
11 Klaus Bohnen, "Produktionsprozeß bei Brecht. Zur Entstehung von *Die Gewehre der Frau Carrar*," *Text und Kontext* 7 (1979): 163-178.
12 Jost Hermand, "Herr Puntila und sein Knecht Matti," *Brecht Heute—Brecht Today. Jahrbuch der internationalen Brecht-Gesellschaft* 1 (1971): 117-136.
13 Wolfgang Gersch, *Film bei Brecht* (Berlin: Henschel, 1975) 238-241.

14 Herbert Knust, "Brechts Galileo-Evangelium," *Euphorion* 79 (1985): 207-225.
15 Brecht, *Gesammelte Werke in 20 Bänden*, vol. 15, 105, 179.
16 For some of the earliest systematic discussions of Brecht's techniques of adaptation, including *Gegenentwurf* and *Umfunktionieren* ("reutilization"), see Reinhold Grimm, *Bertolt Brecht und die Weltliteratur* (Nürnberg: Hoffmann, 1961) and Hans Mayer, *Bertolt Brecht und die Tradition* (Pfullingen: Neske, 1961).
17 Klabund [Alfred Henschke], *Der Kreidekreis* (Wien: Phaidon, 1929); Friedrich Wolf, *Tai Yang erwacht* (Berlin: Chronos, 1930). See the editorial note on *The Good Person of Szechwan* in Bertolt Brecht, *Collected Plays*, ed. Ralph Manheim and John Willett, vol. 6 (New York: Random House, 1976) 376; Berg-Pan 183-185.
18 This view was first expressed by Reinhold Grimm, "Bertolt Brecht: *Der gute Mensch von Sezuan*," *Germanistik in Forschung und Lehre*, ed. Rudolf Henß and Hugo Moser (Berlin: Schmidt, 1965) 184-191.
19 Elisabeth Frenzel, *Motive der Weltliteratur* (Stuttgart: Kröner, 1980) 285-297.
20 Manfred Karnick, *Rollenspiel und Welttheater* (München: Fink, 1980) 214-230.
21 Karnick sees a specific link between Wang's "Song of the Water Seller in the Rain" and a passage spoken by the farmer in Calderon's play; see Karnick 218.
22 Similarities were pointed out, more or less tentatively, by Marianne Kesting, *Vermessung des Labyrinths: Studien zur modernen Ästhetik* (Frankfurt a. M.: Fischer, 1965) 136; Frenzel 296; Karnick 219.
23 Even the names suggest similarities: Agnes means "holy," "pure"; Shen Te means "divine efficacy" or "divine virtue," as pointed out by Tatlow, *The Mask of Evil* 269.
24 See Strindberg's letter of May 13, 1902 to Emil Schering, his co-editor for his collected works, quoted in *Strindbergs Werke. Deutsche Gesamtausgabe*, 4th ed., Abteilung I, Band 8 (München, Leipzig: Müller, 1914) 234.
25 See Brecht's statements on the easiness of being good and the difficulty of being bad to others (if one also wants to be good to oneself) in his notes to the play in Knopf, ed., *Brechts "Guter Mensch von Sezuan"* 14, 17, 18.
26 See my study "Brecht's Dream-Playing: Between Vision and Illusion," *Critical Essays on Brecht*, ed. Siegfried Mews (forthcoming).
27 Bertolt Brecht, *Tagebücher 1920-1922. Autobiographische Aufzeichnungen 1920-1954*, ed. Herta Ramthun (Frankfurt a. M.: Suhrkamp, 1975) 180.
28 See *Strindbergs Werke*, Abteilung I, Band 8, 144. My English version combines the translations of Elizabeth Sprigge, *Six Plays of Strindberg* (Garden City: Doubleday, 1955) 193; and of Harry G. Carlson, *August Strindberg: Five Plays* (Berkeley: Univ. of California Press, 1983) 206.
29 See Sprigge 193 and Carlson 205.
30 In her double role, Shen Te/Shui Ta ("Mater"/"Materialism") grows bigger (with child/with capital).
31 Brecht, *Gesammelte Werke*, vol. 4, 1563-64. The text for this source is included in Knopf, ed., *Brechts "Guter Mensch von Sezuan"* 115-116.
32 Brecht, *Gesammelte Werke*, vol. 4, 1565.
33 Brecht, *Gesammelte Werke*, vol. 4, 1594.
34 "Ware Liebe" was the early title of the project; see Knopf, ed., *Brechts "Guter Mensch von Sezuan"* 13. The "celestial" connection in the pun on "true love" and "merchandise love" recurs in the title of a later project: "Coelestina oder die

Ware Liebe"—see the reference in Reinhold Grimm, *Bertolt Brecht* (Stuttgart: Metzler, 1971) 66.

35 This critical counter-stance would pertain also to the "Hindu" element in Goethe's "Der Gott und die Bajadere," which some critics see as a possible reference for Shen Te's relationship with the gods, e.g., Bernhard Greiner, *Welttheater als Montage* (Heidelberg: Quelle & Meyer, 1977) 126-127.

36 Brecht, *Gesammelte Werke*, vol. 4, 1550.

37 My translation; see Brecht, *Tagebücher* 140.

38 Critics who emphasize the autobiographical significance of Strindberg's work, point out that the Hindu elements in *A Dream Play* were influenced by the dark beauty of the actress (to become Strindberg's wife) Harriet Bosse as "Hindu goddess," playing Indra's Daughter, who embodied Strindberg's "own agony at being earth-bound, chained within life's limitations" (see Sprigge 188).

PAGANS AND SARACENS IN SPENSER'S *THE FAERIE QUEENE*

Mark Heberle, University of Hawaii

In *Orientalism*, Edward Said has shown how the development of Western colonial imperialism, from the eighteenth century to the present, has been accompanied by a scholarly enterprise that appropriates the non-Western world as a stage or theater upon which British, French, or American cultural and political hegemony has defined itself.[1] Employing a parochial perspective assumed to be normative if not universal, such Orientalism finds the societies that it studies to be incomplete, inferior, or simply alien. Said points out that these scholarly distortions have both reflected and reinforced Western political and literary images of the Islamic world in particular, and that the effective power of both policy and poetry rests to some extent upon such misrepresentation.

These attitudes antedate the formation of Orientalism as an organized body of thought, however, and are particularly characteristic of Renaissance epic, a genre in which it might be said that Europe defined itself as a civilization marked by expansive nationalistic imperialism, whether of political organization, ideology, or culture. Spenser's *The Faerie Queene* (1596), the last major European imperial epic and the heir of a coherent Western epic tradition profoundly concerned with cultural and ideological anxieties and pretensions, presents these powerful distortions in a peculiarly distinctive form, consistently employing its Islamic allusions as recognizably proto-orientalist tropes to validate its ethical and ideological ideals.

The Western epic is a fundamentally conservative genre, a long formal poem that idealizes the values of a contemporary aristocratic elite in the guise of a historical narrative set far in the past. From Virgil's *Aeneid* onward, however, the epic also reflects a historical crisis and transition in the very culture whose ideals the poem attempts to elaborate and conserve. Thus, the eloquence and insistence with which the *Aeneid* represents *romanitas* stems from the internal breakdown of the Roman state itself during the century of civil warfare that preceded the Augustan peace as well as the external danger posed by the Asiatic power of Antony and Cleopatra that had been so recently overcome at Actium. In the image of that battle in Book VIII, this threat from the East is graphically represented as alien, a barbaric power with a woman as its joint commander, calling upon hideous, inhuman divinities: "Every kind of monster / god—and the barking god, Anubis, too— / stands ready to cast shafts against Minerva / and Venus and at Neptune."[2] Although Caesar's victory is represented as a culmination of Roman history, the East remains a non-Roman other, imaginatively unassimilated, which anticipates its representation in subsequent Western epics. Nevertheless, the poem celebrates the historical transition from war to peace, and from republic to empire, by outlining a vast cultural and political movement from east to west and back again as Aeneas and his immediate descendants found a New Troy on the banks of the Tiber and Rome, in turn, brings law and order to the East, while Virgil's poem itself, in both transmitting and transcending Homeric epic, duplicates culturally what Roman imperialism has done politically. By the end of the *Aeneid,* the entire world presented by the poem (including the heavens and underworld, past, present, and future) has become a stage that celebrates Roman supremacy, fulfilling what may be called an imperial cycle.

The great Renaissance epics follow the Virgilian pattern of cultural conflict and resolution as they reflect contemporary internal and external crises. Thus, Ariosto's *Orlando Furioso* reflects the ceaseless internecine warfare that plagued the Italian peninsula in the wake of the epochal French invasion of 1494; Tasso's *Jerusalem Delivered,* as well as the poet's ceaseless revisions of it, is heavily influenced by the Counter-Reformation; Camões' *The Lusiads* anticipates not only the competitive scramble for colonies that characterized European foreign policies from the sixteenth century onward but also suggests that Portugal's age of glory already lies in the past. Yet such internal divisions within European Renaissance civilization remain subterranean in these poems. Instead, this crisis, the breakdown of the relative ideological conformity of medieval Christendom into a fragmented network of adversarial nation states (and churches) is suppressed and converted into an imagined unity against the perceived external threat, which is situated geographically and/or culturally in the East. That threat, Islamic political power and influence, had expanded nearly continuously for a millennium and reached its height under the Sultan Soleiman the Magnificent (1520-1566).

The model for overcoming the threat from the East is not the *Aeneid,* however, but the medieval *chansons de gestes,* the *Song of Roland* in particular. Written down near the beginning of the two centuries of Crusades against the East, it recasts that crisis by converting the French setback at Roncevaux two centuries earlier into an epic struggle between Christian and Muslim civilizations. Roland and the *douze pers* are not the only costs of Charlemagne's triumph, however; another casualty is any objective understanding of Islam. Everywhere, the poem dynamically dramatizes Roland's simple battle cry, "Paynims are wrong, Christians are in the right!" (stanza 79),[3] defining the Muslims as morally evil despite their martial courage. Possibly out of ignorance but certainly with malicious glee, the poet blasphemously deforms Islam itself into an idolatrous religion, worshipping vainly a bizarre anti-trinity of gods, including Mahoun (the Prophet himself), Tervagant (English "termagant"), and Apollyon. This proto-Crusade ends with total victory, unlike most of its historical antitypes, and the forced conversion of all the surviving unbelievers. Of course, Charlemagne, like Christendom itself, has more battles to fight after the end of the poem.

Such ideological distortions and inventions contribute powerfully to the poem's effectiveness. They are carried over into the more sophisticated Renaissance epics as well, each of which culminates with a victory over an

Islamic enemy. Like Virgil, Ariosto and Tasso also associate the Eastern foe with a powerful and bewitching woman (Angelica and Armida), and characterize the enemy warriors variously as cruel, lustful, treacherous, arrogant, and blasphemous, while admiring their strength and courage. Tasso and Camões also dramatize an imperial movement from west to east as Goffredo wins Jerusalem and Vasco da Gama reaches India. Moreover, in the quasi-Virgilian prophecies and retrospective histories of *The Lusiads,* Camões sketches a full imperial cycle that establishes the Portuguese commercial imperium from Brazil to China. All three writers urge a unified Christian assault upon the Islamic world, to be led by their dynastic patron, an ideological crusade that is realized in epitome by the epic poems themselves.

The Faerie Queene transmits the Renaissance epic tradition into English and situates itself within that tradition by incorporating what is fundamental to each of its predecessors. Like *Orlando Furioso, The Faerie Queene* is a romance as well as an epic; like *Jerusalem Delivered,* it is militantly Christian; like *The Lusiads,* it is combatively nationalistic. But the poem is also the first significant Protestant epic and thus explicitly dramatizes through its allegory the great ideological split within Europe itself that the earlier epics had denied. And the threat from the East motif plays a small but significant role in furthering Spenser's sectarian ends. The poem's distortion of Islam takes the form of pagan and saracen characters who represent not only hellish ethical and psychological foes but also the Roman Catholic Church itself and the Catholic political powers of the continent.

In *The Faerie Queene,* there is only one allusion to actual historical conflicts between Christendom and Islam, a reference in Book I.10.40 to the ransoming of Christian soldiers captured by the Muslims. This office is connected with redeeming jailed prisoners, the fourth of the seven corporal works of mercy, charitable activities that Spenser locates in an allegorical hospice staffed by seven holy attendants:

> The fourth appointed by his office was,
> Poore prisoners to relieue with gratious ayd,
> And captiues to redeeme with price of bras,
> From Turkes and Sarazins, which them had stayd;
> And though they faulty were, yet well he wayd,
> That God to vs forgiueth euery howre
> Much more then that, why they in bands were layd,
> And he that harrowd hell with heauie stowre,
> The faultie soules from thence brought to his heauenly bowre.[4]

"Turks" and "Sarazins" are identified with militant Islam in this stanza. Despite the grave political threat posed to eastern Europe throughout the sixteenth century by the Ottoman Turks, however, Spenser refers to them explicitly only here. "Sarazin" and its variant "saracen," a more general term for Muslim, are used as an epithet frequently, however. (Whether Spenser was aware or not, the word "saracen" seems to be derived from an Arabic word for "easterner.") This term characterizes the three "Sans" brothers of Book I—Sans Foy ("Faithlessness"), Sans Loy ("Lawlessness"), and Sans Joy ("Joylessness") as well as Pyrochles and Cymochles ("fire-tossed," "wave-tossed") in Book II, who represent extremes of the irascible and concupiscent passions, or anger and sensuality. However, the term "pagan" (variant "paynim") is also applied to each of these figures, and "saracen" and "pagan" seem to be used interchangeably in the poem. Since several of these characters swear oaths by "Mahoun" or "Termagant," however, Spenser explicitly associates them with Islam, or rather the travesty of Islam that characterizes the Western epic tradition from the *Song of Roland* onward. Only two "pagan" characters are not also identified as "saracens"—the insignificant Bruncheval in Book IV and the Souldan in Book V, whose very name marks him as a saracen.

How do Spenser's saracens and pagans function within his allegorical epic? They appear early in Books I and II as armed warriors spontaneously hostile to Spenser's heroes, but they are destroyed or otherwise dispersed before the culminating episodes of each book. In the broadest sense, they are contraries of the titular virtue—Holiness in Book I, Temperance in Book II. Thus, they are reified personifications of the character traits most evident in earlier misrepresentations of oriental characters in Western epics, impious moral evil and emotional extremes of cruelty and lasciviousness.

The three unholy "Sans" brothers are etymologically linked to deficiency and thus define their allegiance as an aggressive anti-religion (without faith, law, or joy), while the intemperate Pyrochles and Cymochles are creatures of excess, but irrationally subject to fits of anger and lust. More importantly, however, the saracen characters of Book I are significant to its historical allegory, which shows how England (Red Cross Knight) abandoned the true church (Una) and succumbed to Roman Catholicism (Duessa) before being restored to holiness by providential intervention (Prince Arthur). Within that ecclesiastical allegory, Red Cross overcomes the saracen threat posed by Sans Foy and Sans Joy, but these are ironic triumphs, since they are accomplished for the sake of his seductress Duessa, whose faith is false. Moreover, since England has fallen under the sway of Roman Catholicism, the true church is left defenseless against the saracen threat: Una, true religion, is nearly raped by the third brother, Sans Loy, militant Islam seen as lawlessness.

Duessa herself has long been discussed as an antitype of the Great Harlot described in Revelation 17, and Spenser's representation of her and her beast derives from numerous Protestant reinterpretations of the Apocalypse that identified the Roman Church with the Antichrist.[5] But Spenser goes beyond these conventional vilifications to connect her with the threat from the East. Although she claims to be empress of the West, the allegory identifies her with the Whore of Babylon, and, like her counterpart Lucifera in Book I, she is also characterized by Persian luxury and extravagance. Most striking of all, she enters the poem as the mistress of Sans Foy, and she later encourages and comforts Sans Joy both before and after his defeat by Red Cross. By making

Duessa the companion and lover of these saracen knights, Spenser not only associates the Roman Church with faithless whoredom generally, but also suggests that Roman Catholicism and Islam share common interests. This startling connection is directly addressed during Duessa's descent to hell in Canto 5, for an allegorical genealogy there identifies Night as the common mother of Duessa herself and the three saracen brothers, so that all of these children of darkness are part of the same family.

Spenser's attempt to paganize England's Christian enemies is evident in Book V as well. The historical allegory of this book, the book of Justice, provides the poet's closest approach to a full imperial cycle. The knight of justice, Artegall, has the mission of rescuing Irena—a paragram for both "Ireland" and "Peace"—from her oppressor, Grantorto ("great wrong"). After attending to economic and domestic injustice in the first seven cantos, Artegall encounters Prince Arthur, and in the last five cantos the two proceed to rid Faeryland of tyrants and other scoundrels, who collectively constitute all the Catholic political enemies of England. Embedded in the middle of this imperial fantasy is an allegorical idealization of the court of Elizabeth, who is personified as Mercilla. In the first of Spenser's putatively just wars, Artegall and Arthur together destroy the power of Mercilla's greatest foe, the Souldan, who is named after the greatest of all Islamic rulers, the ruler of the Turks. Indeed, the forces controlled by himself and his wife Adicia ("Injustice") are identified throughout as pagans, and Artegall disguises himself in pagan armor to outwit his opponents. Arthur's destruction of the Souldan is a transparent allegorization of the defeat of the Spanish Armada in 1588, however, and the Souldan himself represents Philip II, King of Spain.[6] In this episode, Spenser goes beyond simply associating Catholicism with Islam, as in Book I; he identifies the greatest Catholic prince of Europe with his greatest Muslim enemy. This allegory supports Spenser's ideological mythmaking, but only through a willful distortion of history; after all, it was Philip's forces that defeated the Sultan's fleet at Lepanto in 1571, the most important victory of Christian Europe over the Islamic threat during Spenser's lifetime.

In the final episode of the book, Artegall crosses the ocean to rescue Irena— i.e., the Elizabethan regime moves west to pacify Ireland, that "savage island" in Spenser's words.[7] Spenser participated in this *translatio imperii* as a colonizer himself, accompanying his patron Lord Grey, whose brutal policies the poet enthusiastically defends in his *Short View of Ireland*. Irena's oppressor is Grantorto ("great wrong"), another avatar of Catholic political power, for the Spanish had unsuccessfully invaded the island and were always providing support for Catholic rebels against their English rulers. But the name is also a curious echo of "Great Turk," the term popularly applied to the Turkish Sultan.

Whether or not this identification is plausible, Spenser elsewhere radically redefines the threat to the East in *The Faerie Queene*, as we have seen. The "East" is now Catholic Europe, the crisis of the Elizabethan regime its struggle against much of Christendom itself. By associating Roman Catholicism with Islam, Spenser degrades the former with the distorted image of the latter conveyed through the Christian epic tradition. By merging the two, *The Faerie Queene* portrays an England that is courageously and piously battling against both of these evil religions. In *The Faerie Queene*, of course, Spenser simply assumes his reader's view of Islam as an anti-world, challenging and denying the ethical and ideological values being inculcated by the poem. As Samuel Chew points out in *The Crescent and the Rose*, the only full-length study of Renaissance England and Islam, there was widespread ignorance of the Islamic world in England throughout the sixteenth century, and it is reflected in scholarly and popular literature alike.[8] Even more crudely than in the continental epics, the "Mohammedan" is constituted as the other and characterized by sensuality, idolatry, and cruelty as well as immense and threatening political and material power, an entity defined only with reference to England's image of itself as a norm. For example, the Prophet himself was variously misconceived as a god, an idol, a devil, a religious imposter, a renegade Christian, or a schismatic and heretic. The Shi'ite branch of Islam was seen as a distorted form of Christianity because of its cult of martyrdom, associated by analogy with rites centered upon Christ's crucifixion. Tamerlane, whose own conquests temporarily halted Ottoman expansion in the early fifteenth century, was viewed with admiration, as in Marlowe's two heroic dramas of the 1580s, as a foe of Islamic political power and religious belief, even though he was himself a devout Muslim.

While his saracens and pagans are implicitly invested with all the pejorative connotations of such widespread ignorance, Spenser's association of Romanism and Islam marks the full breakdown of Christendom itself. Both religions are darkened beyond recognition, and the demonology that results anticipates an important characteristic of the Western political perspective on the rest of the world from the sixteenth century through the present. Like its epic predecessors, *The Faerie Queene* powerfully misrepresents Islam, and in doing so it anticipates the Orientalist viewpoint analyzed by Said, which may well derive from such canonical literary texts more than from the actual experience of non-Western cultures. Unlike the earlier epics, however, Spenser's also points to the actual historical course of Western influence throughout its three centuries of subsequent political and cultural hegemony: fierce nationalistic rivalry and conflict combined with aggressive international expansion into and misappropriation of the non-Western world.

NOTES

1. Edward Said, *Orientalism* (New York: Random House, 1978) 63.
2. Virgil, *The Aeneid*, trans. Allen Mandelbaum (New York: Bantam, 1971) 213.
3. *The Song of Roland*, trans. Dorothy L. Sayers (Harmondsworth: Penguin, 1957) 91.
4. Edmund Spenser, *The Faerie Queene*, ed. A. C. Hamilton (London and New York: Longman, 1977) 137.

5   John Hankins, *Source and Meaning in Spenser's Allegory* (Oxford: Clarendon, 1971) 104-105; Elizabeth Heale, *"The Faerie Queene:" A Reader's Guide* (Cambridge: Cambridge UP, 1987) 22-23.
6   Rene Graziani, "Philip II's *impresa* and Spenser's Souldan," *JWCI* 27 (1964): 322-24.
7   Spenser FQ VII.i.9.1 (627).
8   Samuel Chew, *The Crescent and the Rose: Islam and England During the Renaissance* (New York: Oxford UP, 1937) 395-97 and Chapter 9, passim.

IV. EUROPEAN INTERACTIONS

GIOVANNI VERGA'S "CAVALLERIA RUSTICANA": A TRANSLATOR'S NIGHTMARE?

> "We have read the *Cavalleria rusticana*: a veritable blood-pudding of passion. It is not at all good, only in some odd way, comical, as the portentous tragic Italian is always comical." [1]
>
> D. H. Lawrence

Ulrich Weisstein, Indiana University

The present undertaking, which focuses on a quartet of translations into English of Giovanni Verga's striking novella, forms part of a larger project, tentatively entitled "The Medium is the Message: Giovanni Verga's 'Cavalleria rusticana' as a Subject for Comparative Literature and the Comparative Arts," that is designed to encompass the whole range of transformations—translations, adaptations, and transpositions—which this small-scale masterpiece of Italian literature has undergone in the course of its history. The trajectory extends from the publication of the story itself in 1880, by way of the author's own stage version (written for Eleonora Duse) which premiered in 1884,[2] and Pietro Mascagni's one-act opera of 1890,[3] to D. H. Lawrence's 1928 English translation, and beyond.

Having been kept alive in consequence of this triple metamorphosis, "Cavalleria rusticana" could have (and certainly should have) become a canonical work, included in all standard anthologies of modern literature; unfortunately, that is not the case. For, in inverse proportion to its intrinsic merit, the opera, often performed in tandem with Ruggiero Leoncavallo's *Pagliacci* has taken much of the wind out of the novella's sails—to the point where many falsely assume, as did Lawrence,[4] that Verga himself was responsible for the libretto. In actual fact, the linguistically flat and dramaturgically flawed operatic text was written, without the author's knowledge—much less his consent—by G. Targioni-Tozzetti and G. Menasci, who came to Mascagni's rescue when the latter, who wanted to enter a competition launched by the Milan music publisher Sonzogno, was left in the lurch by professional writers. Oddly enough, and much to his own surprise, Mascagni triumphed over the other competitors, more than seventy in all, and was on his way to a successful, though in hindsight not overly distinguished, career as head of the *verismo* School that swept the musical stages of Europe in the final decade of the nineteenth century.

What I shall seek to demonstrate in the more comprehensive study of which this essay constitutes a large and fairly self-contained segment, is the fact that in this instance, as in many similar ones, the further one moves away from the original medium, the greater the loss from an artistic point of view and the less forceful the message. However, redeeming features may surface, from time to time, in the other media in which it finds itself ensconced. More precisely, the translations of "Cavalleria rusticana" which I shall scrutinize in the following pages are, almost across the board and in numerous ways still to be detailed, patently inferior to the model, not only because the resources available in the target language are inadequate but also, and specifically in D. H. Lawrence's case, because the translator's linguistic competence left much to be desired. Thus, it comes to pass that, while creative treason is knowingly committed on occasion, unknowingly perpetrated betrayal (in the form of blunders, slip-ups and stylistic infelicities) carries the day. The fear of falling into such traps engenders, even in the most conscientious renditioners, a translatorial nightmare which is hard to shake off and which must be held ultimately responsible for the work's failure to reach out beyond it's innate linguistic borders.

Whether explicitly or implicitly, creative treason is also bound to occur in the transfer of a work from one medium, and/or genre, to another. Thus, in adapting his novella for the stage, Verga knew full well that he was making concessions to popular taste and to the conventions of late nineteenth-century melodrama; and, for good measure, he added artistically superfluous folkloristic trappings. And Mascagni, ever his true self in hankering after theatrical effect, shamelessly exploited not only the music of Bizet's *Carmen* and Verdi's *Otello* but added a hefty dose of overblown musical rhetoric. Verga himself never doubted that the novella, which manifests an uncompromising "will to style," was superior to the drama of his own making, a view which was shared by his finest critical exponent, Luigi Russo, although not, for example, by Benedetto Croce.[5]

Before engaging in the task of comparatively assessing a foursome of English versions of "Cavalleria rusticana," I must briefly touch upon the prehistory of that novella. As is so often the case with fiction of the veristic kind, of which this is an outstanding example, Verga's novella harks back to a *fait divers* ("historical anecdote") or series of events said to have taken place fifteen years prior to its creation. The sensational happenings which lie at its heart were summarized in the appendix of a memoir written almost a hundred years after the fact by Verga's longtime friend Giuseppe Paterno. I will reproduce it here in full because the account, never before translated into English, is hard to come by even in the original Italian. It runs as follows:

> This, one of Giovanni Verga's best novellas, is based on an actual story that occurred in Vizzini in the year 1865. Its protagonists were: Turridu; Lucia, his mother; Santuzza, an orphan; "Uncle" Cosimo, an old bachelor and Lucia's assistant in her wine shop; Alfio, a *mafioso* and head of the Vizzini carters; and Lola, an eighteen-year old, beautiful and star-eyed girl, the daughter of a rich man.
>
> This is what happened: Turridu, the twenty-year-old son of Lucia, the owner of a wine shop on the *piazetta* Santa Teresa in Vizzini, was engaged to marry Lola after his return from military service which, at that time, lasted between

three and four years. Assigned to the Bersaglieri corps, he departed for Palermo.

In the beginning, the two young people corresponded regularly, but less frequently so after a few months, so that it seemed that Turridu had forgotten Lola, his first love. Lola's parents realized that it would be useless to wait for Turridu, for with the passing years young maidens turn into spinsters. So they decided to give their daughter a husband, in view of the fact that Alfio, a mature and handsome man of forty-two, owner of a horse-and-buggy as well as a stable, and a house with garden and bower, had persistently courted Lola. The marriage was arranged, and the wedding celebrated, in the presence of the parents and their friends and neighbors, with music, dance, and song.

The first years of marriage passed quietly and happily; but unfortunately no child was born to the pair. After four long years, Turridu was discharged from the army and returned home to embrace his old mother who, during his absence, had enjoyed the precious company of the beautiful fifteen-year-old orphan Santuzza, who was helping her like a true daughter while "Uncle" Cosimo assisted her in the wine shop. *Mamma* Lucia had raised Santuzza in every way at her convenience and, in her heart, had prepared a new spouse for Turridu since Lola had married Alfio. The affectionate mother had even prepared a layette for their baby; for she had shrewdly guessed that Turridu and Santuzza were having an affair and hoped that after the imminent Easter holidays their marriage could be sealed.

In the few months that had elapsed since Turridu's return, his first love, never forgotten, had reawakened, and he had entered into the heart of the witch Lola, who enticed him with all the arts at the disposal of an evil woman, deceiving Alfio, who, unaware of her adultery, was busy with his work as a carter hauling wine barrels and foodstuffs from Vizzini to Francofonte, Militello, and Gramichele, spending lots of money to adorn his beautiful Lola with rings, as if she were the queen of the land.

Lucia's fervent attempts to dissuade her son from his wild plans did not succeed, nor did Santuzza's reproofs and admonitions. Finally, racked with jealousy, the latter told Alfio to keep Lola in check. At this warning, Alfio swore vengeance and told Santuzza he would teach her a lesson if she had not told him the truth. Duly forewarned, he verified the facts, and on Easter eve, in Lucia's shop, when Turridu offered him a glass of wine, he replied: "Your wine poisons my blood," threw the glass at his rival's feet, approached him in order to embrace him and kiss him with a small bite on the ear as a sign of his challenge. The challenge was accepted, and on Easter morning, in a rustic duel on the floor of the tannery, Turridu was killed, drowning in his own blood.[6]

It would be interesting to show in detail how Verga used the facts reported in this or some other account,[7] which features he retained, eliminated, or modified, what new elements he added, and how he reassembled the mosaic pieces into his novella. It would be equally interesting to show, with reference to the text of the stage adaptation, for example, how, in the theatrical version, Verga restored certain facts reported in his source, such as Lucia being a prosperous wine seller rather than an impoverished widow, and Santa-Santuzza an orphan rather than the daughter of a wealthy farmer. Both inquiries would, however, far exceed the limits of this paper.

As for the genesis of Verga's novella, it should be noted that, according to Francesco de Roberto, whose article "Stato civile della *Cavalleria rusticana*" is richly illustrated with photographs depicting the pertinent Sicilian localities, the most salient moment of the action, the bite on the ear that signifies the so-called *fida* ("challenge"), was, to use a Goethean term, the *Ur-Erlebnis*, the primitive core around which the narrative crystallized. Nor should we forget that what became an autonomous work fending for itself was originally meant for inclusion in Verga's first major novel, *I Malavoglia*.[8] When Verga decided to remove it from that context, he published it separately in the Sunday supplement of the newspaper *Fanfulla* on March 10, 1880. The evidence, scrutinized by Giovanni Cecchetti and Paolo Marchi among others,[9] shows that this early version of "Cavalleria rusticana" is fairly close to but not fully identical with the standard version found in the volume *Vita dei Campi*,[10] which has formed the sole basis for all subsequent editions and translations, from which it differs in several ways.

There are some minor discrepancies in punctuation and in the use of grammatical forms, for example, as well as in the choice of certain words (*giubba* instead of *farsetto*), phrases ("non fanno farina" in lieu of "non ne affastellano sarmenti"), and entire sentences ("Turridu morse leggermente il lobo dell'orecchio del carretiere" instead of the slightly more refined "Turridu strinse fra i denti l'orecchio del carretiere"). By far the most striking and, in my opinion, subtly calculated emendation concerns the dying Turridu's words at the end of the story. In the *Fanfulla della domenica* version, our protagonist cries "Ah! la mia povera vecchia!" but in the standard text he simply exclaims "Ah! mamma mia!" It could be argued that this change is for the better; for while the first exclamation, consistent with the sentiment expressed throughout the final episode (which offers "la mia vecchierella" and "la mia vecchia" as well), is too predictable and perhaps too much in character to serve as an effective punch line, the latter, at once more banal and more succinct, underscores, in its pointed reference to Santa's repartee at the end of her second conversation with Turridu, the existential irony of the situation.

Let us turn to the novella itself and to its four English offspring.[11] To translate a narrative like "Cavalleria rusticana" successfully demands that the translator convey not only the text's literal, metaphorical, and symbolic meaning, but its stylistic *and* linguistic peculiarities as well; for, with regard to language, Verga's story exists on three different levels which occasionally intermesh: 1) the rarely used Sicilian dialect (some would regard it as a separate language); 2) the pervasive presence of lexical and syntactic Sicilianisms, and 3) the solid underpinning provided by standard literary Italian. If he has an ear attuned to linguistic nuances, the translator will quickly realize that he must find a way of reproducing or recreating the interplay between the second and third levels. (For purists like Luigi Russo and several modern editors of Verga's prose, this cohabitation was a clear sign of artistic immaturity and, hence, a constant source of irritation.[12])

In "Cavalleria rusticana," the actual use of Sicilian parlance is limited to a single proverb ("facemo cuntu ca chioppi e scampau, e la nostra amicizia finiu," meaning, roughly, "let's forget about the past") which the jilted lover Turridu hurls at Lola, terminating their first conversation. What is the translator to do in this instance, given the fact that even Italian editors feel compelled to resort to commentary and/or literal translation? He will want to follow suit, as does the reliable Cecchetti ("Let's pretend it rained, then cleared up, and our friendship is over," footnoted "a Sicilian saying that means 'Let's forget completely about everything connected with the past'"). D. H. Lawrence, on the other hand, by italicizing and thereby estranging the passage, alerts the reader to its special status. For the rest, Lawrence does the author, and his audience, a disservice by refashioning parts of the dialogue in the patois of his native Nottinghamshire. For example, Turridu's words (or, rather, his thoughts) "Voglio fargliela sotto gli occhi a quella cagnaccia" appear as "I'll show that bitch summat, afore I've done," a passage Cecchetti renders straightforwardly as "I'll get even with her right under her eyes, the dirty bitch."

As for the lexical and syntactic "idiotisms" which abound in the novella to the point where, cumulatively, they constitute its dominant stylistic feature, all are fully documented in the apparatus of various scholarly editions. In Gino Tellini's edition of Verga's work, for example, "Cavalleria rusticana" is supported by thirty-nine explanatory footnotes.[13] Luigi Russo, among others, even goes to the trouble of showing how, in the lexical sphere, Verga often wavered between Sicilianisms and Tuscanisms and to what extent his grammatical quirks are reflections of an oral style that is characteristic of the "folk." Thus, while the label *babbo*, which is attached to Santa's father, is common in Florence, *massaro*, the term used to fixate the civic status of Lola's father, has a distinctly Southern ring, and *-ste*, the short form for *queste* used throughout the novella, is used colloquially in both the North and the South.

On the syntactical side, the postpositional repetition of certain words or phrases—"quanto ci siete voi che la gna Lola non è degno di portarvi le scarpe, non è degna" and "Per voi tirerei su tutta la casa, tirerei," for instance—is a particularly effective means of conveying a sense of orality. What are translators (those highly vulnerable amphibious creatures) to make of this stylistic *mélange*, and how are they to convey across the linguistic chasm that separates languages the anomalies caused by the seemingly random interweaving of pure dialect, "stylized" dialect and standard literary Italian? If it is hard for readers from Torino, Venice, or Milan to cope with this problem, how much harder must it be for translators and their public. A solution like the one which Eric Bentley preferred in his early translations of Bertolt Brecht's dramas—that of using the standard language throughout, with only minor deviations—will hardly suffice.

Let us test the waters by scrutinizing the four versions of the phrase cited at the beginning of the previous paragraph, "la gna Lola non è degno di portarvi le scarpe, non è degno." None of the translators offers a literal rendition but, as usual, Cecchetti's apt formulation ("Lola doesn't deserve to carry your shoes, she doesn't"), in its outright colloquialism, comes closest to echoing the spirit as well as the letter of the original, while that of the pseudonymous "Alma Strettel" ("For Mistress Lola isn't worthy to wear your shoes, that she isn't") is marred by a lexical error ("wear" for "carry") and suffers from the rhythmically disturbing use of the emphatic "that" after the comma. Lawrence's "Lola's not fit to bring you your shoes, she is not" brings no improvement, for, in addition to scorning the colloquial ellipsis "isn't" in the second instance, it employs "bring" instead of "carry," and labors under the redundancy "you your." Alexander's version ("Lola is nothing, she is not even fit to clean your shoes"), finally, is altogether out of the running and deserves to be castigated not only by the Beckmessers among the critical *Merker*, who will find it offensive on at least three counts: firstly, for the awkward syntactical parallelism "Lola . . . she"; secondly, for the substitution of "clean" for "carry" ("tie your shoes" might have done the trick); and thirdly, for dropping the repetition.

In order to underscore my second point, I would like to examine a sentence which, as Russo has pointed out, demonstrates how Verga intermingles the Sicilian and Tuscan tongues in "Cavalleria rusticana." The sentence, "La vigilia di Pasqua avevano sul desco un piatto di salsiccia," elicits the following comment from Russo: "That *Salsiccio* is most fortunate, (reflecting) the singular-plural preferred in the Sicilian tongue. (A Tuscan would have seen 'un piatto di salsicci'.) But the *desco* sounds a bit too Tuscan and learned to me and has no Verghian ring to it."[14]

Here, to judge by our fourfold sampling, the translators have thrown in the towel. Thus, even though Italian by birth and sensitive to regional usage, Cecchetti simply repeats Lawrence's bland "They had a dish of sausages on the table" (which, in turn, goes back to Alma Strettel's translation), and Alexander ("They had a plateful of sausages on the table") follows suit. They all sweep the linguistic problem under the rug. In fact, a comparative study of their translations makes it clear that in this case there are simply too many hurdles placed in the path of a perfect translation.

Taken by themselves, simple mistakes or oversights in the rendition of terms, technical or otherwise, may be innocuous; but they can have a devastating cumulative effect, to the point of subverting the overall meaning. In the English versions of "Cavalleria rusticana," we come across various instances of such lexical perversion. Alma Strettel, for instance, takes the word *ballatoio* ("terrace" or "balcony") to mean "dancing floor," on the assumption that it is derived from *ballo* ("dance" or "Ball"). Less offensive but more than mildly annoying is the practice, fairly common among modern translators, of retaining a word in its original form and explaining it in a footnote, presumably because they regard it as untranslatable or wish to stress the Otherness of the setting.

Thus Alma Strettel keeps, but comments on, *mantellina* ("cape" or "small cloak"), Lawrence and Cecchetti explicate the meaning of *ballatoio*, and Cecchetti, for reasons of his own, leaves Turridu's "Ah! mamma mia!" in the original Italian.

While these terms are certainly familiar to Verga's compatriots, some Italian editors have found it necessary to provide a brief semantic analysis of designations like *gna, massaro*, and *compare*, labels and forms of address which serve as indicators of the socio-economic standing of the persons to whom they are attached. The same applies to place names such as Licodia, Francofonte, and Canziria, which will sound just as strange and distant to most Italians as they do to Londoners and New Yorkers.

Both semantically and grammatically, Lawrence was greatly handicapped by his "little Italian and less Sicilian." Due to his patent linguistic shortcomings, he totally missed, among other things, the point made by Alfio in his final words to the dying Turridu: "Ora tua madre lascierà stare le galline" ("Now your mother will leave the chickens alone"). Turning the intended meaning upside down, he wrote: "And now your mother can mind her fowls." And in the phrase "il berretto rosso, che sembrava quello della buona ventura," which occurs in the opening paragraph of the story, he loses sight of the qualifying *dello*, making the fortune teller himself take the place of his cap in the analogy. More significantly, as far as the psychological tone of the narrative is concerned, he misunderstands or misrepresents Turridu's pointed and poignant reference to the far-off place where he was stationed and where "si perdeva persino il nome del nostro paese" ("where even the name of our town was lost," as Cecchetti puts it). Writing "I'd almost forgotten even the name of where I came from," Lawrence changes the perspective; for what Verga meant to say, unquestionably, was not that Lola's lover had forgotten her and the whole affair but that, being so far away, he himself had been lost sight of.

More far-reaching yet easily defined are translatorial choices which affect what one might call the atmosphere of Verga's novella, i.e., the emotional and psychological aura in which the characters are bathed and which cements their personal and social relationship. Lawrence, in particular, shows a startling lack of sensitivity with regard to these more or less intangible but essential values. Perhaps the most striking illustration of this lack of *Fingerspitzengefühl* ("tact") is his rendition of the sentence with which, speaking euphemistically, Alfio invites Turridu to the duel: "Se domattina volete venire nei ficchidindia della Canziria, potremo parlare di quell'affare, compare," which Cecchetti, skipping the concluding form of address, renders "If you want to come to the cactuses of Canziria tomorrow, we can talk about that business."

Throughout "Cavalleria rusticana," *compare* is used noncommittally in polite intercourse: Lola and Alfio greeting Turridu (perhaps with some condescension), and Santa addressing Alfio. Alma Strettel, in whose rendition *compare* usually appears as "Master" (an expression that sounds quaint to the ears of a late twentieth-century reader, who would probably associate it with

British upper middle-class schoolboys) here deviates from her own norm by using "comrade," while Alexander simply italicizes Verga's term. Lawrence, who drops the label in all other instances, here, oddly enough, feels called upon to use a word with strongly contemptuous overtones. In his painfully contorted translation, the sentence reads: "Shall you come to the cactus grove at Canziria to-morrow morning, and we can talk about that bit of business of ours, boy?" By doing so, he conveys a sense of moral superiority on Alfio's part that is distinctly absent from the original, where the two rivals, about to engage in what one may well regard as a tribal ritual, appear as equals. Precisely for that reason, Alma Strettel's "comrade," though somewhat ironic, comes much closer to hitting the mark.

One particularly illuminating example of how translators, regardless of their linguistic skills, are bound to succeed in communicating a weighty *double entendre* due to a semantic kinship between the source and target languages relates to a cluster of diminutives which Verga employs to pinpoint important sentimental and socio-economic aspects of his novella. On the affective side, Turridu, having been jilted by Lola and feeling down in the mouth, is described, early on, as a *poveraccio*—rendered "poor fellow," "poor man," "poor chap," and "poor devil" respectively by Alma Strettel, Lawrence, Alexander, and Cecchetti—but his use of the epithet in regard to his mother also indicates their state of impoverishment and the fact that, in contrast to Santa and Lola, he neither comes from nor will marry into a prosperous family.

Gna Nunzia is, in her own words, not only a *vecchierella* ("poor old woman" [Lawrence, Alexander, and Cecchetti] and "my old woman" [Alexander]) but, quite distinctly, a *poveretta* ("poor mother" [Alma Strettel], "poor old mother" [Lawrence], "mother" [Alexander], and, most propitiously, "poor woman" [Cecchetti]) who, in order to survive during her son's long absence, had to sell her most precious possessions, the bay mule and the small piece (*pezzetto*) of land used for cultivating grapes. To be poor, then, in the world depicted in this narrative, means not only to be an object of pity but also to have a low socio-economic status.

What adds spice and esthetic significance in this case is the realignment of the diminutives which Verga, going back to the historical anecdote, decided to use when preparing his adaptation for the stage. In the drama, these belittling and/or prettifying suffixes are no longer assigned to Turridu and his mother, whose affluence now makes her appear as a veritable pillar of village society, but to Santa (re-)transformed into the pregnant orphan Santuzza. As the Italian scholar Vann Bosco-Malvica has demonstrated in an essay specifically concerned with such *altérés*, the relocation of the diminutives is a telling sign of "la participation affective de l'auteur à un personnage du drame dont il a changé l'importance et le caractère."[15] Artistically, this change of emphasis is harmful in so far as sentiment turns into sentimentality and takes on a maudlin and, at least in Mascagni's opera, a pathetic, if not downright pathological, cast.[16]

In an astonishing variety of ways, translatorial fidelity can be tested with regard to realms other than the linguistic one which, rightly or wrongly, tends to dominate most scholarly analyses of the *traducteur*'s martyrial acts of faith. In the English versions of "Cavalleria rusticana," for example, the observant reader is bound to notice certain inconsistencies on what may be called the micro- or macro-structural levels. To begin with the former: as an author, Giovanni Verga had a special way of paragraphing his text by segmenting narrative matter into units that are not separated in accordance with units of setting or action but manifest a programmatic preference for bracketing contrasting phenomena. In doing so, he creates a shock effect that is felt not so much in the first reading as in the subsequent perusals of the novella.

In all Italian versions of "Cavalleria rusticana," including the original text published in *Fanfulla della domenica*, the first paragraph, here given in Cecchetti's translation, looks as follows:

> When Turridu Macca, Nunzia's son, came back from the service, he used to strut in the square on Sundays in his *bersagliere*'s uniform with the red cap that looked like the one worn by the fortune teller who sets up a bench with a cage of canaries. The girls, on the way to Mass, their noses in their mantillas, eyed him longingly, and the urchins buzzed around him like flies. He had also brought a pipe with a carving of the king on horseback that seemed alive, and he lit his matches on the rear of his pants, lifting his leg as if giving a kick. But in spite of all this, *massaro* Angelo's daughter, Lola, had not shown herself at Mass or on her balcony because she had become engaged to a certain man from Licodia, a cart driver who had four mules in his stable. As soon as Turridu found out, damn it! he was going to tear that Licodian's guts from his belly, he was! But he did nothing of the kind and vented his rage by singing all the scornful songs he knew under the girl's window.

The actions and events which Verga telescopes into a single paragraph—Turridu's return from military service, his braggadocio, the townspeople's behavior, the explanation for Lola's absence, and finally Turridu's rather violent reaction to the news that Lola is about to be married—could easily have been divided into a number of distinct segments. What, in a "realistic" account, might have required four or five pages of elaborate description and psychological analysis, is here, thanks to the author's art of concision, imbibed from his great model, Guy de Maupassant, and the sparing use of characteristic detail crammed into a single paragraph occupying less than twenty lines on the page.

None of the four translators of the novella whose efforts we are scrutinizing seems to have found this authorial *tour de force* to his or her liking; for none of them has stuck to Verga's guns. Thus, while Cecchetti divides the paragraph into two halves of approximately equal length (from "Turridu Macca" to "kick," and from "But in spite of all this" to "window"), Alma Strettel and Lawrence, adding a *fermata* after "stable," opt for a tripartite scheme, and Alexander, breaking after "canaries" as well, a quadripartite one.

In the case of a similarly sutured paragraph—"Turridu went back to greet her so often that Santa noticed it and slammed the window in his face. The neighbors pointed out the bersagliere with a smile or a nod when he passed. Lola's husband was making his round of the fairs with his mules"—there are no traitors, perhaps because the translators realized that three one-sentence paragraphs in a row would look odd. But in this instance, the usually alert Cecchetti "nods" when he attaches Lola's final words in the preceding dialogue ("If you want to greet me, you know where I live") to the auctorial narrative which follows it, thereby disrupting the carefully calculated rhythmic alternation of narration and dialogue which is a hallmark of Verga's style.

On a more modest scale, the test of "beautiful fidelity" can be applied to the handling of two ellipses in the text of "Cavalleria rusticana." As the evidence shows, one of these, marking a significant gap or *Leerstelle*—to use a term associated with Wolfgang Iser's version of reader response theory—has been uniformly retained, whereas the other was just as uniformly ignored. The translators' adherence to the model manifests itself with regard to the proverb "Le volpe quando all'uva non ci poté arrivare . . . " ("when the fox couldn't reach the grapes . . . ") whose conclusion Santa aborts and which the quick-witted Turridu completes capriciously: "Disse: come sei bella, *racinedda* mia" ("he said: how beautiful you are, my sweet little grape!"), turning the situation to his own advantage.

The second use of ellipsis, following Lola's remarks "lasciate mi raggiungere le mie compagne. Che direbbero il paese se mi vedessero con voi . . . " ("let me catch up with my friends. What would they say in town if they saw me with you?"), seems to have been overlooked because it is much less conspicuous, although perhaps no less important; for it seems to be the author's way of indicating that her answer, perfectly reasonable within the context as a reflection of the prevailing social norms, is decidedly inconclusive in so far as Lola, newly attracted to the youth, would much rather continue the conversation.

One of the most challenging tasks awaiting the translator as "structuralist" is that of charting and conveying whatever patterns the author of the original text may have established, whether in the form of central images or the repetitive use of key words or phrases. To ignore such constellations, whether out of indifference or in the presumed knowledge that it would be hard, if not impossible, to retain them in the target language, is tantamount to ignoring authorial intentions and thus to subverting, in certain instances, the inherent sense of a passage or even the entire piece. In a narrative as succinct as "Cavalleria rusticana," where such constellations abound, they are obviously significant and must be re-created.

Verga uses simple but "loaded" repetitions which can be divided into two different but related groups: one occurs within a given dialogue where a key word or phrase is bounced back and forth between two speakers like a ball; the other is usually re-introduced toward the end of a narrative section, and prods the reader to measure the distance between two points. "Cavalleria rusticana" offers two striking examples of the former kind, one in a quick-fire exchange between Santa and Turridu, and the other in the less animated but extremely poignant conversation between Lola and her ex-fiancé. In the first instance, the pivotal verb is *mangiare* ("to eat"), and in the second *salutare* ("to greet").

As one Italian critic has noted, the metaphorical use of *mangiare*, endemic throughout the novella, is eloquent proof that Verga sought to keep his figures down to earth while concurrently investing their speech with symbolic strength. In the bantering exchange between Turridu and Santa, application is made when, the girl having rebuffed her impetuous suitor's advances ("Ohé! quelle mani, compare Turridu!" ["Hey! watch those hands, Turridu!"]), the following battle of wits ensues:

> Turridu: Avete paura che vi mangi?
> Santa: Paura non ho, ne de voi ne del vostro Dio.
> Turridu: Eh! vostra madre era di Licodia, lo sappiamo. Avete il sangue risosso. Uh! che vi mangerei cogli occhi!
> Santa: Mangiatemi pure cogli occhi, che bricciole non ne faremo . . .
>
> (Turridu: Are you afraid I'll eat you?
> Santa: I'm not afraid of you or your God.
> Turridu: Eh! your mother was from Licodia, we know that you've got fighting blood! Uh! I'd eat you with my eyes!
> Santa: Go ahead and eat me with your eyes, and we won't leave any crumbs!)

The eating here is done figuratively with the eyes rather than, literally, with the mouth—with obvious implications. In any case, our four translators had no difficulty being consistent on both levels; for in both Italian and English, as in most Western languages for that matter, the cannibalistic implications of kissing and loving signify male possessiveness.

The verb which dominates the other interchange is more subtly shaded, and at least two of the four translators failed to see, or at least express, the inherent sexual innuendo. Here is the text of the passage I have in mind:

> Lola che ascoltava ogni sera, nascosta dietro il vaso di basilico, e si faceva pallida e rossa, un giorno chiamò Turridu.
> "E così, compare Turridu, gli amici vecchi non si salutano più?"
> "Ma, sospirò il giovinetto, beato chi può salutarvi."
> "Si avete intenzione di salutarmi, lo sapete dove sto di casa" rispose Lola.
> Turridu torno a salutarla così spesso che Santa se ne avvide e gli batte la finestra sul muso.
>
> (Lola, who listened every evening, hidden behind a pot of sweet basil, and turned pale and red, one day called Turridu.
> "And so, Turridu, old friends don't greet each other any more?"
> "Well . . . " sighed the young man, "it's a lucky person who can greet you!"
> "If you want to greet me, you know where I live," answered Lola.

> Turridu went back to greet her so often that Santa noticed it and slammed the window in his face.)

Surely, the reader is given to understand that Lola, to use an expression introduced by Santa when she broaches the matter to Alfio, the carter, is inviting Turridu to "adorn his house for him." This is confirmed by the narrator's ironic stance ("Turridu tornò a salutarla così spesso") as well as by subsequent events.

Further improving his record of accuracy, Cecchetti gets the message and safely conveys it by using "greet" consistently throughout the passage. Alma Strettel does not lag far behind but slightly mars her record by using the circumlocution "if you have any intentions of bringing me your greetings." Lawrence, missing the point, substitutes "speak" for "greet," while Alexander, settling on the sequence "know . . . say hello . . . see . . . see" upsets the apple cart. (He could have exploited, instead, the Biblical sense of "knowing.")

The second kind of repetition, bracketing, is exemplified by the recurrent use of an idiomatic expression denoting anger and shame. The first time Verga brings the phrase into play, he does so in order to characterize Lola's socially correct behavior in her first encounter with the newly discharged Turridu: "Finalmente Turridu imbattè in Lola, che tornava dal *viaggio* alla Madonna del Pericolo, e al vederlo non si fece ni bianca ni rossa" ("He finally ran into Lola, who was returning from a pilgrimage to Our Lady of Peril, and, seeing him, she turned neither white nor red, as if it were none of her business"). The telling phrase resurfaces when Lola, hiding behind the pot of basil, turns both pale and red (*pallida e rossa*). The distance between two points in the narrative measured here is that between a girl formally promised to a man other than the one she loves but outwardly in full control of her feelings, and a married woman unable to suppress her continued emotional *engagement*.

How have the four translators coped with this, by all appearances, simple problem? Fairly well, on the whole, in so far as three of them—Alma Strettel, Cecchetti, and Alexander—retain the nuance implied by the progression from *bianco* to *pallido*, the one invoking the proverbial maiden color and maiden blush, and the other denoting the anguish and wrath of a woman chastened by marriage. True to form, Lawrence botches the matter; for his Lola, rather than turning red and white/pale, never "turn(s) a hair" and goes "hot and cold by turns."

Let us round out the survey by glancing at three additional cases of bunching in "Cavalleria rusticana" and their equivalents in the four English-language versions. A small grouping of terms that is more than a mere *quantité négligeable* pertains to Sicily's flourishing oenoculture. I have mentioned the relevant passage in connection with the proverb that is left hanging, with the expected word *uva* ("grape") being replaced by *racinedda* ("little raisin" or "sweet little grape"). But this is not the only time that grapes are mentioned, as Lola later tells her reinstated lover, who seeks to dissuade her from going to confession, that she has dreamt of black grapes, an evil omen, and must therefore do penance: "Domenica voglio andare a confessarmi, che stanotte ho sognato dell'uva nera." We thus get the sequence *uva, racinedda, uva nera*, which propels us from the grape, Lola, whom the fox, Turridu, cannot obtain, to the sweet Santa, whom he takes to be easier prey, and the self-fulfilling prophecy of a nightmare.

It is easy to see why this would be a real crux for the translator. To begin with the well informed and usually reliable Cecchetti, in his version we have "grapes," followed by "sweet little grapes," and then by the ominous "black grapes," which are duly footnoted, as they are in two of the other renditions. Not quite sure what to make of the slightly awkward *racinedda*, Alma Strettel moves from "grapes" to "little cluster" and on to "black grapes," while Alexander has "grapes," "sweet little thing," and "black grapes" respectively. The test of translatorial strength thus comes clearly with the term of endearment applied to Santa. All's not well with the above solutions, and one cannot help but admiring Lawrence for his bold choice of "little gooseberry," on the grounds that, by introducing this vulgar designation for the female breast, the English author, although roughening the discourse, succeeds in conveying the sexual overtones.

Still another frequently mentioned item on the list of familiar things which collectively make up the world in which Verga's characters live (and with which the narrator, in truly veristic fashion, seeks to identify as closely as possible) is the *berretto* ("cap"), which, so the Italian editors tell us, is worn in the country side, unlike the *cappello* ("hat"), which is worn by city dwellers. In "Cavalleria rusticana," two kinds of *berretto* are featured: the red "fez" of the *bersagliere* Turridu, which becomes an object of universal admiration; and the ordinary white one worn by the carter Alfio.[17] Proud man that he is, the latter initially wears it over his ears, but at the end, on the way to the duelling place, he pulls it over his eyes, so as to blot out the world and, presumably, hide his shame. Thus, the reader must cope with the sequence *berretto rosso, berretto, berretto sull'orecchio*, and *berretto sugli occhi*, introduced in that order.

Regardless of whether the translators render *berretto* with "cap" (Alma Strettel and Cecchetti), "fez cap" (Lawrence) or "red cap" (Alexander), nothing will prevent them from being literal in the first two instances, while in the fourth, that of the *berretto* worn *sugli occhi*, it is more or less a matter of phrasing. The crucial link in the chain, linguistically speaking, is the cap worn *sull'orecchio*; for here the literal translation preferred by three members of our quartet—"cap on the ear" (Alma Strettel), "cap over the ear" (Lawrence) and "caps right over their ears" (Alexander)—will not strike the anglophone reader as familiar and will make sense only in context. Only Cecchetti's rendition ("chip on their shoulders") does justice to the idiomatic phrase, albeit at the price of breaking the mold, which seems worth paying in this instance.

The most comprehensive and pervasive pattern by far is that which relates to the act of seeing. It offers relatively few problems to the translator of "Cavalleria rusticana" in so far as its word field is, for all practical purposes, limited to the verb *vedere* ("to see") and the pertinent sense organ, *occhio* ("eye"), which, used for weeping (*piangere*) as well as viewing, functions in a variety of ways. It not only serves to confirm the patent truth of external reality ("ho visto co miei occhi") but also as a channel for desire ("ti mangerei cogli occhi"). On the opposite pole of the semantic spectrum, the obverse condition, that of blindness, prevails, signaling the muting of the world, either literally or figuratively.

Verga makes especially cogent use of this web in the concluding portion of the novella, where he describes the duel between Alfio and Turridu, preceded by their common walk. Turridu opens the conversation by telling his rival that he has decided to fight it out, rather than let himself be killed as the guilty party he is, because he has *seen* his mother feed the chickens ("Ho visto la mia vecchia che si era alzata per vedermi partire, col pretesto di governare il pollaio"). He continues to see her in his mind's eye as he opens the duel by stabbing Alfio, emblematically, in the groin: "Ora che ho visto la mia vecchia nel pollaio, mi pare di averla sempre dinanzi agli occhi" ("Now that I've seen my old mother in the chicken coop, she seems to be always before my eyes"). Alfio responds, first by asking him, sarcastically, to *open his eyes* ("Apriteli bene, gli occhi!") and then by blinding him with a handful of dust he has gathered from the ground ("Acchiappò rapidamente una manata di polvere e la gettò negli occhi dell'avversario"). In so doing, he inflicts upon Turridu the very punishment which, earlier, he had threatened to mete out to Santa and her entire family should she have falsely accused his wife ("Se non avete visto bene, non vi lascierò gli occhi per piangere, a voi e a tutto il vostro parentado"). As we can see, this is an exceptionally rich pattern, but one that, fortunately, even the least able of translators is unlikely to distort beyond recognition.

I have reached the end of my journey. What this comparative study of four English versions of "Cavalleria rusticana," although by no means complete, has shown, with the help of a large number of illustrations meant to characterize the various levels of discourse with which the translator has to cope, is that in spite of the many pitfalls, whether lexical, grammatical, syntactic, semantic or structural, the original can, after all, be satisfactorily rendered, as is the case with Cecchetti's translation. While Alma Strettel's rendition strikes one, at least in hindsight, as being rather coy and slightly prettifying, Alexander's version sins by its inconsistency, which at times borders on capriciousness, while Lawrence's attempt, marred by many lapses and some overly bold deviations from the original, strikes one as being more of a recreation than a translation in the ordinary sense. None of these texts are complete disasters, however; and the real translatorial nightmare they might have engendered begins only when the transfer is not merely from language to language, as is here the case, but from one genre or medium (novella to drama, and drama to opera) to another. It is there that, a veritable Doppelgänger, the Mephistophelean *traditore* steps out of the shadow of the well-intentioned but easily side-tracked *traduttore*.

NOTES

1 D. H. Lawrence, *Letters*, ed. J. T. Bolton and A. Robertson, vol. 3 (Cambridge: Cambridge UP, 1984) 53.
2 On Verga, the playwright, see especially Anna Barsotti, *Verga drammaturgo: Tra commedia borghese e teatro verista siciliano* (Florence: La Nuova Italia, 1974), and Siro Ferrone, *Il teatro di Verga* (Rome: Bulzoni, 1974). Eric Bentley's translation of the dramatized *Cavalleria rusticana* first appeared in the first volume of the series *From the Modern Repertory* (Garden City, N.Y.: Doubleday, Anchor Books, 1954).
3 Especially useful information about the genesis of Mascagni's opera is found in the volume *Cinquantenario della "Cavalleria rusticana" di Pietro Mascagni MDCCCXC-MCMXL: Le lettere ai librettisti durante la creazione del capolavoro (inedite)*, ed. Carlo Ravasio (Milan: Edizioni d'Arte Emilio Bestetti, 1940), which reproduces the letters the composer wrote while he was working on the piece. A rather detailed account of the latter's genesis, as well as of the circumstances surrounding the dramatic adaptation made for the Duse, is given by Alfred Alexander, *Giovanni Verga: A Great Writer and His Work* (London: Grant & Cutler, 1972) chapters 6 and 7. Chapter 8, entitled *"Cavalleria litigata,"* deals with the legal action taken by Verga against Mascagni in order to secure some of the profits from the successful and widespread performances of the opera.
4 "Everybody knows, of course, that Verga made a dramatised version of 'Cavalleria rusticana,' and that this dramatized version is the libretto of the ever-popular little opera of the same name. So that Mascagni's rather feeble music has gone to immortalise a man like Verga, whose only *popular* claim to fame is that he wrote the aforesaid libretto. But that is fame's fault, not Verga's." From Lawrence's introduction to the volume *Cavalleria rusticana* (London, 1923), reprinted in his *Selected Literary Criticism*, ed. Anthony Beal (New York: The Viking Press, 1956) 291.
5 In his article "Stato civile della. 'Cavalleria rusticana,'" which is primarily concerned with Verga's own dramatization of his novella, F. De Roberto states emphatically: "il Verga preferiva e preferisce di gran lunga la novella al dramma" (*La Lettura* [Milan], January 1921: 10).
6 Translated from Giuseppe Paterno, *Giovanni Verga: Scrittore, Romanziere, Novelliere* (Catania: Tipografia Etna, 1974) 37-39.
7 A parallel story is adduced by Vanna Bosco-Malvica in her essay "La Fonction de quelques *altérés* dans 'Cavalleria rusticana' di Giovanni Verga," *Revue des Etudes Italiennes* 23 (1977): 63.
8 The matter is discussed by V. Perroni in an essay entitled "Sulla genesi de *I Malavoglia*" in the journal *Le Ragioni critiche* Oct.-Dec. 1972: 471-526, especially pp. 483 and 514, as well as in "Storia de *I Malavoglia*," *Nuova Antologia* 75 (1948): 105-131.
9 Following the success of the drama, the volume was renamed *Cavalleria rusticana*, the title under which it has been reprinted ever since.
10 After having perused Gian Paolo Marchi's *Concordanze Verghiane: Cinque Studi con un appendice di scritti rari* (Verona: Fiorini, 1970), which contains a chapter entitled "Per una storia del testo," as well as the chapter "Il testo di *Vita dei Campi* e le correzioni verghiane" of Giovanni Cecchetti's book *Il Verga*

maggiore: Sette studi (Florence: La Nuova Italia, 1968), I managed to obtain a copy of the original text through the Indiana University Interlibrary Loan Office.
11 They are, in order of appearance: 1) Alma Strettel, trans., *"Cavalleria rusticana" and Other Tales of Sicilian Peasant Life* (London: T. Fisher Unwin, 1903) 7-22; 2) D. H. Lawrence, trans., *"Cavalleria rusticana" and Other Stories* (London: Cape, 1928); 3) Giovanni Cecchetti, trans., *"The She-Wolf" and Other Stories* (Berkeley: Univ. of California Press, 1962), 10-18; 4) Albert Alexander, *Giovanni Verga: A Great Writer and His World* (London: Grant & Cutler, 1972) 100-106. Lawrence's version has been discussed by Cecchetti, in an essay entitled "Verga and D. H. Lawrence's Translations," *Comparative Literature* 9 (1957): 333-344), and by G. M. Hyde in the chapter "Lawrence and Verga: The Short Stories" of his book *D. H. Lawrence and the Art of Translation* (London: Macmillan, 1981) 36-59.
12 Luigi Russo (*Giovanni Verga*, 4th ed. [Bari: Laterza, 1947] 146) speaks of the "fraseggiare dialettale che il Verga non riesce ancora a tradurre nella sua originalissima lingua," and of his "crudezze dialettali" (378); and in his edition of Verga's *Opere* (Milan/Naples: Ricciardi, 1955) 118, he castigates the author for his inability, in these novellas, to rise to the level of the ideal Platonic language which transcends the inferior dialectal sphere.
13 Giovanni Verga, *Le Novelle*, ed. Gino Tellini (Rome: Salerno, 1980) 113, 122.
14 "Quel salsiccio è felicissimo, singolare-plurale preferito nella lingua di Sicilia. (Un toscano avrebbe visto un piatto di salsicci.) Ma quel desco mi suona troppo toscano e dotto, e poco verghiano" (Russo 389).
15 Bosco-Malvica 68.
16 In "Una traduzione tedesca del dramma *Cavalleria rusticana*," *Rivista di Letterature moderne e comparate* 28 (1975): 7, Raffaela Bertazzoli quotes (in German) from a letter in which Verga admonishes a German stage director to avoid excessive pathos at all costs.
17 For a more detailed explanation, see Verga, *Le Novelle*, ed. Gino Tellini 119.

THE VICTIM AS OPPRESSOR: MIRROR STRUCTURES IN MOTHER-DAUGHTER RELATIONS IN RECENT GERMAN WOMEN'S FICTION

> With your milk, Mother, you fed me ice. And if I leave, you lose the reflection of life, of your life. And if I remain, am I not the guarantor of your death? Each of us lacks her own image; her own face, the animation of her own body is missing. And the one mourns the other. My paralysis signifying your abduction in the mirror.
>
> Luce Irigaray, "And the One Doesn't Stir without the Other"

Maria-Regina Kecht, Hamilton College

Ever since the mid-seventies there has been a steady flow of women's writing—fictional as well as non-fictional—that has centered on the formerly marginal issue of mother-daughter relationships. Adrienne Rich's *Of Woman Born* (1976), a sensitive analysis of the institution of motherhood in the context of Western patriarchal society, was just as influential as the socio-psychological study *The Reproduction of Mothering* (1978) by Nancy Chodorow. Signe Hammer's commentary on extensive interview material, entitled *Daughters and Mothers: Mothers and Daughters* (1975), was followed by a very similar enterprise carried out by Judith Arcana under the title *Our Mothers' Daughters* (1979). The general currency of the topic was heightened by the appearance of Nancy Friday's autobiographical *My Mother, My Self* (1977). Literary criticism took up the subject-matter in Lyn Lifshin's edition of mother-daughter poems, *Tangled Vines* (1978), and Cathy Davidson's and E. M. Broner's collection of critical essays with the suggestive title *The Lost Tradition: Mothers and Daughters in Literature* (1980).

All these publications have also had a wide reception in the German-speaking countries, where a number of sociological and psychological book-length studies have further highlighted the growing interest in the problematics of mother-daughter relations. As examples I just want to mention Erika Schilling's impressive documentation of interviews called *Manchmal hasse ich meine Mutter* (1981), Jutta Menschik's volume *Ein Stück von mir: Mütter erzählen* (1985), and Karin Spielhofer's discussion of the bonding between mother and daughter in *Sanfte Ausbeutung* (1985).[1]

In the absence of a thorough analysis of the origins of the new interest in mother-daughter relations, I want to put forth my own speculative explanation: with the raising of feminist consciousness and the breaking of many taboos concerning family life and family relations, women have dared to step back from their own caretakers, their life-givers, their most powerful individual influences, in order to critically scrutinize the effects of the mother-daughter bondage and to comprehend their own identities in the light of the (s)mothering they have experienced. The distinctness of that primary relationship was suddenly admitted to be of paramount importance for our understanding of women's self-definition, and their relation to the other; and its importance has led to our recognition that it is mothers who frequently perpetuate and reinforce the patriarchal structure of our Western societies.

When reading any of the aforementioned books, one cannot help raising the question whether all these critical attempts at coming to terms with the dangers of mother-daughter symbiosis, stifling over-identification, and the concomitant difficulty of separation and female individuation are not narcissistic exercises in intellectual objectification. It is remarkable that in their preface or introduction, most authors explain how their analysis has been motivated by personal problems with their own mothers, and how these problems have been alleviated by the process of their investigations. Such objectification is typical of the Western logocentric mode of coping with human experience. It is also telling that the examination of mother-daughter relations—rooted as it is in specific socio-cultural patterns of thinking—cannot avoid posing the male development towards selfhood as the standard and the model to be emulated. The maternal barriers to a daughter's autonomy and her free will are lamented and bemoaned in all the empirical studies as well as in the fictional representations of mother-daughter relations.

No matter how personalized a fictional depiction of the problem may be, women writers still intend a certain degree of sensible detachment and objectivity. Indeed, such narrative distance seems a necessary prerequisite for public articulation and sharing of a very private experience. Writing about mother-daughter relations—in a largely autobiographical mode—generally assumes the force of self-therapy, a purgative cure, a final attempt at dis- or re-covering one's self.[2] The hope that such writing entertains cannot be fulfilled, however. In contrast to the socio-psychological investigation of the conflict in mother-daughter relations, usually concluding in rational suggestions for a successful resolution of the conflict, the fictional treatment leads to different findings: the author comes to realize that reason and analytical reflection are ineffective when confronted with the very strong emotional and biological forces that characterize any mother-daughter relation. The conflict cannot be resolved through thought processes. This leaves us with the dilemma of a modern tragedy where the heroine is doomed to reproduce her mother, to be hopelessly caught in a cycle of transmitted identity. Thus she becomes the victim of a kind of socio-biological destiny, deprived of the power of free will.

In her classic work *The Second Sex*, Simone de Beauvoir astutely describes the nature of the conflict that turns the mother-daughter relationship into a struggle for maternal domination and self-extension, leaving behind a victim who has absorbed rather than developed a self, who has internalized the behavior of maternal oppression and imitates it whenever the occasion permits.[3] It is this double identity of tyrant and sufferer, of victim and oppressor in one person, that represents, in my opinion, the most disquieting aspect of, perhaps not quite ordinary, mother-daughter relations. The double identity is linked to an extreme mutual dependence and a powerful drive towards the merging of egos, a bonding that turns out to be a crippling confinement for both mother and daughter.

Such bondage is the central issue of the two German novels I have chosen to use as examples for my discussion of the fictional treatment of mother-daughter relations: Elfriede Jelinek's *Die Klavierspielerin* (1983) and Anna Mitgutsch's *Die Züchtigung* (1985) are both vivid and compelling illustrations of the physical and psychological violence of which maternal love is capable, and the schizophrenic duality of submissive-rebellious behavior on the part of the daughter. Sadism and masochism convert the family nest into a prison full of mirrors without any exit. The role reversals of victim and oppressor are psychologically conditioned and socially motivated. One cannot survive without the other, a sense of identity is only established in the conflict-laden dynamics of blind assertion of power and total subordination.

As different as these novels may be—and I will touch upon those differences—they are strikingly similar in that both are largely autobiographical accounts of pathological mother-daughter relations. The perverse union of mother and daughter excludes the father figure, who is reduced to an object of contempt and ridicule, posing as a negative model for men in general. The child is debased to an object, a piece of precious property, guarded and locked up, or to a marionette on strings, whose desire for autonomy and struggle for separation are squelched with shocking brutality. The successful suppression of the daughter's development, keeping her at an infantile stage of utter dependence as long as possible, leads to her inability to express and experience love and sensual pleasure; and creates self-hatred, depression, and aggressiveness which, in turn, finds its outlet in oppressing others in order to finally gain recognition and respect.

The narrative contexts for this theme are different in Jelinek and Mitgutsch. *Die Klavierspielerin* provides us with a glimpse into the small world of Erika Kohut, a 36-year-old piano instructor who has spent her entire life with her mother, a housewife who has always harbored great dreams and high aspirations for her daughter's career, none of which have been fulfilled. We behold Erika's "good" public image and her quite amazing, secret private life full of voyeurism and experiments in masochism. A brief and rather perverse sexual interlude with Walter Klemmer, one of the piano students, serves to illustrate Erika's crippled personality, her infantile dependence on her mother, and her utterly distorted notions of human affection.

In contrast to Jelinek's mere excerpt from the Kohuts' family life, Mitgutsch's novel *Die Züchtigung* presents the sad life story of three generations of daughters who are scapegoats for their mothers' profound frustrations. Marie, the abused daughter of a rich but tight-fisted farmer, marries a man whom she does not love and of whom she is ashamed. Her daughter Vera is to become the realization of all ambitious wishes, dreams, and hopes, even if this means daily use of the rod; she is to restore the lost self-image of her mother. Once Vera in turn has experienced motherhood, she attempts to give her little daughter everything she herself has been deprived of. But having never learned to love, Vera recognizes that she fails to make her child happy.

As scant as such a depiction of the difference in plots may be, it should suffice to get an idea of the authors' distinct approaches to the central theme of the mother-daughter relation. Jelinek focuses on two aspects: the grotesque symbiosis of the adult daughter and her rather old mother, who still treats Erika like a small child and takes violent revenge whenever she disobeys; and, second, Erika's perverse modes of sexuality and cruelty as the consequences of life-long repression and permanent supervision. *Die Klavierspielerin* is a *post festum* account of what has gone terribly wrong in the raising of the daughter—we are confronted with Erika's neuroses, the shocking results of maternal overprotectiveness and domination.

Mitgutsch, however, presents us with a process, a development that delineates causes and effects, origins and outcomes. We witness the tribulations and humiliations that Marie, the narrator's mother, suffers when she grows up on a farm. Such knowledge is meant to explain, if not excuse, the unfathomable degree of sadism exercised by Marie in bringing up her daughter Vera. Complexes, obsessions, and neuroses are the heritage that Vera, in turn, offers to her own daughter.[4] *Die Züchtigung* portrays what a German critic perspicaciously called "the banality of evil," versions of childhood where "perfect training aligned to horror is internalized."[5]

Mitgutsch and Jelinek choose different narrative perspectives which allow us to infer different degrees of personal distance from the autobiographical problem of the fictionalized subject-matter. In Mitgutsch's novel, the story is presented by Vera in the first person; sixteen years after her mother's death Vera feels compelled to reflect upon her relationship to her mother when her own little daughter demands answers to an issue that has hitherto been consigned to oblivion. In addition to masterfully playing with the distinction between *erzählendes Ich* ("narrating I") and *erzähltes Ich* ("narrated I"), with their respective views and insights, Mitgutsch has the narrator frequently disappear behind the voice of the mother, thus emphasizing the mother's emotional usurpation of the daughter's self.

Jelinek's *Klavierspielerin* is told in the third person from the perspective of a partly omniscient narrator who assumes a rather sarcastic, cynical position towards the described events. Irony modulates the tone of presentation; and not a single character in the story is spared caustic comments. The narrative detachment from the undoubtedly freakish plot is a preferred strategy of Jelinek's because, as she has stated in interviews, in her artistic work she tries to come to terms with her personal obsession with sado-masochism.[6] Perhaps one can also relate the choice of narrative distance to Jelinek's free admission that she comes from a family with a very authoritarian mother who excelled in the use of sexually repressive pedagogical measures. It might be worth adding that Mitgutsch, on the other hand, has avoided commenting on the experiential sources of her first novel, *Die Züchtigung*; her weak disclaimer (placed at the beginning of her book) of any similarity between her fictional characters and real life may fulfill some legal obligations but hardly blurs the distinct impression of profound personal suffering and intense, even obsessive, preoccupation with motherhood and daughterhood.

Style and language are radically different in Jelinek and Mitgutsch. Whereas the former indulges in a stark, colorful, at times even outright vulgar, language full of eccentric and bright metaphors, the latter affects the reader by the poetic simplicity and powerful rhythm of her language.[7] Jelinek consistently undercuts the horror and the tragedy of the events through black humor and irony, but the seriousness of Mitgutsch's realism forces us almost to share the pain and the misery of her protagonists.

Within the scope of this essay it is impossible to enumerate and discuss all the parallels in the thematic representation of the mother-daughter conflict in Jelinek and Mitgutsch. Therefore, I want to single out two major aspects of the conflict: the confinement of mother and daughter in a closed environment and the nature of violence as a constant training measure. Both appear to be the main conditions for a situation in which free choice finds no room for exercise, thus determining the tragedy of the daughter's destiny. Furthermore, confinement and violence set off these two recent novels from more mainstream representations of the tensions between mother and daughter.

As mentioned before, in both *Die Klavierspielerin* and *Die Züchtigung* a mother is the sole adult responsible for the upbringing of an only daughter. The father figure is either locked up in a psychiatric ward, as in Jelinek's book, or he is totally excluded from the possibility of parenting, as in Mitgutsch's book. In both cases, the fathers are deemed to be utter social failures (void of any ambition) who have not managed to satisfy their wives' needs, whether these are economic, social, or sexual. The hegemony and omnipotence of the mother become something like natural givens; and they are not questioned as long as the daughter lives with her mother; nor are they ever contested by the fathers, since child-rearing is accepted to be a female chore.

The mother's tyrannical, possessive nature finds its expression in a variety of ways. Any form of socialization beyond the mother-daughter interaction is made practically impossible: contacts with peers—through kindergarten, school, or work—are screened carefully and always judged negatively; relatives are also considered to be dangerous intrusions into the "family idyll," and possible boyfriends or lovers are presented as incarnations of evil long before they even appear on the scene. In both works, the mothers are shrewd enough to provide their daughters with a rationale for the necessary social exclusiveness. They continually stress the daughter's superiority, her ostensible individualism, and their own better experience in choosing the daughter's company. Disobedience or unsatisfactory performance in school or in the chosen career are always attributed to negative influences from outside. The mothers camouflage the daughter's social isolation as distinctness. Such a strategy achieves two results: first, the daughter cannot avoid internalizing such views as a mere defense mechanism to cope with her loneliness; and second, solidarity with her mother becomes essential, a *sine qua non* for survival, because there is nobody else she can fall back on. The mother becomes indeed the sole being with whom the daughter can share anything. And—as in a self-fulfilling prophecy—the daughter rushes back into her mother's strong arms every time she suffers a disappointment in her encounter with the "outer" world.

Since there is absolutely no space set aside for privacy out of which upsetting signs of autonomy might develop, the daughters are under constant surveillance. They share a bed with their mothers;[8] they have no keys to lock a room; their letters as well as their briefcases, closets, or drawers are routinely checked; their wardrobe and hairstyle are chosen for them; their leisure time activities are determined and imposed; and their study or work schedules are closely scrutinized—coming home late is reason for severe punishment. If the daughter tries to challenge her mother's authority—her prison-guard's prerogatives—by trying to conceal anything, she faces even more repressive measures.

Economic dependence is another powerful mechanism to manipulate the daughters' behavior. In both novels the mothers are in charge of the finances and the bookkeeping; they are very thrifty and decide how the money should be spent, even if, as in the case of Jelinek, the daughter earns her own money. As the mothers dream of a large condominium or a house (the reason for their thrift), they constantly reproach their daughters for not being sufficiently considerate and selfless. Their own economic sacrifice is a perennial theme in creating guilt-feelings in their daughters. Such a sacrifice requires gratitude and strengthens the ties due to the daughter's bad conscience.

The ultimate burden of guilt is placed on the daughter when she is told that her mother worries about having to move into an old people's home or, as in Mitgutsch, that she will definitely die if, or when, her daughter leaves her alone. Life-long devotion and selfless sacrifice are invoked in order to gain reassurance and renewed, exclusive loyalty. These mothers want their daughters to admit that they could not possibly survive without them, that they owe everything to their care-takers (which, in an ironical way, they in fact do). This leaves the daughters without an image, a self of their own.

The "bell jar syndrome" of such mother-daughter relations is vividly captured in Jelinek's comparison between her protagonist and a fossilized insect in amber: "Erika is an insect in amber, timeless, ageless. Erika has no history and she is not going to make history. This insect has long lost its ability to scramble and to crawl. Erika is baked into the cake pan of eternity."[9] In *Die Züchtigung*, the image of being crippled, unable to move, and arrested in stasis is also frequently conjured up when describing the daughter's situation.

Confinement engenders the daughter's infantile dependence, loneliness and social isolation, and it produces repressed wishes and desires which turn into compulsion and aggression. It also causes neurotic arrogance and deep-seated inferiority complexes which result in violence, as exercised by Erika Kohut's and Vera Kovacs's mothers. This brings about dejection, self-hatred, and an obsessive search for oppressive authority figures as well as for helpless victims.

In an attempt to exculpate her mother, the narrator of Mitgutsch's novel wants to understand the roots of her authoritarianism, and she gives us a life-story full of humiliation and emotional deprivation. Red-haired Marie is a horribly abused outcast in her family, the victim of her siblings' brutal pranks, her mother's jealousy and hate, and her father's blind, violent rage; she is the backward farmer's kid in parochial school, the neglected young woman who ends up marrying a man who is a laughing stock for her family. As much as her home was hell, Marie, proudly defining herself as a rich farmer's daughter, experiences life with her economically and socially inferior husband as even more painful and devastating. His sexuality is an insult, and his lack of ambition a constant source of aggravation and bitterness. Having a daughter, not a son, by this man is the worst kind of punishment Marie can imagine.

So this daughter has to be molded and trained in order to redeem her mother's life-long victimization. Physical violence is done to Vera from her earliest infancy, and it stops when she is fourteen.

> A beating: it never meant a spontaneous burst of anger, which might be followed by awkwardness and reconciliation. It began with a look that transformed me into a vermin. And then a silence in which nothing had been decided yet and which nevertheless was past escape. The offense was swallowed up by the silence; it was never discussed. There were no alibis, explanations, excuses. There stood the misdeed, whether it was a banana stain on a dress or food refused—unatonable—and suddenly the misdeed was only a symbol for such an enormous wickedness that no amount of punishment sufficed. "Get me the carpet beater," she commanded; "get me the cudgel." This was a wooden stick the thickness of an arm, which split in two during the course of my education. The broken cudgel was itself significant evidence of a culpability so great that it could never be punished fully. Had she been completely just, she would have had to beat me to death. I owed the fact that she continued to let me live to her sacrificial mother love, which, like the grace of God, was not earned and could never be repaid.[10]

No matter how much Vera tries to please her mother with good behavior, excellent performance in school, and expressions of gratitude, she can never satisfy her mother's expectations. Craving for love and recognition, Vera lives in constant fear of arousing her mother's anger and of being punished. Daily vomiting on the way to kindergarten and school is just one symptom of the emotional wounds inflicted on Vera's psyche. Later on bulimia and anorexia develop as additional symptoms of self-hatred. Any sign of femininity and sexual attractiveness is extinguished since sexuality has been judged to be the worst of all evils.

Vera's suppressed anger and hatred find their open manifestation in the violence she exerts on her dolls. She beats them for their defiance, their bad manners, their unworthiness. Later, as a school kid, she takes delight in terrorizing a weak little boy, and when she is briefly married she catches herself repeating her mother's degrading behavior towards her husband. Trying to avoid physical coercion of her own daughter, Vera nevertheless ends up emotionally manipulating her and quelling her process of individuation.

The tie between victim and oppressor is renewed in every relationship that Vera enters into with a man. Torture and love have become synonymous—and she is regularly drawn to men whose affection, she thinks, is to be won by self-humiliation. This form of internalization also characterizes Erika Kohut's relationship to the other sex. Giving her piano student and subsequent rapist Walter Klemmer a letter in which she enumerates different kinds of esoteric physical torment she would like to experience at his hands, Erika not only expresses her desire to obey unconditionally, but also her hope of being in sole control of the relationship. She wants to enforce her ideas, wants her will to be obeyed. She needs others on whom she can exercise her power, who would be victims of her perverse mind. One possibility is chastisement, playing the stern, authoritarian piano instructor who scolds bad performance as well as bad morals; another one is vindictiveness, like putting tiny glass shards into a young musician's coat pocket in order to punish her for being attractive; and yet another possibility is masochism. Cutting into her own alienated body with a razor blade or a knife, pinching it with dozens of clothes pegs, and sticking needles into it provides Erika with the pain she needs to experience some thrill, to experience herself. Erika is a living incarnation of "musts" and "must nots"—an exemplary product of her mother's upbringing.

In Jelinek's and Mitgutsch's novel, the heroines cannot free themselves from their mothers' strong bonds. They have become doubles, extensions of their mothers' punitive personalities; and the conclusions of both books give evidence that every attempt at rebellion and breaking away is followed by surrender and remorseful return to the woman to whom one owes everything. It is hard to say whether the authors have been more successful than their protagonists. As much as the process of writing may a be an act of self-therapy, it is also a source of guilt about publicly divulging family secrets. And it is difficult to assess whether establishing a public identity as a writer helps the daughter to divest herself of the inherited maternal robes. Mitgutsch ends her novel with an unforgettable paragraph, which I would like to quote here in its entirety, because it turns the self-purging effort of writing and confessing into a futile endeavor of self-exoneration and liberation.

> For sixteen years I buried her over and over, but she always rose and followed me. She caught up with me long ago. She looks at me with the eyes of my child; she observes me from the mirror when I think I'm unobserved; I meet her in my lovers, and I run off with her own arguments. Then she punishes me with loneliness, and I try to win her back through achievement, brilliant achievement, the epitome of achievement. I never please her. I married her and then divorced her, but she transformed herself and lay in wait for me. Her embrace, granted so hesitantly and only in exchange for perfect behavior, always turns into a grip in which I suffocate. I push her away and feel pushed away. I am her and say, You are worth nothing, and sink into grief for my loss, my loss of I, my loss of Thou, the loss of all the love in the

world. Because there are only the two of us. She is everything that is outside, night and the sun, sleep and the rain, love and hate and every person who crosses and darkens my life, and most of all myself. She has transformed herself into me; she created me and slipped inside me; when I died sixteen years ago, when she beat me to death thirty years ago, she took my body, appropriated my ideas, usurped my feelings.

She rules and I serve her, and when I gather all my courage and offer resistance she always wins, in the name of obedience, reason, and fear.[11]

The success of their novels was a surprise to both Mitgutsch and Jelinek. Bearing that in mind I would like to raise some questions for further consideration as a conclusion: Are these portrayals of aberrant, pathological mother-daughter relations compelling because we watch "with pity and fear" events that are largely autobiographical, and therefore so horrifying? Is the reading experience so profoundly disturbing because extreme, abnormal examples of family relations are presented in a straightforward, realistic mode of narration, thus blurring the boundaries between fact and fiction? Do these stark pictures strike a chord in us because we have experienced the effects of overbearing, possessive mothers? Are we impressed by the authors' courage that enabled them to distance themselves critically from the source of their pain and the cause of their humiliating identity crisis? Or, is the key to success perhaps to be found in the shift in reading audience, which has grown tired of the post-romantic self-expressions put forth by men who claimed to be speaking for all of humanity? Does the contemporary reader demand a different paradigm of self-expression, and respond favorably to a woman's voice articulating the *conditio humana*?

NOTES

1   It is relevant to enumerate the earlier American works on the topic because, from its inception, the German women's movement has followed the development of the movement in the United States. It is not surprising then that the German publications on mother-daughter relations started appearing only in the early eighties.

2   This is true for my selected examples of German literature of the eighties, and it also holds true for works of the seventies, as for example, Angelika Mechtel's *Die Blindgängerin, Geschichte einer alleinstehenden Frau* (1974); Karin Struck's *Die Mutter* (1975); Gabriele Wohmann's *Ausflug mit der Mutter* (1976); Brigitte Schwaiger's *Wie kommt das Salz ins Meer* (1977).

3   Simone de Beauvoir discusses the issue of mother-daughter relations in various parts of her book, *The Second Sex* (New York: Vintage, 1974), especially 317, 444, 571-584, and 654.

As an apt characterization of the problem as it presents itself in the two novels I have chosen for exemplary discussion, Jelinek's *Die Klavierspielerin* (1983) and Mitgutsch's *Die Züchtigung* (1985), the following quotation from *The Second Sex* may be instructive: "[T]he daughter is for the mother at once her double and another person, the mother is at once overweeningly affectionate and hostile toward her daughter; she saddles her child with her own destiny: a way of proudly laying claim to her own femininity and also a way of revenging herself for it. . . . [The daughter] imitates her mother and identifies herself with her: Frequently she even reverses their respective roles: . . . the real child is also an *alter ego* for the mother" (317-318).

4   Mitgutsch's story is indeed a haunting exemplification of Simone de Beauvoir's words: "Deeply scarred by their early home life, their [= the parents'] approach to their own children is through complexes and frustrations; and the chain of misery lengthens indefinitely. In particular, maternal sado-masochism creates in the daughter guilt feelings that will be expressed in sado-masochistic behavior toward her children, and so without end" (584).

5   On February 24, 1986, Matthias Jung delivered a "Laudatio" when Anna Mitgutsch was awarded the "Claassen Rose," an annual literary prize of the publishing house Claassen in Düsseldorf. My translated quotation is taken from the unpublished typescript of the speech.

6   Compare Georg Biron's interview with Jelinek in *Die Zeit* 5 October 1984, where she states: "Sado-Masochismus ist mein Thema Nummer eins. Das geht durch alle meine Texte. Das ist mein bisher ungelöstes Problem. Wenn ich die Kunst nicht hätte, als Ventil, würde ich mich wahrscheinlich in Dinge verstricken, die sehr zerstörerisch wären. . . . Gerade daß ich diese Obsessionen literarisch aufarbeiten kann, hält mich überhaupt noch halbwegs in einer normalen Existenz." (Sado-masochism is the number one topic for me. It pervades all my texts. It is a still unresolved problem for me. If I did not leave it as a way out, I would probably get entangled in something that could be very destructive. . . . The fact that I can come to terms with these obsessions in a literary way allows me to lead a halfway normal life.) The English translation is mine.

7   In his "Laudatio," Matthias Jung describes Mitgutsch's language as follows: "Die Sprache . . . ist sachlich, einfach, direkt, konstatierend, nicht anklagend, straff, fast ohne Metaphern, voll poetischer Kraft und Intensität." (The language is factual, simple, direct, not openly accusatory, tight, almost without any metaphors, full of poetic force and intensity.) The translation is mine.

8   In Mitgutsch's novel, the daughter always takes a bath with her mother to make sure that she does not ever touch her own body; the mother puts on an apron while sitting in the tub so that her daughter cannot see her breasts or her pubic hair. It is certainly not surprising that both Vera and Erika secretly explore their bodies through masturbation under the bed covers when their mothers are sound asleep. Thus, even the possession of their own bodies becomes a rebellious act.

9   Elfriede Jelinek, *Die Klavierspielerin* (Hamburg: Rowohlt, 1983) 20. The translation is mine.

10 Anna Mitgutsch, *Three Daughters*, trans. Lisel Mueller (New York: Harcourt Brace Jovanovich, 1987) 83-84.

11 Mitgutsch 215-16.

TEMPORALITY AS A FICTIONAL DEVICE IN BIOGRAPHY: SOME PUSHKIN AND BYRON BIOGRAPHIES

> To control time is to control oneself and others.
>
> Peter Hartocollis, *Time and Timelessness*

Anna Makolkina, University of Toronto

Biography is usually associated with reality and a genuine reconstruction of time. Although nearly every biography claims that the reconstruction of the lifetime of its subject is its main purpose, the claim can never be taken literally. The task of recreating fully and completely the time of the "Other" is a biological and, consequently, discursive impossibility. Thus, a biographer may only create an illusion of a complete temporal reconstruction. Readers of biographies have noticed how a biographer may summarize several years in the life of a subject in one sentence or may devote a whole chapter to a single day. Does this constitute a complete reconstruction? Obviously, the time record in a temporally dependant discourse is selective and incomplete. I would like to suggest that time record in biography is a source of fictionality in a notionally non-fictional genre.

The Russian biographer P. V. Annenkov, for instance, covers the first twelve years of Pushkin's life (1799-1837) in a chapter which is only nine pages long.[1] The first three sentences account for the events that occurred in Pushkin's family more than a hundred years earlier. The reader is informed about the several hundred years preceding the subject's birth. The assumed temporal universe (1799-1811) is expanded to include 1656, the year marking the death of one of the poet's ancestors. Twelve years in the life of the Russian poet are transformed into 178 years in the lives of Pushkin, his ancestors, his parents, and his nurse; Annenkov's chapter represents what one may call *compressed* time. Occasionally he prolongs his descriptions of certain periods in the life of his subject; the second chapter is devoted to the period 1811-1817. The next eight years of Pushkin's life are covered in twenty pages of the biography. The discursive time is unequally distributed between the various temporal segments described.

Sometimes the biographer resorts to a discursive phenomenon defined by Gerard Genette as *prolepsis*, i.e., anticipating future events.[2] According to Genette, *prolepsis* is rare in Western literature. However, the practice of biography proves quite the opposite. Biographers frequently resort to prolepsis in their attempts to cover the lifetime of the subject, the past of his compatriots or national group, and the present of the biographer and his reader.

If Annenkov's biography of the famous Russian poet is an attempt to recreate Pushkin's time, D. M. Petrov's version of the same subject, written a century later, represents more of an account of the past time of the national group, i.e., history of the Russian people.[3] Petrov, unlike Annenkov, focuses on the "lived experience" of the social group rather than that of the individual. The description of Pushkin's literary taste in his childhood leads the Soviet biographer to a long digression that summarizes the intellectual mood of eighteenth-century Russia and conveys his own view of the period. For instance, describing Pushkin's return to St. Petersburg in 1924, Petrov generalizes about the development of the Russian theater, mentions the rebellion in Spain, the Italian Carbonari movement, and the mutiny in Greece against Turkish occupation. The "lived experience" of the subject is extended by Petrov to the analogous experience of several national groups. Petrov's historical perspective dominates the narration, and the nominal central focus of the discourse—the hero—is moved to the periphery. The readers (or biographees) and the subject are separated from each other by the temporal universes of several groups as well as biographer's view of time. Such rearrangement of temporal planes enables Petrov to reach the desired time or extend the narrative possibilities of his biographical discourse. Time, a constrictor and a censoring device, is transformed by a biographer into a liberating device, which permits an escape into another time. The past time of the hero is an opportunity to dwell on the removed past of the national group.

Paul Graham Trueblood wrote Byron's biography in a classical chronological mode.[4] His discourse commences with the traditional beginning of the temporal matrix (the poet's birth in 1788) and ends with its final point (his death in 1824). Nevertheless, Trueblood presents two sets of time—the uninterrupted summary of the temporal matrix (from birth to death) and divided or segmented time in his discourse. Despite the apparent natural chronology, the biographer resorts to various digressions. For instance, in the first chapter, intending to describe the period of 1788-1805, Trueblood "recalls" the events of 1768 when Byron's grandfather "endured hammering adventures of shipwreck and hardship."[5] Being unable to equally cover all the temporal universes, a biographer maneuvers through the given time, selecting and combining the data from the given temporal matrix—the life of the subject from birth to death. Even when a biographer adheres to the chronological patterns of the narration, temporal maneuvering is unavoidable. First, Trueblood extends the temporal universe of 1788-1805 back to 1768, then as far back as 1571, in order to describe the history of Harrow, where Byron studied. This permits the biographer to be present in several centuries simultaneously. The forces of *analepsis* (Genette's term for "flashback") move the line of the natural chronology in the opposite direction:

```
                    1788 ---------------------------->1824
                    (Byron's birth)        (Byron's death)

   1571<--------------------------------------
```

Here and elsewhere, the line of analeptic digressions is consistently opposite to that of the temporal matrix—Birth-Death.

If Trueblood's biography is temporally rich and built within the "natural" chronology, Emilio Castelar's biography of Byron represents a temporal anomaly.[6] This life story puzzles the reader with a nearly complete absence of dates. The invisible chronological markers create an impression that time does not exist, and Byron, a Victorian hero, is in an atemporal universe. The avoidance of time in a biography founded on a temporal matrix is possible, thanks to euphemisms used by the Spanish biographer. Castelar expects readers to form their own chronological associations. When he introduces Byron's genealogical story, he refers to historical events without any indication of time: "His family is of Scandinavian origin. His genius sprung from the foam and the winds of the Northern ocean, borne on the leathern barks of the Normans."[7] "Normans" implies a temporal universe in the atemporal setting. Time is represented by the event which is presumably known to the biographee (reader). Castelar does not even provide the time of Byron's birth but merely states: "The genius of Byron, which appeared at the beginning of this century is like a funeral torch sculptured on our cradles."[8] "Beginning of the century" is a rather vague temporal marker, but the biographer does not measure time with respect to the movement of the Earth around the Sun but to spiritual evolution and human activity. Castelar views history as a succession of periods; a century is seen not as a concrete numerical category but as an indicator of a certain phase or cycle in continuous human movement. Occasional temporal markers refer to the turning points of fate rather than concrete events. For instance, 1750 is mentioned as a year that brought poverty to the Byron's because of the shipwreck that the poet's grandfather had suffered.

Castelar sees his hero's movement through time as a series of disastrous events and focuses on their dates:

1750	1765	1805	1808
shipwreck	killing	loss of love	boy became youth

The date of Byron's marriage is not given either. The biographer's attitude to the event and the subject's state of mind are conveyed through vivid landscape markers:

> He rose on his marriage morning in such a depression of spirits. To pass the time, he sought according to custom, a refuge from trouble in the arms of Mother Nature, and took a long walk in one of those English woods at this season leafless, cold and melancholy as death.[9]

Castelar processes the calendar dates metaphorically and the hermeneutics of time is more important to him than the recording of the actual flow of time. Likened to Apollo, Napoleon, Newton, and Michelangelo, his Byron is a special being who lives in a different temporal universe, where "time passes on." Such a hero rebels against natural chronology and lives in his own heroic time, which produces giants, conquers tragedies, and creates immortality.

Byron's real time, or the temporal matrix of his biography, serves as a temporal stock out of which the biographer chooses his *"desiderative time,"* using Cesare Segre's term.[10] Castelar's desiderative time is Chronos subordinated to the myth of a giant which predetermines the temporal strategy of the teller of Byron's life. Since his giant is immortal, the death of the English poet is not mentioned among other omitted dates. His Byron defies death and time.

If Castelar's strategy is a temporality subordinated to the myth of the hero, Eileen Bigland's perception of time is adjusted to the psychoanalytical motifs, death anxiety in particular.[11] Her biography of Byron begins and ends with the same temporal marker (1824), like a black mourning frame in an obituary notice. However, discussing the death of the biographical subject early in the narrative is not typical of most biographies. A biographer, much like a detective story-teller, delays disclosure of the known end. Usually a biographer deliberately "retards" the process,[12] but Bigland, on the other hand, defamiliarizes the known pattern and discloses the unavoidable ending, death, at the commencement of her discourse, specifically, in the "prologue in Missolonghi, April 1824." The date of Byron's death is a proleptic marker that introduces death before birth, thus inverting the biographical temporal matrix and changing its temporal axis.

After a sad proleptic reminder (1824), Bigland resorts to analepsis ("flashback") into Byron's family past prior to his birth. The direction of the analeptic axis, similar to Trueblood's biography, inverts the general temporal discursive axis:

1824------------------------1788------------------------1824

The analeptic digression, which covers events over several centuries, occupies three pages of discursive or "representational time."[13] Once again we see the familiar temporal strategy of compression. Bigland, like other biographers, selects her temporal focus, her "desiderative time," which reflects the dominant themes in her biography of Byron—his death and his sexuality. Frequently her temporal digressions are accompanied by psychoanalytic commentaries. For instance, referring to an 1821 entry in Byron's diary, Bigland interrupts the temporal universe 1788-1802 when she writes: "who knows, their relationship may have been tinged with the homosexual ideas which often accompany adolescence."[14] Time and temporal markers serve as tools in analyzing the subject's sexuality, and the temporal universe 1798-1801 becomes the psychoanalytic territory. The subject's biological time is subordinated to the chosen interpretation which contributes to a certain temporal organism on the body of time.

Chronos is the foundation of a biographical narrative, and various temporal markers which form special temporal universes indicate temporal omnipresence.

That which a linguistic code fails to mediate is supplemented by temporal symbolism. Each biographer chooses certain dates or temporal markers out of the given temporal matrix, Birth-Death, and introduces them in a specific order, which rejuvenates the biographical discourse about the same subject.

Yury Lotman, who rewrote Pushkin's life in 1982, possesses a novel temporal vision.[15] The novelty of his temporal strategy lies in his dichotomy of signs, i.e., temporal markers and capitalized signifiers such as Home, Love, Childhood. The signifiers frequently replace the temporal markers and indicate temporal universes. In his case, the chosen temporal strategy is subordinated to the dominant theme of the poet as an immortal being. Lotman proposes a new interpretation of time—poet as conqueror of Chronos—which is a revival of Carlyle's myth of the Poet-God[16] or an echo of Sartre's idea of an artist oblivious of time.[17] The fantastic fairytale motif of a *Bogatyr'* ("hero") is given a new life within the economy of a documentary genre. Lotman, who started at the pole of the temporal axis, where real birth and death occur, has returned to the same point, where myth time and the other world dissolve in their fantastic otherness. What started as a Chronos-dependent discourse emerges as a Chronos-free tale, overcoming birth and death. The reality of biographical discourse attests to the fictionality of a notionally non-fictional genre. Biography, much like any other artistic text and, despite the temporal biographical imperative (Birth-Death), possesses the power to extend the fictional boundaries of a presumably unchangeable reality. With the biographical Chronos, foundation and visible structure are simultaneously the source of temporal illusion and artistic freedom. A biographer, confined to a specific time, choses a certain temporal focus in order to create his version of the time of the hero. In using this technique, a biographer is akin to any writer of fiction who can "arrest time."[18] Focusing on a selected temporal fraction, a biographer makes this portion of time salient to the receiver and exercises control over the "Other" just as any writer does. Arresting a certain moment, a biographer exercises his discursive freedom. From a given time to selected time, such is the route of temporality in a biography, which, unlike fiction, originates from the opposite pole of the discourse. Despite the different points of temporal departure, both a biographer and an author of fiction express themselves via Chronos.

The temporal matrix embraces the temporal universe, which can never be exhausted. Each biographer has his or her own preferences for certain temporal focal points, while birth and death remain the invariants of the ongoing biographical discourse. The matrix contains an inexhaustible storage of information preserved for a never-ending biographical discourse about the "Other." The temporal matrix (Birth-Death) alternately regulates, restricts, and frees the narrative forces in a biography. The restrictive power of the matrix manifests itself via the two stable temporal points, birth and death, which constitute the temporal biographical imperative. The matrix is eventually developed into a multi-layered temporal structure:

B------------------------   ------------------------D

        a) time of the hero (subject);
        b) past time of the group;
        c) time of biographer;
        d) present time of his group;

abcd) time of the biographees (readers).

The time of the group influences the life of the hero, as well as its interpretation after his death. To differentiate the time of a group pertaining to a hero from the similar category referring to a biographer, it may be appropriate to name it "past time of the group." This temporal universe may be brought to the fore if a biographer chooses the role of an interpreter of the past or is more interested in the environment of the subject. The present time of the group is the crucial factor in depicting the past time of the group and the life of a hero. It affects the perception of the past by the biographer, who must process specificities of four different worlds—the world of the hero (subject) and that of his time, the world of the biographer, and the corresponding world of his milieu.

The choice of a temporal universe signifies the personality of a biographer, and therefore the "I" reveals itself through the "Other" via other time. The time of the "Other," whether chronologically or non-chronologically processed, is subject to expansion or contraction, which assists a biographer in sustaining his/her relatedness to art. The biographical Chronos features these two most important qualities, which connect the biographical discourse with what is traditionally understood as fiction.

NOTES

1. Pavel Vasilievich Annenkov, *A. S. Pushkin. Materialy dlia izucheniia ego biografii* (St. Petersburg: n.p., 1873).
2. Gerard Genette, *Narrative Discourse*, trans. Jane E. Lewin (Ithaca: Cornell UP, 1980) 40, 51, 74-74, 75-78.
3. Dmitry Mitrofanovich Petrov, *A. S. Pushkin* (Moscow: Prosveshenie, 1973).
4. Paul Graham Trueblood, *Lord Byron* (New York: Twayne Publishers, 1969).
5. Trueblood 18.
6. Emilio Castelar, *Love of Lord Byron*, trans. Miss Arthur Arnold (New York: Harper & Brother Publishers, 1876).
7. Castelar 12.
8. Castelar 12.
9. Castelar 121.
10. Cesare Segre, *Structures of Time* (Chicago: Univ. of Chicago Press, 1979) 76.
11. Eileen Bigland [Lady Cynthia Mary A. Evelyn Asquith], *Lord Byron* (London: Cassel & Co., 1956)
12. Meir Sternberg, *Expositional Modes and Temporal Ordering in Fiction* (Baltimore: Johns Hopkins UP, 1978) 50; Sternberg describes the delayed

ending as "retardation," though he is speaking of detective stories, the term may be applied to biography equally well.
13 Leonard William Doob, *Patterning of Time* (New Haven: Yale UP, 1971).
14 E. Bigland 29.
15 Yury (Jurÿ, Lury) Lotman, *Aleksander Sergeevich Pushkin* 2nd ed. (Leningrad: Prosveshchenie, 1983).
16 Thomas Carlyle, *On Heroes and Hero-Worship* (New York: n.p., 1893).
17 Jean Paul Sartre, *L'idiot de la famille*, 3 vols. (Paris: Gallinard, 1971).
18 Leonard William Doob, *Patterning of Time* (New Haven: Yale UP, 1971).

CHRISTINE DE PIZAN AND BOCCACCIO: REWRITING CLASSICAL MYTHIC TRADITION

Judith L. Kellogg, University of Hawaii

Christine de Pizan, the remarkable late medieval French writer, often called the first professional woman of letters,[1] began her experimentation with Classical mythology early in her career. One of her first non-poetic works, the *Epistle of Othea*, is an extended work of mythography. Even in this early work, Christine stresses the necessity of qualities represented by mythic female figures for developing both a fully rounded moral character and an enlightened spiritual awareness. In addition, she insists that women as much as men are responsible for the intellectual, cultural, religious, and even agricultural evolution of civilization. The idea that women's achievements are interwoven into the very fabric of civilization is more systematically, entertainingly, and elegantly developed in Christine's later work, the *Book of the City of Ladies* (*Le Livre de la Cité des Dames*),[2] and here I wish to explore how in that work Christine reshapes the mythographic tradition, previously a tool used to develop an androcentric view of human history, in the service of her feminist stance. By mythography we mean the medieval impulse to read the mythological and legendary figures of ancient tradition as moral and spiritual allegories affirming Christian truths.

Understanding Christine's use of mythography depends upon understanding her attitude toward mythology, and an examination of her handling of her primary source, Boccaccio's *Concerning Famous Women* (*De Claris Mulieribus*),[3] will identify the underlying assumptions and feminist principles she brings to her reinterpretations that allow her to reconstruct fresh symbolic associations around traditional pagan figures.

But let me first briefly describe Christine's work. The *Book of the City of Ladies* is structured as a reaction to a moment of intense anger and frustration, when Christine, after picking up a misogynist diatribe, laments that she was ever born a woman. She muses that if this author and so many other learned men have so vigorously insisted on women's basic depravity, then it must be true, though her own experience has never given her cause to share their views. As a response to her doubts about her self-worth, three luminous allegorical ladies appear to her: Reason, Rectitude, and Justice. They explain that they have come to console and teach her. And so, the narrative proceeds in what is really a double structure.

In the beginning, the narrative progresses through questions and answers. Systematically, Christine catalogs the traditional arguments of the misogynist tradition. And with each entry in the catalog, Christine is answered with examples of women who in their substance and actions defy these negative views. This encyclopedic collection of portraits is drawn from myth, ancient and medieval history, scriptures, and Christine's contemporary milieu. In the progression, which forms the first structure, we have a fairly complete defense of women.

But the answers to Christine's doubts and questions are not simply responses, for the portraits of women are packaged as building blocks for the construction of an allegorical edifice—the City of Ladies. Reason supervises the laying of the foundation and wall, but before the first block is put in place the ground must be cleared. Using the "pick of cross-examination," Reason assists Christine in removing basketfuls of misogynist misconceptions so that the philosophical edifice can be built flawlessly, not weakened by faulty assumptions. Then, in laying the blocks for the foundations, Reason insists that Christine look no further than her own experience and use no more than common sense to recognize women's capacity for strength, courage, and learning.

Rectitude takes over to build the fortifications, palaces, and mansions, and with righteous indignation she stresses that men are not simply unreasonable in maligning women, but morally wrong. She counters their misogynist claims with portraits of women beyond moral reproach. She also begins to populate the city with exemplary pagan, Biblical, and living women. Justice decorates the turrets and high roof, and then introduces the Queen, the Virgin Mary, accompanied by her entourage of female saints.

In devising the portraits that make up the building material for her city, Christine relies heavily on Boccaccio. In fact, three fourths of her examples can be traced to his *Concerning Famous Women*. The pattern of Christine's borrowing is established even in the first portrait, that of Nicaula. Boccaccio describes her as a wealthy and learned Ethiopian Queen. Marveling at the fame of Solomon for wisdom, she travels to Jerusalem to hear him. He, in turn, marvels at her magnificent display of wealth, wealth which she shares with Solomon as a tribute to his greatness. So in Boccaccio we have a woman, the mark of whose intellect is that she can recognize the greater wisdom of a man. The fact that such a talented woman is so ardent an admirer of Solomon is really a testimony to his greatness and not hers. In their interchange, he offers wisdom, she offers gifts, and no mutual recognition of talent is suggested. The resulting portrait does not in the end glorify a woman as much as a man.

And women cannot really even partake in the qualified praise Boccaccio offers Nicaula. For Boccaccio reminds his readers here, as he does so often elsewhere, that Nicaula only attains her learning by rejecting her female nature, her "womanly softness." He states in his preface that most women "are endowed with tenderness, frail bodies, and sluggish minds by Nature," though a few have acquired "a manly spirit," and thus have accomplished noteworthy deeds.[4] Among Christine's priorities in her work will be to correct two of Boccaccio's assumptions: first, that Nature has created in woman an inferior piece of handiwork; and, second, that a woman must be manly to be worthy.

In praising certain women, Boccaccio is, in essence, reinforcing a male value system and reproaching women generally, for women become remarkable precisely when they have overcome their natural female frailty and act like men.[5] Christine, by contrast, makes her Nicaula second to no man. Reason asks Christine if "there was ever a king endowed with greater skill in politics, government, and sovereign justice, and even with such lofty and magnificent style as one can read about the most noble Empress Nicaula."[6] Christine expands upon Nicaula's legal, political, social, and intellectual accomplishments, and never mentions Solomon. She adds at the end, "she had so lofty a heart that she did not deign to marry, nor did she desire that any man be at her side."[7]

Boccaccio's treatment of mythological women reveals the same veiled ambivalence and backhanded praise as his portrait of Nicaula. For example, with Ceres, he inherits a tradition in which she invents plowing and the sowing of seed. Through the art of cultivation, "wild, wandering men were led out of the woods and into cities," and the savage earth "was changed into a place of beauty and usefulness for men." That is, Ceres provides the basis for civilized life. But Boccaccio's praise is grudging. Because of Ceres' accomplishments, he continues, "the door was opened to vices which had been in hiding for a long time, afraid to come out into the open, and assurance was given them that they might proceed." Certainly the idea of the fall from the Golden Age was a commonplace in Boccaccio's time, but his linking it with Ceres in this way turns a powerful and generous woman into a Pandora/Eve figure.

Like Boccaccio, Christine also links Ceres' cultivating the land to the civilizing of humankind. But where Boccaccio sees the establishment of community marking a lost innocence, Christine sees the possibility for community as Ceres' greatest gift. She remarks that, whereas people had lived "scattered here and there in the forest and wilderness, wandering like animals," by gathering them together in "towns and cities of permanent construction," Ceres led the world "away from bestial conditions to a rational, human life." Where Boccaccio has Ceres' contribution to humankind precipitate a sinking into an abysmal state, Christine's Ceres does the opposite, for she lead us upwards "from the caverns of ignorance to the heights of contemplation and proper behavior."[8]

For Christine, the idea of a civilized community is a compelling one, as she makes clear by her clustering of Ceres with Isis and Minerva. Isis, like Ceres, a woman of great learning, invented an alphabet, taught the Egyptians how to plant gardens and to graft trees, and brought social order out of social chaos for "she instructed the people of Egypt, who had until then lived like savages without law, justice, or order, to live according to the rule of law."[9]

Minerva, by her "subtle mind, [and] profound understanding,"[10] invented a shorthand Greek script, numbers, woolen fabrication, the process of extracting oil from "the fruits of the earth," the making of wagons and carts, and the flute. Even more remarkably, she not only invented armor, but taught men how to deploy their armies. That is, she invented chivalry, that bastion of male privilege and the foundation of the social order as the medieval world understood it.

These three women have an allegorical place in the foundation of Christine's city, but she makes clear that these three are also historical figures on whom her civilization depends, women who provided humans their most necessary technologies and most cherished institutions. Though many of the basic facts of the initial portraits come from Boccaccio, in the selection of detail which emphasizes community, in the grouping of the three to suggest their similar contributions, and in the subsequent elaboration of their significance, Christine's radically different attitude becomes apparent.

Christine's women created the civilized life that men enjoy, and they created it strong, and pure, and sufficiently complete to sustain human life comfortably. They invented agriculture as an economic base, and added just laws and a social structure (chivalry) designed to maintain order. Christine highlights the collective contribution of women to civilization by insisting that no male contribution, not even that of Aristotle, the most revered ancient authority, is more important. As she says,

> It seems to me that neither in the teaching of Aristotle, which has been of great profit to human intelligence and which is so highly esteemed and with good reason, nor in that of all the other philosophers who have ever lived, could an equal benefit for the world be found as that which has been accrued and still accrues through the works accomplished by virtue of the knowledge possessed by these ladies.[11]

If the order women have created has degenerated, as Boccaccio claims, then it is because men took it over and corrupted it. Christine's City then turns one from faulty interpretations of history to the original facts of history so that women can reclaim the social order they created, their legitimate birthright. The further implication is that, if left to themselves, their community will never degenerate—their age will be a continual golden one.

These three are not the only mythological figures that Christine uses to build her edifice. She scatters them throughout her narrative, the most startling being those, such as Medea and Circe, who are transformed from sorceresses of terrifying power and destructive passion into women with considerable talent, learning, and virtue to offer the feminine community.

So Christine has chosen, like Boccaccio, through euhemerizing her mythological figures, to make them like all her other figures—actual historical women. Yet the resulting message is nothing like Boccaccio's. Whereas Boccaccio's women are didactic models of virtue and vice, Christine's women are uniformly virtuous. Whereas Boccaccio's virtuous women are isolated examples beyond the reach of most women who are by nature flawed, Christine's are representative of the natural virtue, courage, and talent shared by all women. They send a message that women as a whole must recognize their collective strength. Whereas Boccaccio's underlying message is one of reproach to most women that they fail to measure up to the models he offers, Christine's is one of recognition of the power, goodness, generosity, intelligence, ingenuity and loyalty of the female spirit.

We can see, then, that in these portraits, Christine makes no distinction between her mythological and historical figures. And here, using criteria described by Alicia Ostriker, I would say that all Christine's portraits of ancient figures can really be called mythic. Ostriker points out that whenever a poet employs a figure or story which is interpreted and defined by a culture, the poet is using myth, so that quasi-historic figures like Napoleon and Sappho are in this sense mythic. As she says,

> like the gods and goddesses of classical mythology, all such material . . . exists or appears to exist objectively, in the public sphere, and consequently confers on the writer the sort of authority unavailable to someone who writes "merely" of the private self. Myth belongs to "high" culture and is handed "down" through the ages by religious, literary, and educational authority.[12]

And certainly, grouped as they are, these portraits conform to what Jesse Gellrich calls the "mythologizing" impulse of medieval thought—the desire to make all experience fit into a pattern which affirms absolute spiritual truth as defined by a culture, a perspective which "'reads' existing phenomena as connected by a preexistent design and then catalogs and indexes from a seemingly unquestioned sense of the unity and continuity of the universe."[13]

And as solidly medieval as her mythologizing perspective is, Christine also has much in common with modern feminist revisionist mythmakers, and a brief comparison is useful here. For although Christine presents her figures as real women, paradoxically, she reinfuses them with their primal, archetypal power reflecting the original resources given to every woman. Adrienne Rich recounts a similar attempt to return to the source of myth in "Diving Into the Wreck." Rich's poem gives voice to women's frustration at trying to situate their own experience within a male mythic framework. As she dives, she descends through the layers of her own consciousness, and encounters "the wreck and the story of the wreck / The thing itself and not the myth."[14] Just so, Christine seeks to disengage her mythic figures from their traditional associations and to retrieve "the thing itself," the goodness, richness, and astuteness of essential female nature.

Unlike Rich, Christine does not reject the myths. She leaves the myths intact, but infuses them with new significance. As she lets fall the veil of male cultural authority to validate her own experience, she begins to understand the process whereby women are devalued as the systematic imposition of an ideology of male dominance. To counteract that, she uses the same set of myths men had used, and creates revised images which carry and perpetuate a markedly different ideology supporting historical female power and strength.[15]

If in revising Boccaccio's individual portraits we can see the workings of her feminist mythology, it is with her three allegorical ladies and the city they oversee that we can see her original feminist application of mythography, mythography being the Christian moralization and allegorization of pagan myth.[16] Christine is certainly practiced and adept at this process. Her early prose work, the *Epistle of Othea to Hector*, is a straightforward work of mythography.[17] And, in fact, the *Book of the City of Ladies* as a whole is structured remarkably like each individual section of the *Epistle of Othea*. The *Epistle of Othea* is composed of 100 segments, each consisting of three parts, what Christine labels her text, gloss, and allegory. The text, the literal level, tells the basic story, often including a euhemeristic explanation. The gloss provides the moral interpretation, and the allegory the Christian spiritual interpretation.

In the *Book of the City of Ladies* we find that Christine's edifice as a whole is itself a neat mythographic construct following just this pattern—a text, gloss, and allegory based upon one large portrait, in this case the collective portrait of women. Reason presents the text, the literal story, describing women as they were originally created by Nature, who herself is an active partner of the other allegorical ladies. Nature is, in this sense, the author of the text which Reason presents. Reason tells of women who did as much as is humanly possible to improve life and uphold secular values without the aid of Christian revelation.

Rectitude glosses women morally, and finds them superbly able to make proper ethical choices. Since Rectitude measures out the parameters of the city with her ruler of righteousness, it is fitting that her interchange have a tropological flavor. The fact that Rectitude is Christine's original allegorical creation strongly suggests that she was devised specifically so that the city would work as a neat mythographic structure.

Justice reveals women's potential for salvation and blessedness through their fierce and loving essential piety. The vessel she carries which measures each person's rightful portion attests to her anagogical significance. With Justice, revelation does not focus on Christ directly, but upon contemplating the beneficence and magnificence of the Virgin. In reigning over a city which includes not merely Christian women, but is built upon a foundation of remarkable pagans, the Blessed Mother reminds women that a community which binds them has been shared since creation, irrespective of the incarnation of Christ. By binding the universal feminine community together, she allows women to do as Virginia Woolf was to describe many years later, to think back through their mothers, not shamed continually by the sin of Eve, but rejuvenated by examples of virtue, culminating in the Virgin mother herself.[18] Certainly Christine means to be orthodox and to preserve the legitimacy of God the father, sitting behind the rest, orchestrating the universe. She does not wish to challenge Christian doctrine or belief, but she does intend to identify and validate the creative feminine power of that universe. In this she has much in common with modern feminist mythmakers, who, again to cite Ostriker, seek "to retrieve, from the myth of the abstract father god who created the universe *ab nihilo*, the figure on which he was based, the female creatix."[19] Though Christine does not intend the Virgin to be a replacement for God, she does certainly insist on the creator's delight in his female creation. And Christine affirms the feminine creative principle by making her ladies, Reason, Rectitude, Justice, and here I must add, Nature, the forces who give humankind shape and substance and make possible life's moral and spiritual richness.

So we can see that Christine's feminist revision of myth begins with her lending fresh symbolic weight to traditional figures she borrows from Boccaccio, but culminates in her mythographic vision, the allegorical edifice itself of the city. Thus, by using mythological figures to identify the natural worthiness of women and a mythographic superstructure to affirm the feminine creative principles at work in the universe, she is able to provide what Jane Schulenberg has identified as "compensatory history," a figurative refuge for women from the demeaning assumptions made about them by men in medieval society.[20] Christine's moment of crisis has turned instead to one of joyous self-affirmation, which every woman could share.

NOTES

1. The best recent critical biography of Christine de Pizan, which includes an extensive bibliography, is that by Charity Willard, *Christine de Pizan: Her Life and Works* (New York: Persea, 1984).
2. The only modern edition of the French text available is that of Maureen Cheney Curnow, "'Le Livre de la Cité des Dames' de Christine de Pisan: A Critical Edition" diss., Vanderbilt University, 1975. French citations are from this edition. English renditions are from the translation by Earl Jeffrey Richards, *The Book of the City of Ladies* (New York: Persea, 1982).
3. Citations are from Giovanni Boccaccio, *Concerning Famous Women*, trans. and ed. Guido A. Guarino (New Brunswick, N.J.: Rutgers UP, 1963). For many years Christine was viewed simply as a mechanical borrower of received notions. See, for example, Gianni Mombello, "Quelques aspects de la pensée politique de Christine de Pizan d'après ces oeuvres publiées," *Culture et politique en France à l'époque de l'humanisme et de la Renaissance*, ed. Franco Simone (Torino: Accademia delle Scienza, 1974) 43-153. On her borrowing from Boccaccio, see A. Jeanroy, "Boccacce et Christine de Pisan: le *De Claris Mulieribus*, principale source du *Livre de la Cité des Dames*," *Romania* 48 (1922): 93-105. Several recent studies have attempted to identify her original handling of Boccaccio, notably Richards xxxv-xli; and Liliane Dulac, "Un Mythe Didactique chez Christine de Pizan, Semiramis ou la Veuve Héroique," *Melanges de Philologie Offerts à Charles Camproux*, vol. 1 (Montpellier: C. E. O., 1978) 315-343.
4. Boccaccio xxxvii.
5. See Valerie Wayne, "Zenobia in Medieval and Renaissance Literature," in *Ambiguous Realities: Women in the Middle Ages and the Renaissance*, ed. Carole Levin and Jeanie Watson (Detroit: Wayne State UP, 1987), for an illuminating study of the process by which women in medieval and Renaissance texts "were sometimes damned not with faint praise, but with extensive and effusive adulation . . . affirming an association of strength and virtue with men and masculinity" (48). Focusing on the figure of Zenobia, Wayne demonstrates that typically, when male medieval and Renaissance writers "set out to praise women, the norms they use presuppose male superiority so fully that they denigrate women even as they praise them" (55).
6. *Book of the City of Ladies* 32.
7. *Book of the City of Ladies* 33.
8. *Book of the City of Ladies* 79.

9   *Book of the City of Ladies* 77.
10 *Book of the City of Ladies* 73.
11 *Book of the City of Ladies* 81.
12 Alicia Ostriker, "The Thieves of Language: Women Poets and Revisionist Mythmaking," *Signs* 8 (1982): 72.
13 Jesse Gellrich, *The Idea of the Book in the Middle Ages: Language, Theory, Mythology, and Fiction* (Ithaca: Cornell UP, 1985) 43.
14 Adrienne Rich, *Diving Into the Wreck: Poems 1971-1972* (New York: Norton, 1973) 23.
15 Joan Kelly, in assessing Christine's contribution to early feminism, remarks that the opposition "to male ideology has remained central to subsequent feminist thought, as has the creation of adequate empowering images of women" ("Early Feminist Theory and the *Querelle des Femmes*, 1400-1789," *Signs* 8 [1982]: 28). Ostriker makes the point that in creating these empowering images, "women writers have always tried to steal the language" (Ostriker 69). Here Nadia Margolis' comments are particularly relevant, "Christine de Pisan: The Poetess as Historian," *Journal of the History of Ideas* 47 (1986): 361-77. She describes Christine's shift from using a traditionally feminine form of discourse, poetry, to a traditionally masculine form, history, and how in so doing, Christine is able masterfully to craft this masculine discourse, while developing a distinctive feminine stance and style. She suggests that Christine's reasons for writing history in the early fifteenth century can be compared to "reasons for women dominating novels in the eighteenth and early nineteenth centuries" (364). That is, both genres provided certain room for self-examination and for rebuilding a different story of humanity.
16 For an overview of the mythographic tradition, see Jane Chance, "The Origins and Development of Medieval Mythography from Homer to Dante," *Mapping the Cosmos*, ed. J. Chance and R. O. Wells (Houston: Rice UP, 1985) 35-64; see also John McCall, "The Backgrounds," *Chaucer Among the Gods* (University Park: Pennsylvania State UP, 1979) 1-17. For a useful discussion of the relationship between mythography and the iconographical tradition into the Renaissance, see Jean Seznec, *The Survival of the Pagan Gods*, trans. B. Sessions (Princeton: Princeton UP, 1953).
17 The only modern edition of the Old French text available is that by Halina D. Loukopoulos, "Classical Mythology in the Work of Christine de Pisan, with an Edition of 'L'Epistre Othea' from the Manuscript Harley 4431," diss., Wayne State University, 1977. For a translation, see Curt Bühler, "The Epistle of Othea": Translated from the French Text of Christine de Pisan by Stephen Scrope (London: EETS, 1970).
18 For a fuller comparison of Virginia Woolf and Christine de Pizan, see Sheila Delany, "A city, a room: the scene of writing in Christine de Pisan and Virginia Woolf," in *Writing Woman* (New York: Schocken, 1983) 181-97.
19 Ostriker 75.
20 Jane Schulenburg, "Clio's European Daughters: Myopic Modes of Perception," in *The Prism of Sex: Essays in the Sociology of Knowledge*, ed. Julia Sherman and Evelyn Beck (Madison: University of Wisconsin Press, 1974) 35.

POLITICS OF MIS-TRANSLATION: THE ARAGON AFFAIR

Svetlana Boym, Harvard University

In 1930 the surrealist group voted unanimously to re-name the journal *La Révolution Surréaliste* and call it *Le Surréalisme au service de la Révolution*. They dedicated the central article of the first issue to the suicide of Soviet Russia's most famous revolutionary poet—Vladimir Mayakovsky. The title *La Révolution Surréaliste* suggests the transformation of the world through the surrealist "practice of poetry," while *Le Surréalisme au service de la Révolution*, by reversing priorities, insists on poetry's engagement in the practical struggle for social change. Five years later, Louis Aragon, who by then had broken his ties with the surrealist group and became a "party-line communist," proclaimed that it was not enough to re-name the journal: the times demanded action, "poetry in the revolutionary march," and a "return to reality."[1] These shifts from the "surrealist revolution," to "surrealism in the service of the revolution," and finally, to the revolutionary "return to reality" reflect the tensions between surrealists and the French Communist Party, between revolutionary politics and revolutionary poetics, between writing and acting. It would seem that in the American academic context of the 1980s these issues lack historical urgency. In fact, many crucial questions that emerged out of the complex political and poetic context of pre-war France, are echoed in contemporary critical debates, particularly in the arguments between Marxists and deconstructionists, and in discussions regarding the limits of the text and the limitations of textual criticism. My paper will focus on the intertwining of poetics and politics in "poetry in the revolutionary march"—the genre developed by Vladimir Mayakovsky and "translated" from Russian by Louis Aragon. I will attempt to do a culturally intertextual reading of Aragon's controversial poem "Front Rouge" and expose a hidden "Russian connection" in Aragon's "translations" of the words "revolution" and "reality."

The Aragon Affair, which occurred shortly after Mayakovsky's politically controversial suicide in the heart of Soviet Russia in 1930, finalized the split between the surrealists and the communists. The scandal was sparked by Aragon's poem "Front Rouge," written in the Soviet Union during the Second International Congress of Revolutionary Writers. At the congress, Aragon and Sadoul were supposed to expose the political position of the surrealists, but instead, they pleaded *mea culpa,* and denounced surrealists, Trotskyists and "Freudianists" as dangerous counter-revolutionary idealists.[2] Upon his arrival in Paris, Aragon played a double game, vacillating between the surrealists and the communists "in the line," flirting with both and periodically denouncing one to the other. "Front Rouge" stirred up controversy not only between the conservative bourgeoisie and revolutionary intellectuals, but also between different "theorists" of the revolution. On the one hand, the bourgeois press read the poem "literally" as a piece of communist propaganda, a direct appeal to start a Russian style proletarian revolution in Paris, for which Aragon was threatened to be put on trial. On the other hand, the surrealists, particularly Breton in his "Misère de la poésie," argued that a poem cannot be interpreted "literally."[3] Moreover, Breton criticized "Front Rouge" for being artistically conservative, for not staging a poetic drama alongside the social one. The poem was regarded as a return to "the passionate subject" and a step back from the surrealist "revolution in the poetic language"—to borrow a term from Julia Kristeva.

The history of the composition, genesis and exegesis of "Front Rouge" exemplifies the ambivalences inherent in the expression "revolutionary poet." Indeed, should it be read as a tautology, a reiteration of the same, or an oxymoron, a combination of the mutually exclusive adjectives? In other words, is a poet a revolutionary by definition if he practices revolution in the poetic language, or is it his engagement in a social struggle that matters? What is more "revolutionary," to be socially engaged or to be disengaged but faithful to the only truly "dissident" ideology—poetic anarchism? What is understood by "revolution"? What language is it translated from?

In Breton's use, "revolution" is hardly a borrowing from Russian Leninism or German Marxism, but rather a French avant-garde concept which can be easily turned into a neologism—*surrevolution*. The exemplary "revolutionary poet," such as Vladimir Mayakovsky, is a revolutionary in poetics and a poet in the revolution who rebels against the murder of poetic language by the bureaucratic officialdom.[4] Breton maintains that there is a mutual attraction between poetry and social revolution, and yet he wishes to preserve a suggestive white space between them, a mark of irreducibility of one to the other.

Louis Aragon, on the other hand, understood it to mean, first and foremost, a revolutionary in a Marxist-Leninist sense, a revolutionary with a Russian accent, and only then a poet. Mayakovsky was instrumental in Aragon's conversion to Communism "in the party line" and his radical break with surrealism. The dead Russian poet became Aragon's "beacon that illuminate[s] reality"—a Socialist realist reality as opposed to the "sur-reality" of the avant-garde nightmare. (The ideological shift is located, in fact, in a different choice of derivatives from the most ambiguous, authoritative, and rhetorically persuasive root—"real.")

In his essay "Mayakovsky and Shakespeare," written in the 1950s, Aragon pays special attention to the ideology of translation from Russian, and the political dangers of mis-translation, which might give us some clues to reading "Front Rouge." He bases his theory on the example of Mayakovsky's famous poem "Левый марш" ("Left March").[5] Aragon vehemently argues against the practice of rhyming translation, because it emphasizes "the formalist" elements in poetry rather than "the sense." According to Aragon, it is important to recognize "the predominance of the content over the poetic form." Thus, the "real" is associated with "content" and historical reference. The translation of Mayakovsky's poem "Left March"—written in 1918, a year after the revolution, and an example of "poetry in the revolutionary march"—exposes the dangers of the "formalist" approach. Here is the beginning of the poem in Russian, quoted by Aragon, next to its verse translation into French, followed in turn by an English translation:

Разворачивайтесь в марше!	Allons, en marche à tour de rôle!
Словесной не место кляузе.	Assez de chicane bavarde!
Тише, ораторы!	Silence, orateurs!
Ваше	La parôle
Слово,	Prends-la
Товарищ маузер.	Mauser, bon camarade!
Довольно жить законом,	Assez de loi, vieilles et fausses
данным Адамом и Евой.	Depuis Eve et Adam, bancroches!
Клячу истории загоним.	Cavale-toi, Histoire, eh! rosse!
Левой!	Tous gauche,
Левой!	Gauche!
Левой!	Gauche!

Rally the ranks into a march!
Now's no time to quibble or browse here
Silence, you orators!
You have
the floor
Comrade Mauser!
Enough of living by laws
that Adam and Eve have left.
Hustle old history's horse
Left!
Left!
Left![6]

Here Aragon notes a minor rhetorical slippage, done for stylistic purposes. The substitution of Mayakovsky's "Довольно жить законом, данным Адамом и Евой" ("enough of living by the laws that Adam and Eve have left") by "assez de loi, vieilles et fausses" ("enough of living by the laws" in general) jeopardizes the ideological meaning of the poem: from a Bolshevik Marxist revolutionary it "transforms Mayakovsky into an anarchist."[7] Aragon demonstrates that an infatuation with poetic devices here leads to political mistranslation. This slippage also discloses the incredible fragility of the Marxist-Leninist "true sense of the poem," since it shows how easily it is obscured by a simple syntactical substitution. In Aragon's view, "Left March" has to be controlled: by marching too far to the left, one can become vulnerable to formalist and idealist attacks and fall victim to the arms race of rhetoric.

From Mayakovsky's "Left March," mis-translated into French, I would like to move to Aragon's own march, written in the year of Mayakovsky's death. I will attempt to read in it Aragon's desire to give a true and ideologically correct poetic translation of Mayakovsky's "poetry in the revolutionary march" which would ensure the poet's permanent revolutionary role as commander-chief of the "army of art"—to use Mayakovsky's image—giving orders about which foot goes first. The poem, however, was written more than ten years after the revolution and after Mayakovsky's triumphant "Left March," at a time when the representation of revolutionary enthusiasm in Soviet art had become strictly codified and had gone through significant modifications, too subtle perhaps for an enthusiastic and well-meaning foreign poet.

"Front Rouge" presents a challenge to structuralist criticism because it problematizes the relationship between the "literal" and the "figurative" meaning of the text, between the written text and the act, between text and its political and historical "con-text," between the French text and its Russian "inter-text," exposing different dimensions of cultural translation. My reading will be a double movement between the analysis of the text and the examination of Russian historical references suggested in it, a double movement which will point at certain inconsistencies in Aragon's practical poetics of the "real."

The lyrical persona of "Front Rouge" tries on Mayakovsky's mask of the revolutionary poet "in the line," playing the roles of the "agitator of [the] masses" and the "loud-speaker." We witness Aragon's change of make-up: a covering up of the surrealist split subject—that of a semi-awake automatic writer—with the confidence of a "proletarian poet," both a participant in the revolutionary march and its leader: "J'assiste à l'écrasement d'un monde hors d'usage / J'assiste avec enivrement au pilonnage des bourgeois / . . . Je chante la domination violente du Prolétariat sur la bourgeoisie."[8]

The poet optimistically projects a feeling of continuity between his aspirations and those of the revolutionary proletariat, and a sense of a perfect reconciliation of his artistic and political engagement. In section four there is a meta-poetic moment in which the poet defends his program against the epigones of pure art with "quelques mots bien simples." What follows is a documentary fragment—somewhat similar to what in Mayakovsky's avant-garde group *Left Front* was called the "literature of facts"—a story of the foreign conspiracy around Soviet Russia and of General Vrangler's plans of invasion. It is a reference to the events of the Russian Civil War of 1918-1920 which served as a context for Mayakovsky's "Left March."

However, the rest of the poem is quite different from the direct and straightforward documentary passage. "Front Rouge" has a skillful rhetorical construction: it is built on the principle of symmetry and analogy. Each section acts out the conversion or the correct ideological translation from French into Russian: from URSS into SSSR—the Russian version of the abbreviation of the Union of the Soviet Socialist Republics. SSSR, SSSR, SSSR serves as a refrain which ends each section. The poet, using one of Mayakovsky's favorite devices, alliteration, attempts to motivate the whistling sound of the name of the first revolutionary state: "SS un air joyeux comme le fer SS / SR un air brûlant c'est l'es / perance c'est l'air SSSr c'est la chanson d'Octobre aux fruits éclatants / Sifflez sifflez SSSR SSSR la patience s'aura qu'untemps SSSR SSSR SSSR."[9]

There appears to be a perfect continuity between the French sound and the Russian, the expression of the "true poetic sense" ("la vérité révolutionnaire en marche") a continuity between the triumphant Russian revolution and the immanent French revolution, between the revolutionary and the post-revolutionary struggle against traitors and conspirators.

The poem proceeds through a number of iconic poster-like images characteristic of Russian poetry of the 1920s and of the art of visual propaganda. Here everything is in black and white, or rather in red and white; the "bad guys" are: an aristocratic Parisian madam, a cliché-embodiment of the ruling classes, the "traitors of the revolution"—a whole bestiary of them—"les ours savants de la social-démocratie," and "les loups," who together with "les chiens" enter into an anti-proletariat conspiracy. "L'image du Communism vainquer" also has a carefully elaborated iconography: "Marx et Lenin dans le ciel / rouge comme l'aurore," and the Revolution whose "yeux bleus brillent d'une cruauté nécessaire." ("In spite of the fact that the Soviet Union is a multinational state, the revolution, which is always called Russian, ought to have a Slavic look and Slavic blue eyes.")

"La cruauté nécessaire" of the revolution deserves special attention. It is not a surrealist theater of cruelty, but programmed revolutionary violence, violence "in the line." It is interesting that the Marxist critic Roger Garaudy, generally profoundly sympathetic to Aragon, criticizes the poem for what he calls "surrealist anarchism," precisely that anarchism which Aragon feared the most in the mis-translations of Mayakovsky.[10] Indeed, we see in the poem a certain intoxication with "À bas" slogans which sometimes lead to quite unexpected syntactical paradoxes. For instance, at the very end of the poem we read: "À bas l'impérialisme à bas / SSSR SSSR SSSR."[11] It is, of course highly unlikely that Aragon would wish to proclaim "down with" the revolutionary state which he glorified throughout the poem. Garaudy's example of "the surrealist anarchism" does not concern rhetoric. Rather, the critic sees it as "the anarchist theme of the destruction of churches," which is a surrealist exaggeration. Unfortunately, this is one of the most realistic and documentary elements of the poem, a "literature of fact" if compared with a not so surrealist Soviet reality of the 1930s. Aragon's statement was, in fact, prophetic. On the personal order of Stalin, many churches, which, in addition to their Religious function were important architectural monuments, were demolished in the process of constructing new communist Moscow. Among them was the famous Passion Monastery right in front of the monument to the greatest Russian nineteenth-century poet, Pushkin. It was considered inappropriate for the national genius Pushkin to face the citadel of religion, so his monument was turned around and the old monastery pulled down. This proves that "literal" and "literary" meanings of any utterance can be defined only in context: what is an outrageous avant-garde metaphor, or an expression of overwhelming revolutionary enthusiasm in bourgeois France becomes a grotesque reality in Stalinist post-revolutionary Russia.

Some other historical references in the poem have controversial political implications. One of the Russian historical references in the poem is an image of the marching troops of Boudenny, the hero of the Russian Civil War of 1918-1920. They are represented as "la conscience en armes du Prolétariat," and the heralds of "la Révolution Universelle." However, in the 1930s, ten years after the Civil War, the Stalinist slogan "beware of the enemies of the revolution," repeated by Aragon in his appeal to fight those who endanger "les conquêtes d'Octobre" and threaten to "sabotage le Plan quinquennal," acquires a different meaning. At that time it was no longer a struggle against the abstract "madame" and the bourgeoisie, but rather against fellow-revolutionaries, particularly revolutionary intellectuals, who were accused of all kinds of conspiracies allegorized by Aragon. Among them were fellow-writers from Mayakovsky's avant-garde group *Left Front*; for instance, Tretjakov was accused of cosmopolitanism and formalism. Aragon himself persecuted the émigré Russian dadaist Ilja Shershnevich for having left the "cradle of the world revolution" by sabotaging his collaboration with Matisse and other French communist artists. There is a sad irony in the fact that in the year of Mayakovsky's death, Aragon, in his sincere desire to adopt the Russian poet's revolutionary mask, ends up repeating the official post-revolutionary clichés, foreshadowing the Stalinist paranoia that lead to the epoch of the great purges. Aragon's "true sense of poetic translation" turns into a blind miming of foreign revolutionary rhetoric, into an intoxication with the optimistic and destructive rhythms of the official revolutionary march, into a kind of revolutionary exoticism. "Front Rouge" stands on a peculiar frontier between bourgeois France and post-revolutionary Stalinist Russia, a frontier where the song of liberation turns into a glorification of oppression. As a reaction to surrealist "automatic writing" and linguistic experimentation, Aragon turns to the automatic copying of the officially sanctioned revolutionary, or rather post-revolutionary, conventions which had a murderous effect on language. According to both John Berger and Julia Kristeva, it was this systematic "murder of the poetic language" in the Stalinist Russia of the 1930s and the consolidation of the official "speak" that can be regarded as a "poetic" reason for Mayakovsky's suicide.[12]

Forty-five years after the publication of "Front Rouge" Aragon described "Front Rouge" as "a poem which I hate."[13] Paraphrasing Proust, this "search for the lost reality" culminated in the final recognition of the compromises and contradictions involved in the act of assuming a seemingly uncompromising, radically political position. In an autobiographical confession-commentary, Aragon describes his state of mind during the writing of "Front Rouge" as "*double vertige.*" The syntax of this autobiographical description is far less coherent than that of the poem. Its numerous significant ellipses, incoherences and vacillations recover the moral, poetic, and political drama erased by the revolutionary optimism and joyful self-confidence of the engaged proletarian writer of "Front Rouge." "*Le double vertige*" enacted in this passage reveals the complexities and contradictions of the situation, and all the difficult compromises which the poet preferred to conceal in his "Front Rouge," and only forty-five years later was able to confront with proper intellectual honesty. It is Aragon's belatedly acknowledged "double vertigo" that leaves us with more questions than answers: What happens during the "transport of the revolution," both political and poetic? Does it lead to internationalism, or to mis-translations? What is more dangerous politically: the active revolutionary idealism of the engaged poet, at times with a tinge of necessary idealization, or the double movements, in-between states, and anarchic poetic subversions of the surrealist intellectual? Where do we locate the cultural mis-translation: in the text or in the context, in rhetoric or in politics? And finally, where does one trace the frontier of what Walter Benjamin called "the foreignness of language"?

NOTES

1 Louis Aragon, "Le Rétour à la réalité," lecture given at the International Congress of Writers in Defense of Culture, republished in *Pour un réalisme socialiste* (Paris: Denoel et Steele, 1935) 69-89.
2 On the circumstances surrounding Aragon's visit to Soviet Russia and the role of Elsa Triolet in his communist conversion, see Maurice Nadeau, *L'Histoire du surréalisme* (Paris: Éditions du Seuil, 1964) 140-147.
3 André Breton, *Misère de la poésie: L'Affaire Aragon devant l'opinion publique* (Paris: Éditions Surréalistes, 1932). "Front Rouge" is quoted from this edition.
4 André Breton wrote an essay on Mayakovsky's suicide entitled in Russian "Любовная лодка разбилась о быт" [Ljubovnaja lodka razbilas' o byt] and published in *Le Surréalisme au service de la revolution* 1 (1930) reprinted in André Breton, *Point du Jour* (Paris: Gallimárd, 1970) 71-84. For a discussion of this essay in connection with Roman Jakobson's "On the Generation that Squandered Its Poets," see my article "The Death of the Revolutionary Poet: On the Russian-French Border," in *Re-Appraisal of Modernism and Avant-Garde,* ed. by D'Acierno and Lekatsas (Ithaca: Cornell UP, [to be published in 1989]).
5 Louis Aragon, "Shakespeare et Maïakovski" in *Littératures soviétiques* (Paris: Denoël, 1955) 323-330.
6 "Left March," in *Mayakovsky,* trans. and ed. by Herbert Marshell (London: Dennis Dobson, 1965) 129.
7 Aragon, "Shakespeare et Maïakovski" 330.
8 Aragon, "Front Rouge" 25.
9 Aragon, "Front Rouge" 25.
10 Roger Garaudy, *L'Itinéraire Aragon* (Paris: Gallimard, 1963) 229.
11 Aragon, "Front Rouge" 25.
12 Julia Kristeva, "Ethics of Linguistics," in *Desire in Language* trans. by Thomas Gora, Alice Jardine and Leon Roudiez (New York: Columbia UP, 1980). John Berger, "Mayakovsky: His Language, His Death" with Anya Bostock, in *The Sense of Sight* (New York: Pantheon Books, 1985).
13 Louis Aragon, "Une préface morcelée" in *L'œuvre poétique,* vol. 5 (Paris: Livre Club Diderot, 1975) 145-152.

SOMETHING ABOUT EMILIA: WOMAN AS LOVE OBJECT IN BOCCACCIO, CHAUCER, ANNE DE GRAVILLE, AND SHAKESPEARE AND FLETCHER

Susan L. Wing, University of Hawaii

In his epic poem *Teseida delle Nozze d'Emilia* (1340-42), Boccaccio presents a tale of two knights, cousins and sworn brothers, whose friendship is put to the extreme test when each falls in love with the Amazon princess Emilia. The unwitting object of their love, Emilia becomes the cause of Palamon and Arcite's love melancholy, the force which severs their sacred vows of friendship, and the prize awarded to whichever cousin wins the chivalric tournament arranged by Theseus, Duke of Athens. Before the contest, each of the principals prays to his or her patron deity: Arcite to Mars, asking for victory; Palamon to Venus, desiring Emilia; and Emilia to Diana, petitioning that, if she cannot remain a maiden, she will be won by the knight who loves her most. Though victorious, Arcite is fatally injured by his horse as he tours the arena in triumph, and Palamon eventually is awarded Emilia. Thus each knight ironically receives his literal request.

As an exciting tale of chivalry and romance, the *Teseida* inspired a number of translations and adaptations, the best known being Chaucer's "The Knight's Tale" (c. 1387). Two additional versions of the tale to be considered here are Anne de Graville's French verse translation and reduction of the *Teseida*, entitled *Le beau Romant des deux amans Palamon & Arcita et de la belle et saige Emilia* (1475), and Shakespeare and Fletcher's collaborative drama *The Two Noble Kinsmen* (1613), adapted from Chaucer's "The Knight's Tale." The relationship between the cousins as they compete for Emilia constitutes the central focus of each version and remains relatively constant. But just as the treatment of Boccaccio's Emilia undergoes radical reduction in Chaucer's hands, so too the Emilia created by Shakespeare and Fletcher bears virtually no resemblance to her Chaucerian prototype. Indeed, though scholars do not know for certain if either Shakespeare or Fletcher was familiar with the *Teseida* or de Graville's version, there are several resemblances between the heroines of the playwrights and Boccaccio that are absent from Chaucer's tale.

This paper will explore the various depictions of Emilia in these four tellings of the story, spanning three languages and cultures and more than 260 years; these adaptations from Boccaccio reflect not only the plot manipulations, styles, and skills of their various authors but also the cultural milieus and the position of women through these times. In spite of their varying portrayals, all four Emilia figures are ultimately powerless victims of Venus' sway over the "civilized" male knights because they are unwilling objects of masculine obsession, an adulation none of them seeks. Controlled by the ruling patriarchal social structure, each must submit to the decree of her brother-in-law Theseus that she marry the victor regardless of her own desires.

At the start of the *Teseida,* Boccaccio announces his determination to show that the accomplishments of Mars and Venus are "con poco bene e pien d'assai martire" ("of little worth and steeped in sorrow" [I.3]),[1] a description that fits all four versions of the tale considered here, most appropriately *The Two Noble Kinsmen.* But unlike its successors, the *Teseida* begins by devoting the first of its twelve books to the uprising of the Amazon women against their husbands. Not wanting to be kept in subjugation, but to govern themselves, "ciascuna col suo telo / de' maschi suoi li spirti sanguinosi / cacciò, lasciando lor di mortal gielo / tututti freddi, in modi dispettosi . . ." ("Each one spilt the life blood of her men with her own weapon, leaving them in the icy embrace of death as the stone cold victims of her spite" [I.7]). The Amazons set up their own government under the leadership of the virgin Queen "Ipolita gentil, mastra di guerra" ("The noble Hippolyta, mistress of warcraft" [I.8]).[2] No men are allowed to enter the kingdom, and those by chance swept into its harbor are forced to pay monetary tribute to escape with their lives. Angered Greeks complain to Theseus, Duke of Athens, who, inspired by Mars, resolves "di purgar cotal peccato" and punish the Amazons' "crudeltate a dismisura" ("to avenge these crimes"; "excessive cruelty" [I.13]). Hippolyta rallies her women, claiming that Theseus deems them troublesome because they refuse to be subjected by and obedient to the whims of men.[3] Yet after a number of fevered battles, Hippolyta recognizes that Venus is justly angry with the women and is conspiring along with Mars against them in Theseus' favor. The Amazons surrender to Theseus, who weds the beautiful, valiant Hippolyta. Only after the fighting is Hippolyta's sister Emilia mentioned, a beautiful young girl whom Theseus decides to give in marriage to his friend Achates. Then finally, halfway through Book II, Theseus returns to Athens in victory with Hippolyta and Emilia, "rosa di spina" ("a rose among thorns" [II.93]). At this point, the mourning queens beg Theseus' aid, and Chaucer, Anne de Graville, and Shakespeare and Fletcher's adaptations begin.

Boccaccio's inclusion of the war between Theseus and the Amazons contributes to a fuller characterization of Emilia than those in Chaucer or de Graville. Although too young to have been personally involved in the Amazons' war, Emilia throughout the *Teseida* refers to "la innata crudeltate / c'ha contro al nostro sangue Citerea" ("the supernal cruelty that Cytherea bears toward our blood" [X.69]) and attributes the death of her betrothed Achates and of the victorious Arcite to the love goddess' vengeance against the Amazons. Though Chaucer omits it, Shakespeare and Fletcher do incorporate variations on the Amazonian themes, as when the Second Queen admonishes Hippolyta for being "near to make the male / To thy sex captive" had Theseus not "shrunk thee into / The bound thou wast o'erflowing" (I.i.80-81, 83-84).[4] With Emilia, the playwrights take quite a different, haunting direction, as we shall see shortly.

In the *Teseida,* the young Emilia, singing amorous songs, habitually goes into the garden, "a ciò tirata da propria natura / non che d'amore alcun fosse constretta" ("drawn there by her own nature, not because she was bound by any love" [III.8]). Both Arcita and Palemone, noble cousins captured by Theseus in his war against the cruel Creon of Thebes, can see the garden from their prison chamber and are wounded by Cupid at the sight of Emilia's eyes and the sound of her voice. Unlike in the later versions of the tale, Emilia hears the "Alas" of the wounded cousins, and, though still "più che non chiede amore intero, / pur seco intese ciò che quello affetta" ("too young for mature love, she understood what it meant" [III.19]); taking pleasure in their pain of admiration, "e più s'adorna / qualora poi a quel giardin ritorna" "[she adorned] herself more everytime she returned to the garden" [III.19]). According to Boccaccio,

> Né la recava a ciò pensier d'amore
> che ella avesse, ma la vanitate,
> che innata han le femine nel core,
> di fare altrui veder la lor biltate;
> e quasi nude d'ogni altro valore,
> contente son di quella esser lodate,
> e per quel di piacer sé ingegnando,
> pigliano altrui, sé libere servando.

("She was not prompted by any thought or feeling of love, but by vanity, which women have innate in their hearts in making others see their beauty. Almost stripped of any other worth, they are satisfied to be praised for beauty, and by contriving to please by their charm, they enslave others while they keep themselves free." [III.30])

Unlike in "The Knight's Tale" and *The Two Noble Kinsmen*, Boccaccio's Palemone and Arcita both love her from afar without fighting over who saw her first or who deserves her more. When the ransomed Arcita must leave Athens to go into exile, Emilia gazes on him in compassion, though she still is too young to understand that she is the cause of his grief. When Arcita returns years later in disguise, love melancholy has so altered his appearance that no one recognizes him except Emilia, who, while remaining mute, wonders "ma ben si maraviglia quale scaggia / di bianco l'abbia così fatto bruno / e dimagrato, che par pur la fame / nel suo aspetto e pien di tutte brame" ("Yet she wondered what illness had altered his complexion from white to an emaciated brown. For his bearing revealed hunger and great desire" [IV.58]). However, she is now old enough to realize that she is loved. Although Arcita ingratiates himself in Theseus' court and is much admired for his prowess in arms and song, and though his secret love for her remains undiminished, Emilia evinces no corresponding feelings of love for him. Glad at hearing of his cousin's return, Palemone immediately desires to possess Emilia, breaks out of prison, confronts Arcita, and, in spite of the other's protests, takes him on in a bloody fight to the death. Enflamed with animalistic passion, wading in blood, they fight even harder when a stunned Emilia unexpectedly comes upon them. Once Theseus arrives and hears their story, his anger at their escape and flouting of his laws gives way to compassion as he recalls how "io già innamorato fui / e per amor sovente folleggiai" ("he once fell in love and committed follies for love" [V.92]). Then, without consulting Emilia, he decrees that Palemone and Arcita, plus one hundred knights each, must fight in a tournament; the winner will be awarded the prize of Emilia. "Nulla rispose Emilia, ma cambiossi / tutta nel viso, tanto vergognossi!" ("Emilia answered nothing, but her face changed completely so embarrassed was she" [V.102]). As in de Graville and Chaucer, though not in *The Two Noble Kinsmen*, Boccaccio's Emilia, loving neither cousin, raises not a word of protest but mutely accepts her status as an object of veneration to be awarded to the victorious knight.

Indeed, we hear little of her until the night before the tournament, when she goes to pray to Diana. She asks her patron goddess first, "Per che se 'l mio migliore è che' tuoi cori / seguiti ancora vergin giovinetta, / attuta gli aspri e focosi vapori / ch'accendono il disio" ("If it is best for me follow your choice still as a young virgin, allay the harsh vapors that inkindle desire in the young men, my lovers" [VII.82]). Then, after praying for those who will be injured for her sake, she asks,

> E se l'iddii forse hanno già disposto
> con etterna parola che e' sia
> da lor seguito ciò c'hanno proposto,
> fa che e' venga nelle braccia mia
> colui a cui più col voler m'acosto
> e che con più fermezza mi disia,
> ché io nol so in me stessa nomare,
> tanto ciascun piacevole mi pare.

("If the gods have already decreed that they accomplish what they have determined to do, grant that the one who loves me more, the one who desires me with greater constancy may come to my arms, for I myself do not know which one to choose, so winsome does each one seem to me." [VII.85])

After Diana's choir tells her that she must be the bride of one cousin, the goddess gives her a sign and Emilia watches the two fires, which stand for the fates of the two cousins—Palemone's brand flickering out and then lighting again, Arcita's burning and seeming to weep tears of blood. Not understanding the significance of the signs, Emilia passes the night in anguish and watches the tournament in great perturbation. Crying out against the evil and suffering Palemone and Arcita's love for her has wrought, she envisions the ghosts of those who died unjustly for her terrifying and gloating over her and asks, "Oh, quante madri, padri, amici e frati, / figliuoli e altri, me maladicendo, / davanti a l'are staranno turbati, / da' loro iddii i miei danni chiedendo" ("how many mothers, fathers, friends, brothers, sons, and others will curse me as they stand wrathfully before the altars, begging their gods to do me harm" [VIII.100]). Finally, she rails against love, "e sanza amare innamorata sono" ("for without loving I am in love" [VIII.109]). Yet once Palemone is defeated, Emilia "già d'Arcita credendo fermamente / esser, l'animo suo sanza dimoro / a lui voltò, e divenne fervente / dell'amor d'esso" ("firmly believed that she belonged to Arcites and without delay she turned her thoughts to him, and became fervent in her love for him" [VIII.124]. Hers is not a freely made choice but one she believes has been determined by the gods (VII.127).

Now that Mars has answered Arcita's prayer for victory, Venus answers Palemone's for Emilia by sending the fury Erinys, which frightens Arcita's horse as he rides the field in celebration so that it falls over backwards onto its rider. Pale as death, experiencing the lovers' pain, Emilia weds Arcita, but he continues to fail for a number of days and gives her to Palemone, swearing he has taken only a kiss. Emilia blames herself for Arcita's death, speaking of the ancient wrath the gods have felt towards her Amazonian blood and ruing the day she sang in the garden. Convinced that she will be a curse on any who marry her, she begs that she be allowed to follow Diana or else to be a bride of Theseus' enemies. At Arcita's death, her grief, and that of all Athens, is overwhelming. Finally, after many days pass, as opposed to Chaucer's "lengthe of certeyn yeares" (2967),[5] Theseus commands that Palemone and Emilia marry, though both protest. Emilia's fears that Diana's anger at her caused violence to Achates and Arcita are summarily brushed aside by Theseus in just one verse: "Questo dire è niente; / ché se Diana ne fosse turbata, / sopra di te verria l'ira dolente, / non sopra quelli alli quai se' donata" ("If Diana were angry, her sad wrath would fall upon you, not on the others to whom you have been given" [XII.43]). Commanded to return to joy, a reluctant Emilia, not yet fifteen, described as an idyllic golden haired, brown eyed medieval beauty, weds Palemone in splendor. Palemone vows to marry her, "e essa, come donna non già gnara, / simil promessa fece immantenente" ("and she, as a lady who was foolish no longer, immediately made a like promise" [XII.69]). Boccaccio's phrase "non già gnara" neatly sums up and dismisses Emilia by implying that any young noble woman would be foolhardy to disobey her duke's orders or to reject such a suitor as Palemone. But on another level, it suggests that Emilia was foolish to believe that the gods would concern themselves with her—in either malevolence or benevolence. Beautiful Amazon princess though she be, and intense though her innocent suffering has been, she is ultimately unimportant, a venerated object placed on a pedestal to be loved or be killed for, whose own feelings and desires are of no consequence. "One may suspect," Thomas G. Bergin notes,

> that the seven penetrations of Palemone on his bridal night, indicative more of machismo than rapturous love, brought less pleasure than pain to his child bride; we are told that he arose the following morning fresh as a rose, but we hear nothing of Emilia's state of mind. Emilia is meant rather to be contemplated than enjoyed.[6]

If Boccaccio's Emilia seems sympathetic yet relegated to secondary status, Chaucer's Emelye in "The Knight's Tale" appears as virtually non-existent, functioning less as a character than as a presence associated with May and speaking only during her prayer to Diana. Described by Norman Eliason as "possibly the most mindless heroine in all literature," subject to "the rival claims of Palamon and Arcite, two equally hare-brained young men,"[7] Chaucer's Emelye perfectly fits the tradition that medieval courtly love, as A. C. Spearing observes,

> is often a one-way affair: it is seen from the point of view of the man, whose feelings are of great interest and may be analyzed at length, while the woman exists as an object arousing those feelings. The arrow is shot in one direction only. . . . The feelings of Emelye are never considered at all.[8]

When adapting the *Teseida,* Chaucer deliberately chose to make his heroine little more than an unwitting catalyst for the Palamoun and Arcite story. As she walks in the garden below the prison, Chaucer's Emelye hears no "Alas!" from the love-wounded cousins; indeed, she doesn't know they exist, as Theseus notes when pointing to the absurdity of Palamoun and Arcite's fighting savagely over a maiden who "woot namoore of al this hotte fare, / By God, than woot a cokkow or an hare!" (1809-10). While Emelye's state of mind receives Boccaccio's attention and commentary, Chaucer effectively ignores it, minimizing her character so that he can better satirize the chivalric courtly love tradition and expose the debilitating effects of passion ungoverned by order or reason. Instead of the frantic despair of Boccaccio's Emilia as she watches the knights fighting over her, Chaucer's Emelye watches the tournament without comment. Once Arcite wins, the Knight rather insultingly and cynically describes Emelye's reaction: "And she agayn hym caste a freendlich ye / (For wommen, as to spek in comune, / Thei folwen alle the favour of Fortune)" (2680-82). Though the great Chaucerian critic E. Talbot Donaldson has noted that "the adaptability of women, their ability to follow fortune's favor and disfavor by making the best of even a very bad situation, is something Chaucer himself seems to have admired" (a characteristic of figures so diverse as Griselda and the Wife of Bath),[9] still the Knight's reduction of Emelye gains uncomfortable prominence simply because so very little else is said about her.

The only time in "The Knight's Tale" that Emelye speaks is in her prayer to Diana. Unlike Boccaccio's Emilia or even Shakespeare and Fletcher's, Emelye asks first that she be allowed to remain a virgin, that Diana turn Palamoun and Arcite's love away from her: "And if so be thou wolt nat do me grace, / Or if my destynee be shapen so / That I shal nedes have oon of hem two, / As sende me hym that moost desireth me" (2322-25). Crying bitter tears because she wants to stay a maid, Emelye watches the burning pyres. Although Chaucer's account of what happens closely resembles Boccaccio's, he hints at an underlying sexual allusion by the repeated use of "queynte" and Emilia's "sore aghast" reaction to the drops of blood:

> But sodeynly she saugh a sighte queynte,
> For right anon oon of the fyres queynte,
> And quyked agayn, and after that anon

> That oother fyr was queynt and al agon;
> And as it queynte it made a whistelynge,
> As doon thise wete brondes in hir brennynge,
> And at the brondes ende out ran anon
> As it were blody dropes many oon. . . .
>
> (2333-40)

To be sure, the meaning of "queynte" in these lines technically does not refer to pudenda,[10] but the repetition of the word four times within five lines stresses it. The description of "wete brondes" running with "blody dropes" perhaps reinforces an allusion to female genitals, particularly to the blood at the loss of virginity. Even though Emelye does not comprehend the specific symbolic meaning of the signs, her feelings of horror may reflect her subconscious sexual fears.

After Arcite's disastrous accident, he sends for Emelye and addresses her with "Alas, myn hertes queene! allas, my wyf! / Myn hertes lady, endere of my lyf!" (2775-76)—a decidedly ungallant remark, as Terry Jones has noted: Arcite "is so bound up in his own misery that he is totally blind to the effect that his words must have on his lady—here she is, a young girl, faced with a dying man, being told that she is the cause of his death!"[11] Although Emelye shrieks at Arcite's death and grieves excessively at his funeral, Chaucer gives her no more words. Eventually, "by processe and by lengthe of certeyn yeres" (2967), as opposed to the days of the *Teseida,* Theseus, declaring it is best to make a virtue of necessity, commands that she and Palamoun marry; unlike their Boccaccian prototypes, neither objects, and they wed in a happily-ever-after ending. As Herbert G. Wright has observed, Emelye, unlike Boccaccio's Emilia, "is not a thinking being who wonders whether she does not bring disaster upon all to whom she is plighted, and so she exhibits no reluctance to marry Palamoun. An angel hovering in the background, a colorless abstraction, she lacks the individuality and the humanity of Emilia."[12] She is, as such, a mere object of male desire—beautiful, passive, and deadly.

Boccaccio's *Teseida* was translated and adapted into a number of Italian and French versions during the fourteenth through sixteenth centuries, though unfortunately some are now lost. Of the two I have seen, *Le beau romant des deux amans Palamon and Arcita et de la belle et saige Emilia,* Anne de Graville's 1475 French verse translation (3648 lines long) and reduction of the *Teseida,* holds the most interest.[13] Yet its editor Yves Le Hir believes that "Anne de Graville n'a jeté qu'un oeil furtif sur le texte italien. Presque toujours imperturbable, elle a tenu son regard rivé à la traduction."[14] That is, de Graville cast only a furtive glance at the Italian text and based her poem on a French translation. But since some of the translations extant do not correspond, and since others are lost, it is impossible to establish her source with certainty.

In any case, my own translation of de Graville's poem has proven both instructive and disappointing: instructive because of certain similarities in diction, phrasing, or invention that lead me to believe that Shakespeare or Fletcher may have known either de Graville's poem or her source; disappointing because, in spite of the title's promising reference to "la belle et saige Emilia," de Graville's heroine does not seem to differ significantly from Boccaccio's. Her prayer to Diana and her reaction to Arcite's death and to Theseus' desire that she marry Palamon are very similar. Like Boccaccio's heroine, she fears that Achates and Arcita died because of the gods' anger at her breaking a vow of chastity. Theseus' reply is similarly abrupt and dismissive: "Nen parle plus & ny metz contredit / A mon vouloir, car tes vaines parolles / Je tiens & sens inutiles & folles" ("Do not speak of it more, and do not contradict my will, since I hold and judge your vain words useless and foolish" [3367-69]).[15] The promise of change implied by de Graville's "saige Emilia" remains unfulfilled, for Emilia's "wisdom" is no more than that, if she must be possessed, it will be by the cousin who loves her best—a rather deflated wisdom since the love has been forced upon her.

In their prologue to *The Two Noble Kinsmen* (1613) Shakespeare and Fletcher cite Chaucer as their source, yet they make a number of additions and changes from "The Knight's Tale." Their Emilia's role is greatly expanded from Chaucer's passive, silent object of love, and she displays considerably more personality and psychological complexity than Boccaccio's. Yet nowhere more than in Emilia are seen the sometimes discordant effects of Shakespeare and Fletcher's collaboration:[16] the naive, chaste Amazon of I.iii bears little resemblance to the coy, courtly maiden of II.ii, just as the scattered, flustered creature of IV.ii trying to decide between Palamon and Arcite differs markedly from the contemplative, sorrowful servant of Diana in V.i. The actress portraying Emilia has a difficult role, for the character vacillates so often that she risks losing dramatic credibility.

The Emilia portrayed in Shakespeare's first act is an Amazon princess dedicated to Diana. In I.iii, Shakespeare invents a scene between Hippolyta and Emilia that has no basis in Chaucer in order to provide clues to Emilia's character and present an innocence-before-experience leitmotif so that Emilia's later fate as the destined bride of the surviving cousin can be given special poignance. The friendship motif introduced with Palamon and Arcite in scene two is extended in scene three to include the strong, manly ties between Pirithous and Theseus and those between the pubescent Emilia and Flavina. Just as the cousins are shown before any sullying of their "gloss of youth" (I.ii.5), so Emilia is portrayed as virginal devotée of Diana as she converses with Hippolyta on friendship and various sorts of love. We are also reminded of Hippolyta and Emilia's status as Amazon warriors when Hippolyta, sending her love to Theseus through Pirithous, reminds him

> We have been soldiers, and we can not weep
> When our friends don their helms, or put to sea,
> Or tell of babes broach'd on the lance, or women
> That have sod their infants in (and after eat them)
> The brine they wept at killing 'em.
>
> (I.iii.18-22)

In Hippolyta's rhetorically complex clauses, the picture of women boiling and then eating their infants in the tears they weep while killing them compacts in three lines the horrible side-effects of war, vividly combining infanticide, cannibalism, and grief. That Emilia and Hippolyta can hear of such savagery without fear or surprise points not only to their ability as trained warriors to put aside the conventional feminine compassion they demonstrated in the play's first scene, but also to their acceptance of expediency and necessity in an often dark world.

Hippolyta and Emilia's discourse on friendship prompts Emilia's memory of her childhood friend Flavina. Full of beautiful language and images, Emilia's description reflects a childhood freshness:

> ... but I
> And she (I sigh and spoke of) were things innocent,
> Lov'd for we did, and like the elements
> That know not what nor why, yet do effect
> Rare issues by their operance, our souls
> Did so to one another. . . .
> (59-64)

This speech echoes Polixenes' memories of his boyhood friendship with Leontes in *The Winter's Tale,* a reminiscence which implies that childhood friendship, free from the intrusion of sexuality, has some advantages over the commitment of man to woman in marriage, a theme explored on several levels in *The Two Noble Kinsmen.* The unconscious sensuality of Emilia's reminiscences, which continues with images of swelling breasts, phoenixes, and musical sensations, leads up to her declaration that "the true love 'tween maid and maid may be / More than in sex [dividual]" (81-82). Although Hippolyta lightly teases her, Emilia's reply, "I am not against / Your faith, yet I continue mine" (96-97), brings a rather touching conclusion to the scene, especially when viewed in the context of the play's plot, for Emilia will have good reason to doubt the felicity and wisdom of heterosexual love when Palamon and Arcite are catapulted into a whirlwind of unchecked passion that allows no compromise, and Emilia is dragged along with them.

But when Fletcher takes over in Act Two, the Emilia who enters the garden and is seen and claimed by the cousins is quite changed. Not Chaucer's vision of May, nor Boccaccio's charming, slightly egotistical young girl, she appears rather to be a conventionally teasing, somewhat boy-crazy maiden exchanging bawdy pleasantries with her waiting women and discussing young men and gowns. Yet woven into the background of Fletcher's pleasing, stereotypical picture of the two young women in the garden are several hints of Shakespeare's darker vision. For instance, her thoughtless declaration that "Men are mad things" (II.ii.126) serves both the immediate purpose of commenting on Palamon and Arcite's sudden succumbing to love at that very moment and also of foretelling the folly to which that love will lead. And as the banter takes a bawdy turn, we see the emergence of the bargaining imagery which links Emilia and the Jailer's Daughter (150-52). Of course, even Shakespeare often employed monetary imagery when speaking of love; but because Emilia and the Jailer's Daughter, who goes insane for the unrequited love of Palamon, are treated as prizes or objects of barter, the mercantile imagery begins to link their fates.

In III.vi, often praised as Fletcher's best scene, Theseus and his court interrupt Palamon and Arcite as they fight over who can love Emilia; as with Chaucer's heroine, Emilia has no idea of their passion. Yet, unlike her prototypes, Emilia must suffer the most because Theseus declares that the losing cousin and his warriors be executed. Emilia is forced to agree to this plan because she will not (and later in Act Four cannot) choose between them and because each cousin will accept no alternative: he must possess her or he will gladly die. Never having felt "the agony of love" (219) that drives Palamon and Arcite, she is helplessly ensnared in it, as her anguished question to Theseus reveals: "Shall any thing that loves me perish for me?" (241). Like Boccaccio's Emilia, she fears reprisals from the families of those who will die for her, showing particularly her continuing concern for mothers and women.[17] Fletcher's depiction of Emilia—understated, dignified, yet sympathetic—arouses our pity here. Yet in her next appearance in IV.ii, when, entering alone with two pictures, she tries to choose between the cousins and so prevent their final battle, Fletcher sacrifices consistency of characterization to theatrical reversals as she pathetically and comically attempts to prefer first one and then the other cousin, abandoning all her earlier words of chastity and appearing as a "sotted, / utterly lost" lovesick maiden ready to "run mad" for first Arcite, then Palamon (45-46, 48).

With the return of Shakespeare's hand in V.i comes Emilia's coldly beautiful prayer to Diana. Unlike the prayers of Boccaccio and Chaucer's heroines, which describe Diana's cruel powers, Emilia's prayer need cite no such examples because the play's depiction of her sad dilemma has been expanded well beyond its sources. The paradox of Emilia's situation, "bride habited, / But maiden-hearted" (150-51), links inextricably to her patron goddess' seemingly contradictory governance over chastity and childbirth and runs as a dark undercurrent through her prayer of praise. "Guiltless of election" (154), Emilia awaits a sign that her prayer has been heard. Rather than with Chaucer's symbolically significant bleeding pyres, Shakespeare's goddess answers with an ascending tree bearing one rose which soon falls. Emilia rightly interprets that she has been discharged from Diana: "I shall be gather'd" (170). Yet, like her predecessors, she does not understand the "mystery" (172) of her goddess' reply.

Unlike her prototypes, however, Emilia refuses to witness the tournament which she knows must result in the death of the vanquished cousin. Although her role degenerates briefly into a grim, desperate comedy as she hears first one and then the other cousin's name called out, her anguish breaks through when, presented with Arcite, who tells her "To buy you I have lost what's dearest to me / Save what is bought, and yet I purchase cheaply, / As I do rate your value" (V.iii.112-14), she asks pitifully, "Is this winning? O all you heavenly powers, where is [your] mercy?" (138-39). And in the final scene, after Arcite's unexpected fall and, in comparison to the sources, relatively quick death, she has little to say before being handed over to Palamon within twenty-five lines. Philip Edwards draws an appropriate distinction between Emilia's earlier, freely given love for Flavina and her later, half-hearted feelings for Palamon. The first stage is "all impulse and spontaneity, the second a forced movement into a love so half-hearted that the object might be either of two cousins, a love so uncentred that a substitute will do as well as the real thing."[18]

Given her prototypes and her role as a princess subject to a duke's will, Emilia cannot choose her own husband, a right that Catherine M. Dunn argues Renaissance women character types were more and more frequently demanding (31). Is that why Emilia in *The Two Noble Kinsmen* is shown as so much more determined than her predecessors to remain a servant of Diana and to resist the cousins? Shakespeare and Fletcher could not change her fate—but they could give her doubts about the felicity of male/female relationships, doubts that could be safely expressed through her rebelling yet "immature" love for Flavina, through the reminders of her Amazonian past, and through her concern with women and mothers. I tend to disagree with critics such as Gwyn Williams and Richard Abrams who view her as a lesbian;[19] rather, her overwhelming sympathy for women counterbalances the preening, homoerotic nature of the Palamon and Arcite rivalry, which seems to exaggerate the friendship tradition. Her protests may be her only way of breaking out; yet her plight is much harsher than in the earlier tales. That Arcite dies accidentally cannot lessen her guilt because one cousin must die; her forced wedding requires a funeral.

Ultimately, the four Emilia figures, so varyingly depicted and realized, fulfill stereotyped female roles to a disquieting extent. To be sure, the retelling of an ancient Greek tale necessitates conformity to the basic storyline; yet Emilia's consistent passivity in all four versions remains somehow disturbing, even if expected. Though the tales vary widely in form and tone and though Emilia's role ranges from important to negligible, she is never given even the self-determination to prefer one cousin over the other. Whether conveyed through an epic romance dedicated to the trials endured for Mars, a rime royal poetic narrative praising chivalry and satirizing courtly love, or a bleak tragicomedy, Emilia's role remains the same: hapless and hopeless, incapable of choice or thwarted in assertion, she stands as a victim of both Venus' dominion and of masculine control. Only in *The Two Noble Kinsmen* is the sources' happily-ever-after ending muted to make her powerless position clear.

NOTES

1 Giovanni Boccaccio, *Teseida*, ed. G.C. Sansoni (Firenze: R. Accademia della Crusca, 1938); Bernadette Marie McCoy, trans., *The Book of Theseus. Teseida della Nozze d'Emilia,* Giovanni Boccaccio (New York: Medieval Text Association by Teesdale Publishing Associates, 1974).
2 Of whom Boccaccio says, "sì rimosse / da sé ciascuna feminil paura, / e in tal guisa ordinò le sue posse, / che 'l regno suo e sé fece sicura" ("Setting aside her

feminine timidity, she disciplined her troops so well that she made herself and her kingdom secure") I.9.

3 She cautions her women,

> "Né vi metta paura conscienza
> d'aver peccato negli uomini vostri,
> ché morte lor la loro isconoscenza
> lecita impetrò nelli cor nostri,
> che non stimavan che d'equal semenza
> con lor nascessim, ma come da mostri,
> da quercie, over da grotte partorite,
> eravam poco qui da lor gradite."

"And do not let your conscience trouble you that you have sinned against your men, since it was their ingratitude that justified their death in our hearts. For they did not treat us as if we had been born of the same kind of seed as they were, but we pleased them little more than if we had been engendered of monsters, or oak trees, or even caves" [I.29]).

4 Shakespeare, Williams, and John Fletcher. The Two Noble Kinsmen. ed. Hallet Smith, *The Riverside Shakespeare,* ed. G. Blakemore Evans et al (Boston: Houghton, 1974).
5 Geoffrey Chaucer, "The Knight's Tale," *The Works of Geoffrey Chaucer,* ed. F.N. Robinson, 2nd. ed. (Boston: Houghton Mifflin, 1957).
6 Thomas G. Bergin, *Boccaccio* (New York: Viking, 1981) 125.
7 Norman E. Eliason, "Chaucer the Love Poet," *Chaucer the Love Poet,* ed. Jerome Mitchell and William Provost (Athens: Univ. of Georgia Press, 1973) 69.
8 A. C. Spearing, ed. *The Knight's Tale,* Geoffrey Chaucer (Cambridge: Cambridge UP, 1966) 11-12.
9 E. Talbot Donaldson, *The Swan at the Well: Shakespeare Reading Chaucer* (New Haven: Yale UP, 1985) 60.
10 Thomas W. Ross, *Chaucer's Bawdy* (New York: E. P. Dutton, 1972) 175-84.
11 Terry Jones, *Chaucer's Knight. The Portrait of a Medieval Mercenary* (Baton Rouge: Louisiana State UP, 1980) 156.
12 Herbert G. Wright, *Boccaccio in England from Chaucer to Tennyson* (London: Univ. of London: The Athlone Press, 1957) 49.
13 The other, held by the Huntington Library (San Marino, CA), is *La Theseide de M. G. Boccaccio, Innamoramento piaceuole, and honesto, di due Giouani Thebani Arcita, & Palemone,* D'ottava Rima nuouamente ridotta In Prosa per Nicolao Granvcci di Lucca. Lucca: Vicenzo Busdraghi, 1579. A reduction in prose of the *Teseida,* this version seems to be very closely based on its Boccaccian source; there are no changes in the depiction of Emilia.
14 Anne de Graville, *Le beau Romant des deux amans Palamon & Arcita et de la belle et saige Emilia,* ed. Yves Le Hir (Paris: Presses Universitaires de France, 1965) 29.
15 My translation.
16 Through my study of *The Two Noble Kinsmen,* I have come to concur with the assignment of authorship generally accepted by contemporary editors. In his Riverside edition of the play, which I shall use throughout, Hallett Smith establishes the following divisions:

I.i. - II.i.	Shakespeare (but I.iv. and v. uncertain)
II.ii. - vi.	Fletcher
III.i.	Shakespeare
III.ii. - V.i.33	Fletcher
V.i.34-173	Shakespeare
V.ii.	Fletcher
V.iii., iv.	Shakespeare

The Prologue and Epilogue are usually given to Fletcher (Smith 1640).

17   The goodly mothers that have groan'd for these
And all the longing maids that ever lov'd,
If your vow stand, shall curse me and my beauty
And in their funeral songs for these two cousins
Despise my cruelty, and cry woe worth me,
Till I am nothing but the scorn of women.
                                        (III.vi.245-50)

18   Philip Edwards, "On the Design of *The Two Noble Kinsmen*," *A Review of English Literature* 5 (1964): 103.
19   Catherine M. Dunn, "The Changing Image of Women in Renaissance Society and Literature," *What Manner of Woman. Essays in English and American Life and Literature,* ed. Marlene Springer (New York: New York UP, 1977) 15-38; Gwyn Williams, "The Loneliness of the Homosexual in Shakespeare," *Person and Persona. Studies in Shakespeare* (Cardiff: Univ. of Wales Press, 1981) 131-41; Richard Abrams, "Gender Confusion and Sexual Politics in *The Two Noble Kinsmen,*" *Drama, Sex, and Politics,* ed. James Redmond (Cambridge: Cambridge UP, 1985) 69-76.

V. ASIAN INTERACTIONS

ALLEGORIES OF THE NOVEL IN ALBERT WENDT'S *POULIULI*

Joseph Chadwick, University of Hawaii

The explicit topic of Albert Wendt's *Pouliuli* is the *matai* ("family chief") Faleasa Osovae's Lear-like attempt to give up through a feigned madness the responsibilities of his chiefly position while still maintaining the privileges and even the power of that position. Through this situation, the novel sets up a microcosmic version of the confrontation between traditional Samoan society and encroaching Western values and practices, a confrontation embodied in the figure of Faleasa and especially in Faleasa's responses to the "corruption" that he discovers or comes to acknowledge within his own familial, religious, and political institutions. This cultural and political confrontation, I will argue, co-exists in *Pouliuli* with a less explicit allegory that centers on the novel itself, an allegory which raises troubling questions about the position of this novel within the cultural conflicts that are its explicit theme.

The novel sets up the problem of cultural transformation first of all through its structure, the alternation between chapters devoted to its post-World War II time frame in which Faleasa is seventy-six years old and chapters devoted to Faleasa's childhood, adolescence, and young manhood. This structure allows the reader to gauge the gradual degrees by which both Faleasa and his village of Malaelua come to be involved in a struggle over cultural transformation. And many flashback episodes foreground this theme, focussing on Faleasa's first encounter with a *papalagi* ("person of European stock"), his first visit to the relatively Westernized city of Apia, and his time spent working for the U.S. military during World War II. The problem of cultural transformation shows up most dramatically, however, in Faleasa's use of his madness to attack powerful village figures who associate themselves with Western practices and values. Within his own family, for example, he acts against his son Elefane and wife Felefele, who, when Faleasa has begun to feign madness, suggest that "'we'd better take him into Apia to see a *papalagi* doctor.'"[1] In the church, he acts against the pastor Filemoni, whose "wife and two children were intolerably spoilt, condescending, disrespectful of the *faa-Samoa* ("Samoan way"), an embodiment of the worst characteristics of the town where his wife was born the daughter of a government clerk."[2] In the political arena, he acts against Malaelua's Member of Parliament Malaga, who, Faleasa believes, "had been the first Malaeluan to go up to form two in the Apia government school," "had worked in New Zealand for ten years, attended night school there, and mastered the use of figures and English; and . . . understood modern government,"[3] but who, as Faleasa's close friend Laaumatua alleges, "never attended the night school he's always talking about," "spent most of his time living off a series of women," and "was deported back here."[4] And in all of these arenas, he acts against himself, or at least the version of himself as *matai* and *matai* council leader—the version summed up by the very title "Faleasa"—which he has worked so devotedly to construct since childhood; for it is that self which, as he acknowledges when he decides to bring down Malaga, "was responsible for having allowed the market system of the town to infiltrate Malaeluan life and taint its very centre with a deadly cynicism."[5] Faleasa's madness, then, can be seen at this level as a device that enables him to try to reverse both the infiltration of Malaeluan life by the market system of the town and all of that infiltration's consequences. That madness, exposing and attacking the "corruption" that accompanies Western values and practices in this society, operates in somewhat the same way as a piece of muckraking journalism or, to bring the analogy closer to home, a novel of social reform. Indeed, that madness operates as a kind of double of this novel in particular and, as I will argue, of novels in general. This doubling between feigned madness and novel is set up at a structural level in that *Pouliuli*'s narrative begins at the exact instant when Faleasa (literally and figuratively) awakens to his feigned madness and ends when the madness goes beyond feigning, with Faleasa "standing on the topmost step [of the church], with his arms outstretched to the dazzling sky, his mouth fixed in a silent scream."[6] This beginning and ending suggest that feigned madness and the novel's narrative are co-extensive, that the former may even be the condition of the latter. Indeed, it is precisely that feigned madness which makes Faleasa the kind of individualized, psychologically complex, self-preoccupied figure which we expect to find as a novel's protagonist. Withdrawing from his family and society by "placing well-aimed pools of vomit in strategic positions (for instance, over the mattress of the only bed), and rearranging everything according to the chaotic freedom of his rebirth,"[7] Faleasa begins the novel by making himself into something very like a Sartrean protagonist nauseated by bad faith and struggling to come to terms with the "chaotic freedom" which he suddenly claims for himself. That feigned madness seems to be the enabling condition of Faleasa's very existence as a novelistic character, and thus of the existence of the novel itself.

The fundamental link between feigned madness and novel set up by *Pouliuli*'s structure and the events of its first chapter allows us to read the vicissitudes of that feigned madness as an allegory for the contradictory position of this novel, and even of novels in general, in relation to traditional Samoan society. And we are presented with a highly condensed and therefore very revealing version of that allegory in the figure of the genuinely mad Old Man or the "German" who Faleasa, as the boy Osovae, meets in the novel's crucial tenth chapter. The old man seems to associate his madness with the "insatiable memory" from which, he claims, literacy liberates us, asking: "Did Osovae know that his type of memory could devour a person bit by bit, bone by bone?"[8] And he goes on to explain that:

> the papalagi missionaries, by bringing the magic of the written word to Samoa, had rescued their people from the brutal nightmare swamp in which their collective memory was rooted and from which it derived its ferocity; had

turned their people's attention from the irrational madness of their vain and violent blood to the humane light of the word. This was a crucial mystery Osovae should contemplate when he grew up: because he was literate he would have no difficulty in unravelling it.[9]

Explicitly linking "irrational madness" to oral memory and opposing both to "the humane light of the [written] word," the Old Man's discourse seems to challenge the link between madness (genuine or feigned) and writing that, I have argued, other features of the novel forge. But that challenge collapses when we learn that the Old Man is by no means illiterate (he was, according to the most plausible rumor, educated in Samoan, English, and German by a missionary couple, and studied theology in England and Germany), and that his madness stems from precisely his literacy: fired by his superiors at the LMS theological college in Samoa for "refus[ing] to speak any other language but German and . . . organising military parades with his students," he "accused them and his dead parents of having stolen his soul and replaced it with the crippled soul of a papalagi."[10] And indeed the Old Man subverts his own praise of the written word even as he delivers it: by telling Osovae that "because he was literate he would have no difficulty in unravelling" the "crucial mystery" of the "magic of the written word," the Old Man constructs an utterly circular argument, asserting that literacy makes its own value self-evident. The Old Man, then, allegorizes the psychic and cultural contradictions that literacy—and the freight of Western values and practices that accompany it in this context—poses for this oral culture. Displacing the blame for his madness from literacy to oral memory, constantly making the little circles of stones that represent an integral cultural tradition, the Old Man desperately tries to deny his own literacy and the cultural alienation to which that form of knowledge and power condemns him.

The figure of the Old Man forges some important links between cultural transformation, literacy, and madness, links which suggest that a fundamental conflict divides the largely oral Samoan culture into which the Old Man is born from the literate culture of the West, the culture whose characteristic form of narrative has become the novel, into which he is imperfectly assimilated by education. But the question of the allegorical implications of Faleasa's *feigned* madness for the novel remains. Those implications can be teased out from the self-defeating consequences of the actions Faleasa takes under cover of that madness: the replacement of the greedy pastor Filemoni by another figure not chosen out of any concern for religious convictions (Laaumatua's cousin); the temporary replacement of Faleasa as *matai* council leader by the vain and greedy Sau; and the imprisonment of Moaula for the killing of the deposed Member of Parliament Malaga, which leaves Elefane and Felefele in control of the *aiga* ("extended family") with Elefane taking over the titles of Faleasa and Member of Parliament and leaves Faleasa in the Old Man's state—and even posture—of genuine madness. These consequences suggest that Faleasa's feigned madness does not offer an effective strategy to counter the Westernizing influences that have accompanied the infiltration of Malaeluan life by "the market system of the town," and that some element of that madness actually remains complicitous with precisely those influences. Laaumatua defines that complicitous element early on when he admonishes Faleasa:

> "The individual freedom you have discovered and now want to maintain is contrary to the very basis of our way of life. Have you considered that? For over thirty years you, Faleasa, and a few other matai have led our village, and your leadership, as was the ancient practice, has been based firmly on the principle that you exist to serve others, to serve the very people you are now branding as cannibals. A good leader doesn't live for himself but for his people."[11]

As this passage shows, a fundamental contradiction haunts Faleasa's feigned madness: that madness may be a means of trying to resist Westernizing influences, but the very effort of resistance is made in the name of a concept of individual, personal freedom central to modern, Western, bourgeois ideologies. Faleasa's effort at resisting the greed and self-interest that he associates with Western influences is precisely an expression of his own self-interest, his placing of his own desires above the interests of his village and family.

A similar contradiction haunts this novel *as* a novel—and perhaps haunts all novels that represent non-literate societies or societies for which the novel remains an imported art-form. For although this novel, like Faleasa in his feigned madness, turns its attention to the ways in which Western values and institutions have changed traditional Samoan life, its very form as a novel tends to constrain it to make a struggle over individual freedom central to its narrative. As a genre traditionally concerned with what Peter Bürger has called "the portrayal of bourgeois self-understanding . . . in a sphere that lies outside the praxis of life,"[12] a genre whose form and themes are deeply shaped—in Europe, at least—by its concurrent emergence with mass literacy and with ideologies of personal freedom and privacy, the novel, like Faleasa's feigned madness, is, as Laaumatua puts it, "contrary to the very basis of our way of life." Just as Faleasa's madness contradicts the very *faa-Samoa* which it is meant to preserve, so a novel like this one, even while representing a village's struggle with the forces of cultural transformation, marks through its very existence the degree to which such transformation has already taken place.

The novel's participation in the very process of cultural transformation which it so deeply questions becomes clear if we look at the novel against the body of oral literature to which it explicitly compares itself: the Pili legend.[13] This legend too is concerned with a decisive cultural transformation which comes about once the lizard-boy Pili, having kidnapped his mortal mother and performed three tasks for his divine father with the help of his friends "Tausamitele—Insatiable Appetite, Lelemalosi—Strong Flight, and Pouliuli—Darkness,"[14] extorts from his father both his own transformation into human form and "a live ember, a fishing-net, and a war club—possessions which mortals did not then have."[15] With these implements Pili introduces agriculture and brings all of the islands of Samoa under a unified rule which lasts until he divides his kingdom among his children, who promptly start fighting among themselves, and then vanishes, perhaps having "jumped up and been swallowed by his friend Pouliuli."[16] The parallels between Pili and Faleasa are obvious: both defy their fathers, perform tasks which their fathers dictate, and introduce decisive technological and political innovations (Faleasa's use of a gun—the first seen in Malaelua—to settle an inter-*aiga* feud exemplifies his use of such innovations). And both suddenly abdicate their positions by leaping into "the dark healing Void" of Pouliuli.[17]

Another parallel, however, set up in the third of Pili's tasks, shows how the novel itself is implicated in the process of transformation which Faleasa's innovations help to bring about. In that task, Pili's father orders him to imitate that actions of two giants, who

> rolled themselves into balls with their feet in their mouths and then, within seconds, swallowed their bodies up to their necks. Pili laughed haughtily. "Watch!" he called . . . and he jumped into the air and vanished completely but continued to talk. He had of course simply leapt up into Pouliuli's huge mouth.[18]

Vanishing completely "into Pouliuli's huge mouth" but continuing to talk is very close to what Faleasa does as he feigns madness but continues to set up the stories which dictate events in Malaelua—such as the rumor of incest that undoes the new *matai* council leader Sau. But it is also a very precise description of the position of the fundamentally novelistic anonymous, third-person omniscient narrator—as we can see by comparing it to the following exemplary definition of that position offered (even while giving that narrator a local habitation and the name Marlow) in Joseph Conrad's *Heart of Darkness*:

> It had become so pitch dark that we listeners could hardly see one another. For a long time already he [Marlow], sitting apart, had been no more to us than a voice. There was not a word from anybody. The others might have been asleep, but I was awake. I listened, I listened on the watch for the sentence, for the word, that would give me the clue to the faint uneasiness inspired by this narrative that seemed to shape itself without human lips in the heavy night-air of the river.[19]

Like Pili or Conrad's Marlow, the novelistic third-person narrator—the narrator of *Pouliuli*, for example—speaks from darkness, from the darkness of his anonymity and invisibility within the story he recounts, from the darkness even of the printer's ink which enables the alienating distance between story-teller and story-receivers which he exists to mediate.[20] And he accomplishes his "magic" through the aid of techniques that allow the disguising of the author's constitutive invention of his story under the veil of the narrator's pretense of objective reportage. Just as Pili's fulfillment of his task allows him to transform radically the social order over which his father had presided, so the novel's anonymous, omniscient narration and focus on an individual struggle for freedom sharply challenge both the narrative techniques and the ideals of leadership of traditional Samoan society.

It is tempting to read these allegories of the novel in *Pouliuli* as Albert Wendt's attempts to work through the contradictions implicit in his personal situation as a writer. But it is more illuminating to focus not on Wendt's personal situation, but rather on what these allegories have to say—in combination with the novel's explicit drama of cultural conflict—about the psychic, cultural, and political consequences of writing a novel in a society, like that of the Samoa *Pouliuli* depicts, where it is not a traditional cultural practice. Writing a novel about such a society can then be seen as a fundamentally transformative and deeply contradictory act: transformative because it deploys narrative techniques radically different from those that structure the stories through which that society has traditionally transmitted its history, culture, and political order; contradictory because the novel's techniques thus prevent it from telling the very stories through which that society has traditionally represented itself. The very act of writing that produces *Pouliuli*, then, makes the novel, like its protagonist, into a reluctant agent of cultural transformation, preserving the forms of traditional society but not the substance. Hence the novel's thematic "resolutions"—Faleasa's frozen, silent scream and the weak Elefane's takeover of the *aiga*—perhaps also figure the fate of traditional Samoan culture in this—or any other—novel.

NOTES

1 Albert Wendt, *Pouliuli* (Honolulu: Univ. of Hawaii Press, 1980) 32.
2 Wendt 4.
3 Wendt 124.
4 Wendt 125.
5 Wendt 128.
6 Wendt 144.
7 Wendt 7.
8 Wendt 104.
9 Wendt 104-105.
10 Wendt 111.
11 Wendt 17.
12 Bürger makes this observation with regard to "bourgeois art" in general, but he also identifies the novel as typifying such art when he defines "reception . . . by isolated individuals" as bourgeois art's characteristic mode of reception and argues that "[t]he novel is that literary genre in which the new [bourgeois] mode of reception finds the form appropriate to it." Peter Bürger, *Theory of the Avant-Garde*, trans. Michael Shaw (Minneapolis: Univ. of Minnesota Press, 1984) 48.
13 As Subramani points out in his account of the Maui myth in Wendt's fiction, "the Maui figure reappears as Pili" in *Pouliuli*, and variations on this myth can thus be found throughout Polynesia (Subramani, *South Pacific Literature: From Myth to Fabulation* [Suva, Fiji: Univ. of the South Pacific, 1985] 124). For a succinct summary of such variations, see Katharine Luomala's chapter on Maui

Allegories of the Novel in *Pouliuli* 161

       in Katherine Luomala, *Voices on the Wind: Polynesian Myths and Chants*, rev. ed. (Honolulu: Bishop Museum Press, 1986) 85-98; for a specifically Samoan variation, see C. Steubel's chapters on Pili in C. Steubel, *Myths and Legends of Samoa*, trans. Brother Herman (Wellington, N.Z.: Reed, 1976) 22-31. Subramani notes that the Pili myth is tied to the themes of "Faleasa's search for a 'human form' and his efforts to reunite Malaelua under a new leadership" (124), but he does not trace the links between that myth and the problem of cultural transformation.
14 Wendt 95.
15 Wendt 97.
16 Wendt 97.
17 Wendt 12.
18 Wendt 96.
19 Joseph Conrad, *The Heart of Darkness* (New York: Signet, 1950) 95.
20 That distance, Jacques Derrida argues, has always operated at an epistemological level not only in written texts but also in spoken ones: "The ethic of the living word would be perfectly respectable, completely utopian and a-topic, . . . it would be as respectable as respect itself if it did not live on a delusion and a nonrespect for its own condition of origin, if it did not dream in speech of a presence denied to writing, denied by writing. The ethic of speech is the *delusion* of presence mastered." Jacques Derrida, *Of Grammatology*, trans. Gayatri Chakravorty Spivak (Baltimore: Johns Hopkins UP, 1976) 139. What renders this argument irrelevant to the implicit conflict between oral and written texts in *Pouliuli* is precisely Wendt's refusal to ground claims for the priority of the oral on what Derrida calls the "ethic of the living word." Indeed, Wendt explicitly acknowledges the problematic status of origin and communication in an oral text when he describes the rumor that undoes Sau as "detach[ing] itself from the general rotting bread-fruit stench and . . . quickly [taking] on highly enriched odours and deviously monstrous shapes, which in turn divided and multiplied in the contented but by then blazing imaginations of the Malaeluans until they reached the infinite possibilities of a true mythology" (87). As this passage shows, Wendt makes no claims for the epistemological priority of speech or the oral text; but as my argument claims, he does insist on the cultural and social differences between oral and written texts generated by the specific historical situation of an oral Samoan culture colonized by literate Western powers.

THE MOLD OF FORCE: MATERNAL TRANSFORMATIONS OF SUBMISSION INTO AGGRESSION IN MODERN JAPANESE WOMEN'S LITERATURE

Victoria Vernon, Hamilton College

Let me begin by citing a poem by Nagase Kiyoko entitled in translation simply "Mother."

> I am always aware of my mother,
> ominous, threatening,
> a pain in the depths of my consciousness.
> My mother is like a shell,
> so easily broken.
> Yet the fact that I was born
> bearing my mother's shadow
> cannot be changed.
> She is like a cherished, bitter dream
> my nerves cannot forget
> even after I awake.
> She prevents all freedom of movement.
> If I move she quickly breaks,
> and the splinters stab me.[1]

This article, like the one by M. R. Kecht, deals with motherhood as a culturally patterned and patterning function—its relationship to societal demands made upon mothers rearing daughters in patriarchy and the effects upon the individual psyches involved. Such issues have become increasingly visible, both in modern literary treatments and in Western feminist criticism, and Japan has one of the clearest and most formalized historical patterns for that relationship. At the same time, Japanese literature as a whole has been impressive in capturing the ambiguous nuances of a subjective response to a world seen largely in terms of society and its restraints. The culture itself has traditionally emphasized relationship to others and submission to social roles as the crucial elements in the formation of personality. It places less stress upon the necessity, indeed the possibility, of the achievement of full autonomous "Individuality"—that free self that in the West is a mythic literary inheritance of Romanticism and a less acknowledged accommodation to the "rightness" of competition in a capitalist society.

Women writers within the Japanese culture are particularly astute in exploring issues now reaching formulation in Western feminist criticism. They need not make the same assumptions upon which examination of those issues is frequently postulated here. More constrained to recognize that their culture endorses extreme gender differentiation, they are conversely less hampered by inherited, if tacit, assumptions about the primary value of the development of an independent separated ego, an assertive individuality most associated in the West, too, if we think about it, with a masculine model. Thus, literary autobiography by women in Japan does fully document the struggles and successes of women who succeeded in breaking free of the traditional restraints that bound their mothers and which their mothers dutifully attempted to instill in them, but the writers acknowledge openly that society is the primary source of those controls and bring less than sole responsibility to bear upon the maternal figure. Even liberated daughters who depict their "own" stories readily concede their inheritance of their mothers' sexual nature, tending not simply to record a pattern of chronological "progress" toward the transcendent value of Western individualism—self-actualization—but rather a cyclic pattern in which the freed daughter can become a once more bound mother. Such accounts need not follow a Western linear narrative model, triumphantly or tragically concluded by the victory or defeat of differentiation. And while in Japan, as elsewhere, direct autobiography inhibits the possibility of recording maternal tensions and antagonisms toward daughters, other forms of literature, such as autobiographical fiction, poetry, and fantasy, permit an extraordinarily frank recognition that such feelings exist.

As is so often the case for a comparatist, I found immersion in this literature an unsettling and transforming experience, forcing questions to the surface: Was not the very self-actualization that maternal constraints demonstrably impeded in the literary accounts in itself a primarily Western value, or worse, a primarily Western illusion? Had not my formulation of the question assumed an answer implied in my own social and cultural conditioning? And would not the Japanese woman writer once more teach me the limits of my own questions, the inadequacy of my assumed answers? Well . . . yes, to all of the above. The literary works demonstrated to me that, despite (perhaps even because of) the intricate and intimate ambiguity of mother-daughter relationships in a society with a history of extreme gender distinctions and enforced submission of women, Japanese writers could depict their experience with a clarity and psychological sensitivity that evade capture within the dichotomizations of Western systems of analysis and classification. We understand what they are saying in a universal sense, but what they say is not reducible to our systems of rationalization.

Nothing in Nagase's poem, for example, necessarily marks it as Japanese in origin, and yet, students in a first-year writing course on the feminine experience rejected this and other Japanese poems as being alien and depressing in their starkness and ambiguity, considering them too disturbing to be acceptable. Perhaps young Americans are inculcated with a sentimental blindness that insulates them; they want to believe in their own individuality and in their separation and difference from mothers who may be loved but have been outgrown. The outright declaration in Nagase's poem of the mother's negative influence no doubt depressed these young readers, but I suspect they found the declaration of the impossibility of breaking free from her to be even more threatening on a cultural level. Nevertheless, the poem reflects an anguish that daughters all over the world are capable of experiencing.

In Nagase's poem, the mother is named only by her function, a practice so universal that we do not question or even notice it. There, as in all literature dealing with this relationship from a daughter's perspective, the writer is inevitably posing a named or personalized individual against the power of a designated social role. Thus, an "I" is posed against an "ominous" and "threatening" presence, seen as both within and without the self. "My mother" is "a pain in the depths of my consciousness," but also an "easily broken shell" with a restraining and wounding power that "prevents all freedom of movement." And yet, the very act of writing constitutes a movement against the shell whose splinters "stab *me*." Because this "I" was "born bearing my mother's shadow," the desired separation motivating the act of writing is also partially impossible of achievement. The mold may be broken, the shell shattered, but the writer's being has been formed within it.

As literary autobiography and autobiographical fiction testify, the societal mold into which mothers attempted to compress their daughters was a particularly rigid one in Japanese culture. A very real sense of the cultural constraints imposed upon women in what might be termed living memory arises from direct accounts of women born in the late nineteenth and early twentieth centuries, women whose socialization was the product of late Tokugawa and early Meiji mothers. Whereas Ishimoto Shidzue's [Shizue's] *Facing Both Ways: The Story of My Life*[2] may be the clearest articulation of the inculcated restraints of a traditional mother's training of her daughter, other autobiographies, such as Sugimoto Etsu's *A Daughter of the Samurai*,[3] also published in English in 1935, bear out the extreme social pressures for conformity exerted upon Japanese daughters. It is not coincidental that both writers broke the mold imposed upon them in early childhood, and that the autobiographies themselves are, in part, a justification of the daughters' turning away from the traditional. Sugimoto's work is subtitled, for example, *How a daughter of feudal Japan, living hundreds of years in one generation, became a modern American.*

What both authors had resisted and wanted to justify resisting was a cultural image of women endorsed by "hundreds of years" of tradition and enforced by the legal codes of the nation—an image of submission so complete that it went beyond every waking moment. Even the optimistic Sugimoto notes that "samurai daughters were taught never to lose control of mind or body—even in sleep. Boys might stretch themselves into the character *dai*, carelessly outspread; but girls must curve into the modest, dignified character *kinoji*, which means "spirit of control."[4] Sugimoto's marriage was to provide her with more than the usual freedom for a Japanese woman, since she was married by arrangement to a Japanese resident of the United States, but Ishimoto's experience was at once more traditional in its early years and more daring in its development. It is she who gives us the more detailed picture of a mother perfect in meeting the expectations of her culture and meticulous in raising her daughters for their roles in that culture:

She never betrays unpleasant feelings. Endurance and repression are her greatest ideals. She says to me, "Endurance a woman should cultivate more than anything else. . . ." She was faithful to the family system. . . She did not wish her daughters to be exempt from the matter of pleasing mothers-in-law as she believed the performance of this obligation makes a woman's virtues brighter. Having inculcated this in her children, she dared to have her eldest daughter [the author] marry into a family with a mother-in-law who was said to be especially difficult to please.

My mother was especially assiduous in educating her children. She made every effort to further their development, but her feudal concept of "man first, woman to follow" was clearly seen in her treatment of her sons and daughters. Of course the daughters took sex discrimination for granted, as they did not know anything else. Mother had never understood the moral beauty of romantic love between man and woman. She regards it as indicative of wild feelings which can be allowed to exist only among vulgar people. "Unselfishness, sacrifice and endurance for woman. That is all-sufficient," my honorable mother maintains.[5]

Although Ishimoto shows respect for her mother's fidelity to the feudal code and subsequently tried to follow the model and fulfill the role for which her mother had trained her as a dutiful wife, obedience to the then liberal views of her husband paradoxically demanded the development of political consciousness and economic self-sufficiency. She was to become a founder of the Japanese birth control movement, a political activist and an advocate of women's rights. After her husband reversed his liberal politics and demanded her return to submissive self-effacement, she attempted to comply for a while, but the marriage ended in divorce. Much of the energy invested in the autobiography is devoted to describing the necessity for breaking free from "the box" in which she states her mother's precepts had enclosed her, even though we can assume that in the breaking free of this shell, she herself was stabbed. No doubt the direct autobiographical mode imposed restraints upon Ishimoto's depiction of her personal reaction to maternal pressures, but more importantly she wishes to use the experience of her own life to testify to the social pressures upon Japanese women in general. Likewise, Sugimoto's portrayal of her mother does not extend to any kind of criticism of the person; her criticism is directed rather toward the social force that requires a mother to prepare her daughter for a submissive life role.

Even the shift to the thinly veiled fictions of the autobiographical novel, however, allows the cost of such socialization to be questioned more personally and permits the exploration of the negative dynamic of the mother-daughter relationship. Thus, Miyamoto Yuriko in her autobiographical novel *Nobuko* allows the title character to confront a mother who, by the conventions of the *shishōsetsu* or "I-novel," is a barely fictionalized version of her own mother. Here, not only the demands of society, but a conflict between identification and differentiation are addressed directly in the course of an argument over Nobuko's marriage.

> Nobuko felt agitated, as if her heart had been stabbed and was now being stirred with a small pointed object. Takeyo knew just how to inject a poisonous needle into the most vulnerable spot of Nobuko's heart; she had a woman's instinct toward another woman, and a mother's toward her daughter.[6]

Despite the ominous nature of the conflict, the daughter is able to draw back to the ground of identification in order to defend the necessity of differentiation, and the argument is resolved with a frank assessment. "Surely you're aware of how much you have hoped for me, my work and my success. You're trying to make me do what you couldn't do with your own life. Isn't that right?"[7]

It is interesting that the fictionalization in such autobiographical works, like the emotional expressiveness of poetry, provides a forum for more direct articulation of the tensions that the daughter experiences. But what would it take, we must ask further, to allow the mother's perspective free articulation? What form could permit a mother's voice to oppose the near absolute demand of the Japanese tradition that a mother sacrifice herself for her husband and children and that, with a daughter, she be stern merely to prepare her for a similar inevitably subordinate adult role. Certainly direct autobiography would never permit a mother to express hostility toward her daughter without labelling herself a monster in nearly any culture.

The fictions of fantasy, however, do provide an avenue for such thematizations, and when we compare two modern short stories, Kōno Taeko's "Ants Swarm" and Takahashi Takako's "Congruent Figures" to the prewar autobiographies, we can see that the loosening of the formal feudal codes of patriarchy following the war has been accompanied by a willingness on the part of the Japanese woman writer to probe into areas partially tabooed or blanked out in the West. Here feelings that resemble those in Nagase's poem are expressed, but it is the mother's voice that utters them. For Kōno uses actual fantasy and Takahashi the power of dreams to release a mother's hostility toward her daughter.

Thus, in "Ants Swarm" a woman involved apparently willingly in a sado-masochistic marriage wherein she is tortured as a routine part of sexual intercourse believes she has inadvertently become pregnant. Although distressed by the prospect of having a child at first, her most vivid projection of interaction with the unborn occurs at the moment when the protagonist, Fumiko, realizes that the child might have been a girl. This realization allows her to indulge with her husband in horrifying fantasies of repression and torture in which she is the principal agent.

> [T]o a girl I will be very strict . . . other people will think I am the stepmother. . . . If it is a girl I will not let her have much education. . . . I will make her stay at home and use her as a maid. Yes, by this time of day she'd be forced to prepare breakfast. . . . She ought to be a child who is incapable of criticism—an idiot-like child.[8]

Her unshared internal fantasies escalate to the point where Fumiko visualizes herself as contemplating pouring hot butter over the already scarred body of her kneeling daughter, but in the projections that she shares with her husband, the final scenario concerns their daughter's life after they have married her off to a man whom they encourage to abuse her. "I will not listen even if she comes to me to complain. I'll show her my body and tell her that her father is such a cruel man, but that her mother endures it. I'll tell her that she must bear it too."[9] The perversity of the fantasy does carry along with it an eerie note of repetition of the dictates of the feudal code—we hear the reverberation of "endurance," "submission" and "repression" again, here distorted into a source of emotional satisfaction, through which the tortured becomes victorious by becoming a torturer in turn, torturing, it seems, an image of herself.

Just so do the dreams of the mother in "Congruent Figures" permit an exploration of the submerged feelings of a denied and denying mother. Takahashi's story begins when Akiko, the protagonist, receives a letter from her daughter, Hatsuko, announcing that she plans to visit after years of separation and alienation from her mother. Hatsuko announces that she will be bringing with her a child whom the grandmother has not yet seen and asks her mother why she has disliked her so intensely.

> What were you angry with me about? . . . Since you were the same old mother to my brother, I thought for a moment that you were merely maintaining our generations-old custom of treating boys with respect but bringing up girls with strict discipline. Sometimes you looked at me with a hard face devoid of emotion, and after that you always looked aside coldly.[10]

Akiko's answer to her daughter's question begins to appear in an initial revery: "It was an emotion which all of the mothers of the world must have felt about their daughters . . . like small white bubbles coming up from the swamp that is called life, where the corpses of their ancestors, related to them by blood, are lying about."[11] Prompted as she is by the recognition that her daughter is like her in body, face, gesture and voice, Akiko begins to verbalize her hostility and the reasons for it, "I felt the existence of a woman beside me, a woman who felt and acted exactly as I did,"[12] and the more she reflects upon this the more visceral the feeling becomes. "I felt as if the contents of my body flowed from me in huge quantities from its external structure while my hands and feet surely remained or that my hands and feet were invaded by Hatsuko's hands and feet."[13] When her daughter begins to menstruate, Akiko feels even more that her own person has been appropriated. Even the odor of Hatsuko's body begins to threaten her own identity: "with Hatsuko's growth, I was forced to smell my body smell even in places where I had not gone. I was forced to have the strange feeling of encountering my body smell outside of myself."[14] In maturing, "Hatsuko had stolen from me the woman whom, although longing for, I had locked up."[15]

Ultimately, however, the protagonist's brooding upon the transmission of the mother's self to the daughter comes to seem more universal and more ominous. An old neighbor woman, whose presence has bedeviled Akiko and who seems to be able to read her thoughts, appears in a dream. Holding out a mirror to Akiko, the old woman shows her a face that overlaps her own. "It is the face of mother," in the old woman's words. To Akiko's objection that "It was not my mother's," the old woman replies "It is the face of mother itself in general," and the dream resolves itself in a shower of blood spurting from the old woman's wrist.

> [A]nd the old woman stretched out her hands and scooped it up saying it was the blood of women, look there is a limitless amount, scooped and scooped and it was still there; it is transmitted to the woman who comes out of your stomach, then to another woman who comes out of that woman, and what is transmitted is woman's karma, here try to scoop it, where can you find maternal love? It is nothing but an illusion manufactured by men.[16]

Thus, when Hatsuko does appear with her child, who is of course a girl, Akiko can only hold the child with "an ominous feeling," and her final comment to her daughter signals the renewal of the cycle once more. "'You too bore a girl,' I said smiling thinly. I checked my impulse to say it will begin with you now."[17]

From within a tradition that has made maternal love an absolute demand of patriarchy, the Japanese woman writer can thus use fantasy as a fictional challenge to such absolutes. Compelled by the strong gender differentiation of her culture to recognize that her experience cannot be subsumed by an essentially male model, she visualizes her experience as female and bound to a cyclic life model. Thus, although direct autobiography may seem to affirm that a daughter can free herself from the specific social restrictions that bound her mother, it does not frame this as a personalized struggle for free individuation from a single other (a particular mother). The story runs deeper than the conflict of a *Mommy Dearest,* and even autobiography testifies to the power of social forces over the individual life. In the fictions of fantasy, moreover, the Japanese woman writer can carry her exploration of biological inheritance far beyond the personal to a degree capable of making more than one small classroom of Western readers uncomfortable. Speaking from behind the mask of "mother itself in general," some Japanese women writers suggest that not one, but two, women are caught within the shell of relationship and that there is pain in the depth of both consciousnesses.

NOTES

1. Nagase Kiyoko, "Mother," in *Women Poets of Japan,* edited and translated by Kenneth Rexroth and Ikuko Atsumi (New York: New Directions, 1977) 90.
2. Ishimoto, Shidzue [Shizue], *Facing Both Ways: The Story of My Life* (New York: Farrar & Rinehart, 1935).
3. Sugimoto, Etsu, *A Daughter of the Samurai: How a daughter of feudal Japan, living hundreds of years in one generation, became a modern American* (New York: Doubleday, Doran & Company, 1935).

4   Sugimoto 24.
5   Ishimoto 112-12.
6   Miyamoto Yuriko, *Nobuko*, excerpted in *To Live and To Write: Selections by Japanese Women Writers 1913-1938*, edited and translated by Yukiko Tanaka (Seattle: Seal Press, 1987) 49-50.
7   Miyamoto 50.
8   Kōno, Taeko, "Ants Swarm," translated by Lippit, in *Stories by Contemporary Japanese Women Writers*, translated and edited by Noriko Mizuta Lippit and Kyoko Iriye Selden (New York: M. E. Sharpe, 1982) 113-114.
9   Kōno 114.
10 Takahashi, Takako, "Congruent Figures," translated by Lippit in *Stories by Contemporary Japanese Women Writers* 155.
11 Takahashi 155.
12 Takahashi 155.
13 Takahashi 160.
14 Takahashi 168.
15 Takahashi 173.
16 Takahashi 177-78.
17 Takahashi 181.

POETORII AND NEW-STYLE POETRY IN THE *SHINTAISHISHŌ*

Lucy Lower, University of Hawaii

The tumultuous events of the opening years of the Meiji era, which began in 1868, and the far-reaching changes these effected in all aspects of Japanese life, at first brought forth fairly little in the way of literary response. Then-current poetic forms were extremely limited in the subjects they could treat and the way in which they might treat them, and innovators from within the traditions of *waka* (native forms which clung to canons of taste and diction a millennium old) and *kanshi* (poetry written in Chinese) were in short supply.

The *Shintaishishō*, or *Selection of New-Style Poems*, published in 1882, was the first step toward the establishment of a new, modern poetry. It is one of the more curious products of Meiji literature, its oddities including the occupations and preoccupations of its three compilers; its mix of translations and (for want of a better word to distinguish them) original poems; the gap between its poetic quality and its critical reception on the one hand and its historical impact and popular reception on the other; the paradox, for that matter, of its immediate popularity in view of the pedantry of its presentation; and the warring impulses evident in the compilers' attempt to introduce a radically new poetry while often relying, rhetorically and prosodically, on the forms of the past to lend dignity and credibility to their efforts. Among the most interesting aspects of this collection are the stated aims of the compilers and what those aims reveal about changing concepts of poetry.

The three compilers were all junior professors at the newly renamed Tokyo Imperial University, and none was a poet. Toyama Masakazu (1848-1900) was a sociologist. He was studying at the University of London when the Tokugawa shogunate fell; he later attended the University of Michigan from which he graduated with a bachelor's degree in science and philosophy. Yatabe Ryōkichi (1852-1899) was a botanist and Cornell graduate. Inoue Tetsujirō (1855-1944) was a philosopher. He graduated from Tokyo University, where he had studied with the slightly older Toyama; he later also studied in Berlin. Toyama and Yatabe, together with two eminent visiting professors, were advocates of the progressivist, evolutionist thought then at the peak of its influence at Tokyo University. Inoue was junior partner in this movement, as he was in the *Selection of New-Style Poems*, where his contributions were significantly fewer than those of Toyama and Yatabe. The visiting professors were Edward Morse (1838-1925)—lecturing in 1877 on Darwinism at the invitation of Toyama, who had heard him at Michigan—and Ernest Fenollosa (1853-1908), introduced by Morse, who lectured in 1878 on a version of political and economic philosophy that synthesized Hegel and theories of scientific progress. All disciplines, including those in the humanities, were affected by the evolutionist argument.

Toyama, for example, used social Darwinist Herbert Spencer's *Principles of Sociology* as a text in a history course, and his "Representative Government" and "Philosophy of Style" in teaching the English language.[1] The influence of these currents of thought was felt not only in the direction taken by scholarly inquiry but also in matters of methodology: evolution was considered to be the basic principle underlying all phenomena.[2] Close ideological as well as collegial ties thus drew the three together as friends, and led them eventually—inevitably—to take the position that poetry, like any other aspect of culture or society, could and should evolve and "improve." Appreciative readers of Western, especially English-language, poetry, they became increasingly dissatisfied with what they felt was limited or outmoded in the native tradition, and they began actively to try to come up with a new form of poetic expression suitable to the new age.

Each of the three compilers contributed a preface to the *Selection*, and these are followed by the *hanrei*, a brief, unsigned digest of the aims and principles of organization of the work. These texts, together with headnotes to certain poems (notably Inoue's translation of Longfellow's "Psalm of Life" and Yatabe's *Kamakura no daibutsu ni mōde de kan ari* ["Thoughts on Visiting the Great Buddha at Kamakura"]), set forth their grievances against the poetries of their day. Basically there are two: that available forms are too short for the development of complex ideas or extended thought, and that they do not use contemporary Japanese.

Inoue—writing, it should be noted, in classical Chinese—begins his preface with a quote from the Sung Neo-Confucian Ch'eng I lamenting how the poetry of his day has become inaccessible; he then quotes the early Edo period Confucian and Neo-Confucian scholar Kaibara Ekken's disparagement of the Japanese practice of writing poetry in Chinese and his insistence that the would-be poets merely make fools of themselves and produce verses that are excessively difficult to understand. Inoue's complaints about the poetry of his own day, of course, parallel these.

Yatabe takes a different tack, developing an argument for cultural relativism in matters of religion and morality. When he veers off into a discussion of the lack of poetry then being composed in ordinary Japanese, we can infer that he believes poetry, too, should be relevant to the issues and experience and language of its age and its culture.

Toyama's argument is the most developed and the most colorful rhetorically. Citing the extreme shortness and simplicity of the three forms of poetic expression then available (the thirty-one-syllable *tanka*, the seventeen-syllable *haiku,* and short, T'ang-style lyrics), he complains that the ideas expressed therein must also of necessity be extremely short and simple, and "of no more substance than incense smoke or a shooting star." He is also appalled by the practice, then widely current, of composing verses in Chinese and reading them in Japanese, as a betrayal of Chinese prosody as well as being outlandish on its face. He compares it to the willful playing dumb of one who can speak, or the imitation of a marionette by a human being—that is, one who has the power of independent movement. Rejecting the strictures on prosody, diction and imagery imposed by both the *waka* and *kanshi* traditions as too constricting and too arcane, he pleads for a form that will accommodate "extended thought" in "aurally pleasing, native Japanese." In the headnote to his Longfellow translation, Toyama mounts another of his rhetorically famous appeals, that "a Meiji verse [*uta*] should be a Meiji verse, and not a verse of ancient times; a Japanese poem [*shi*] should be a Japanese poem, and not a Chinese poem; this is what it means to compose a new-style poem."

Although it was, even in the 1880s, somewhat anomalous for three such academics—neither professional poets nor even scholars of literature—to undertake to "modernize" a poetic tradition, it is less so than it might seem from the perspective of Western literary development. I am not sure whether to point to the Confucian tradition's assumption of a familiarity with literature, specifically poetry, for any educated man—that tradition certainly shaped the early education of all three compilers, and they draw upon it variously, as we have already seen, in their essays and comments—or to the spontaneous, universally accessible version of the *waka* tradition that was supposed to represent the natural expressive outlet for human feeling. The three prefaces to the *Selection* progress from Inoue's classical Chinese through Yatabe's intermediate style—heavily Sinified Japanese but with the native inflections written out—to Toyama's more nearly modern Japanese. In addition to Inoue's references to Confucian and Neo-Confucian thinkers, we have Toyama quoting the T'ang official and man of letters, Han Yü; even the *hanrei* alludes to the *Shu ching* (*Classic of History*). On the other side, Yatabe echoes the seminal document of *waka* poetics, the preface to the 10th-century *Kokinshū* anthology, when he anticipates poetic achievements by future generations of new-style poetry that will "cause the gods and demons to weep." Toyama, once again the most exuberant rhetorically, in the last third of his preface shifts into a rhythmic alternation of five- and seven-syllable phrases, heightening the intensity of his prose much as this same technique does in the lyric climax of a Nō drama. Moreover, the poems in the *Selection* are invariably cast in alternating lines of seven and five syllables, some variation of which defines virtually every utterance in the Japanese-language poetic tradition. Both the term *shintaishi* and its meter recall the *imayō*[3] of the Heian period, and some of the martial poems (Toyama's *Battōtai* ["Drawn Sabres Regiment"] is an example) were indeed widely recited, or transformed into popular songs. It would be a mistake to dwell overmuch on the new style's affinities to *imayō*, however, in view of the former's at least theoretical embrace of other meters, as outlined in point two of the *hanrei*. Closer models for the singing or recitation of new-style poems can, at any rate, be seen in the recitation, as was then very popular, of poems written in Chinese and in the metrically similar translations of Christian hymns. If the classical education of Toyama, Yatabe, and Inoue was as evident in the substructure of the *Selection of New-Style Poems* as their Western learning was in its inspiration, we should not imagine that they themselves were unaware of it. It was poetic evolution they advocated, not utter rejection of the past. This is implicit in Yatabe's cultural relativism and explicit in both Inoue and Toyama (I quote again from the latter's preface): "we disdain neither old nor new, elegant nor common; mixing Japanese, Chinese and Western styles, we are intent primarily on making ourselves understood and we have spared no effort to be understandable."

The first point of the *hanrei* offers an ambitious redefinition of the Chinese ideograph *shi* that links the new style with existing forms: "in China one calls these *shi*, in our own country one calls them *uta*, and there is not as yet a general term applying to both *shi* and *uta*. In this book are neither *shi* nor *uta*, yet our use of the word *shi* for these works is in the sense in which it corresponds to the general Western term 'poetry [*poetorii*],' which includes both *shi* and *uta*, and not as it has been used from olden times." The introduction of this term as signifying a unified concept of poetry that included not only traditional forms *and* the new style of the present *Selection*, but other styles yet to be invented, is at the center of what the compilers were attempting to do, and it provides a kind of figure for the fate of their efforts. The abstraction was not particularly difficult for anyone to understand, on the other hand it appears not to have been particularly congenial. It didn't stick. The compound term *shiika* had previously served as inclusive of both *waka* and *kanshi*, but it is a compound term in which the component parts retain their separate identities; it is equivalent to saying "*waka* and *kanshi*," not "poetry." As poetry in Chinese gradually died a natural death during the early decades of this century, *shi* has come to refer routinely to the descendents of new-style poetry (*shintaishi*), namely modern poetry (*kindaishi*) and contemporary poetry (*gendaishi*). (These are general terms, but in practice refer only to poetry based on Western models.) These *shi* have become simply another, separate genre of poetry. "*Shi*" tends to be used alone, in fact, only when it is clear from the context what kind of poetry— *kindaishi, gendaishi,* or even *kanshi*, its original designation—is under discussion. *Waka* remains inviolable, unassimilable; it comes under the *shi* rubric only in a large study with a title like, for example, *Nihon kindaishi shi* (*A History of Modern Japanese Poetry*), in which modern *waka* might be allotted a chapter or two near the end.

As the science and philosophy background of the compilers is reflected in their attempt to reconceptualize Japanese poetry, so is it most evident in their original poems. And as they failed in the one attempt, to redefine poetry, so did they in the other, to compose it, largely due to the distortions that background produced. In their eagerness for a poetic forum that could accommodate "ideas" and "extended thought," they tended to drag in poetically undigested tracts of discursive thought, pausing only to trim them into five- and seven-syllable phrases (not a difficult thing to do in Japanese). These were mixed with passages of uninspired poetic conventionality that frequently resulted in "poems" that were unintentionally hilarious when they were not merely tedious. Notable examples are Toyama's *Shakaigaku no genri ni daisu* ("On the Principles of Sociology"), originally written, in meter, as an introduction to Noritake Kōtarō's translation of Spencer's essay in 1882. Toyama extols the brilliance of

Darwin and Spencer and their theories of survival of the fittest, but breaks midway into a catalog of plants and animals culled straight from traditional poetry. We get deer inevitably belling for their mates, and a play on the traditional association of peonies and lions. Yatabe's "Thoughts on Visiting the Great Buddha at Kamakura" provides another example: he observes blandly that what had formerly been the object of religious pilgrimage was now principally a tourist attraction. This leads to a plodding recapitulation of his theme of cultural relativism and how the diversity of the world's values and ideas, through evolution, fuel its progress. The compilers were right in their insistence on bringing into poetry topics that had not in the past been admitted, but their treatment of those topics betrayed the limits of their understanding of poetry. Ironically, their *poetorii* was insufficiently abstract: it applied only to the grouping of various *poetic forms* under a single umbrella and failed to distinguish between poems and poetry as an essence. Their *poetorii* could not be used metaphorically, for example, as in "the poetry of a bird in flight."

The translations in the *Selection* are slightly more successful poetically, the originals being works of proven merit. But here too the compilers' phrasing tended to carom between the outright clumsy and the simply pedestrian. A qualified exception might be Yatabe's translation of Thomas Gray's "Elegy Written in a Country Churchyard," which has received grudging praise from critics and was a great favorite with readers.

The translations cover a considerable range temporally and stylistically—from Shakespearean soliloquies to Longfellow and Tennyson, for example—as befits the compilers' desire to expand the range of possibilities for Japanese poetry. There was also a range of topics. Discursive discussion of current ideas dominated the compilers' original poems; explorations of the nature and meaning of human life were more appropriately treated in paired translations of *Hamlet's* "To be, or not to be" soliloquy (by Toyama and Yatabe), and of Longfellow's "Psalm of Life" (by Toyama and Inoue). There was a nature poem: Charles d'Orléans' "Sur le Printemps," via an English version by Longfellow. And there were poems reflecting current events, most notably war: translations of Tennyson's "Charge of the Light Brigade" and Robert Bloomfield's "The Soldier's Home" (both by Toyama), and of Thomas Campbell's naval ode, "Ye Mariners of England" (by Yatabe). It was, of course, a time of burgeoning nationalism in Japan, full of martial expressions of patriotism, with a taste for war poetry inspired by such conflicts as the American Civil War and the Crimean War abroad and Saigō Takamori's revolt at home.

Fourteen of the nineteen poems in the *Selection of New-Style Poems* were translations, and all but one of the poems that gained any degree of popularity were translations (Toyama's "Drawn Swords Regiment" is the exception). Obviously the importance of Western models in establishing this new style of poetry was overwhelming. But it is illuminating to contrast this importation with the importation of Chinese poetry a dozen centuries earlier: while poetry in Chinese remained poetry in Chinese and, in addition to following Chinese prosody, grammar, syntax, and vocabulary, tended to restrict reference to what was appropriate historically in a Chinese poem, the development of the *shintaishi* involved the transformation of foreign models, eventually, into an authentic Japanese poetry. Translations of Christian hymns and children's songs, similar in structure to the foreign *poetic* models made available in the *Selection of New-Style Poems* and in some cases predating them, were also factors in the development of modern poetry. These, however, were not presented or intended primarily as literary works; they were, rather, pedagogical or intended to express religious sentiments. The compilers of the *Shintaishishō*, for all their failures, can be credited with fathering a new style of poetry, one indeed that would predominate in the modern era.[5]

Finally, I would like to say a word on the critical reception, or rather receptions, of the *Selection of New-Style Poems*. All three of the compilers, in their individual prefaces, anticipate adverse criticism of their efforts, at least by poets. In defending themselves they betray something of the scope of their ambition as well as their sense of their own historical significance. Inoue fears that the world's poets will consider these "new-style" poems amateurish, but notes that new poetic styles have since ancient times arisen "spontaneously" and not as a result of endless polishing and refining, an assertion we may take as an indictment of the conservatism that characterized Meiji poetry circles.[6] Yatabe expects the public at large to find their poems "freakish and vulgar" because they are not in one of the familiar forms, but immediately reverts to the cultural relativist argument that he has developed throughout his essay and predicts the new style's acceptance should a great master of the form emerge in a future generation. And Toyama, though he expects "discriminating" readers to laugh at what sounds to them like the "babbling of someone talking in his sleep," quotes the familiar proverb: "Every worm to his taste; some prefer to eat nettles."

There had been, previous to publication of the *Selection*, stirrings toward reform in a few remote corners of the contemporary Japanese poetry establishment, but these generally took the form of reviving the *chōka*, or long poem, that had last truly flourished in the eighth century. Predictably, the innovations of the *Shintaishishō* were rewarded with derision beyond the compilers' wildest fears. A good deal of the criticism was directed, justifiably, at the quality of their translations and their poems. But some also addressed the very foundation of the new style, criticizing it for not being what it set out not to be; that is, attuned to the standards of the *waka* tradition. However, the popularity attained by certain poems—the translation of Grey's "Elegy," for instance, or Toyama's "Drawn Swords Regiment"—increasingly drew the more imaginative (as well as some of the more outraged) poets toward experimentation themselves. Long pent-up responses to the momentous cultural changes of the new era, not quite suited to expression under the old rules and suddenly finding an outlet, positively poured forth. Within the next seven years eight more major collections of mostly original "new-style" poems were published by poets, with the movement reaching its peak achievement in the translations of *Omokage* (*Vestiges*) under the editorship of Mori Ogai and others in 1889 and in Shimazaki Tōson's romantic *Wakana shū* (*Seedlings*) in 1897.

That such a dim view of the new style should prevail initially among established poets whose livelihoods and reputations were at stake is hardly surprising. Nor is their resistance to change generally. They were insiders, keepers of a highly conservative—in the early years of the Meiji era, practically moribund—tradition, and among the last to have their educations contaminated by exposure to the flood of new ideas from the West. Among the first, as we have seen, were our three compilers. Such a radical redirection of a poetic tradition would almost necessarily have had to come from outside established poetic circles, and as the compilers were outsiders, so were their poetic models. So was the substance of their ideas of what poetry should be and do. Yet, although Western, and particularly English-language, poetry provided examples of what could be done, and although Western scientific ideas provided the rationale for change, the issues that drove Toyama, Yatabe and Inoue, and that ultimately shaped modern Japanese poetry, sprang from problems inherent in Japanese poetry at the time rather than from Western poetics—the need for longer poetic forms and the greater freedom length in part conferred, and the need for a language that mirrored modern life.

NOTES

1 Kurihara Hisae, in Nakajima Kenzō, Ota Saburō and Fukuda Rikutarō, eds., (*Hikaku bungaku teki kozā II*) *Nihon Kindaishi: hikaku bungaku teki ni mita* (Tokyo: Shimizu Hirobumi dō, 1971) 292-98.
2 Ota Saburō, in Nakajima Kenzō and Yano Hōjin, eds., *Kindaishi no seiritsu to tenkai: kaigai shi no eikyō o chūshin ni* (Tokyo: Yūseidō, 1969) 19.
3 *Shintai* ("new form style") and *imayō* ("modern style") express very nearly the same idea.
4 Written in the phonetic script used for foreign words.
5 It would eventually even inspire the revitalization, to some degree, of native *waka* forms.
6 Ie repeats this claim almost verbatim in his introductory comments to his translation of Longfellow's "A Psalm of Life."

TYPOLOGY IN TRADITIONAL JAPANESE POETICS: THE RECEPTION OF CHINESE BUDDHIST MODELS

Arthur H. Thornhill III, University of Hawaii

In recent years, the relationship between Buddhism and the literary arts of Japan has received increased scholarly attention. Nowhere is this connection more evident than in classical court poetry, or *waka*, where critics often note the strong influence of such Buddhist concepts as *mujō* ("impermanence") upon aesthetic ideals and poetic sentiment. Much of the new *waka* scholarship investigates the adoption of certain attitudes toward the avocation of writing poetry which derive from the Buddhist paradigm of spiritual cultivation (*shugyō*). For example, William LaFleur has analyzed the use of the term *shikan*—a form of Buddhist meditation practiced in the Tendai sect—by the poet Fujiwara Shunzei (1114-1204) to describe intense mental concentration upon one's poetic materials.[1] In a similar vein, Konishi Jin'ichi has written about the adoption of the ideology of *michi* ("the Way") by medieval artists and poets.[2]

I would like to suggest, however, that we might profitably examine an earlier juncture in the history of *waka*, when, in my opinion, Buddhist-derived conceptions of the art of poetry emerged for the first time: the age of the *Shūishū*, the third imperial anthology, which took shape between 1005 and 1011. This is the age dominated by the "reign" of the statesman Fujiwara Michinaga (966-1027), the age when the *Tale of Genji* was composed. Konishi has termed this period the age of *fūryū*,[3] when the ideals personified by the young Genji—the genteel mastery of poetry, music, and the art of love—reached their apex. Nevertheless, it is important to remember that the later chapters of the *Genji* reflect a mature understanding of such Buddhist concepts as the law of karma, and the ideal of renunciation is presented therein as an alternative to the life of *fūryū*. In addition, this is the age of Izumi Shikibu, perhaps the first *waka* poet to have internalized a mature Buddhist dialectic. In order to document a parallel development toward Buddhist ideals in *waka* criticism, I would like to examine the adoption of Buddhist typological models in the critical writings of Fujiwara Kintō (966-1041), the dominant poet of the *Shūishū* and probably its main compiler.

In the history of Japanese poetry, the seminal work of criticism is the Kana Preface to the first imperial anthology, the *Kokinshū*, composed by Ki no Tsurayuki in the early years of the 10th century. This preface contains statements which become the basis for the composition and reception of all poetry within the formal *waka* tradition. The early critical models are derived from Chinese poetics, most notably the Great Preface to the *Shih ching* (Book of Songs). The famous opening statement, "Japanese poetry takes as its seed the human heart and burgeons forth in the myriad leaves of words," provides the central concepts of *kokoro* (emotional content, meaning, conception) and *kotoba* (diction, expression, style). In a later section, Tsurayuki presents critiques of the "Six Poetic Geniuses" in terms of *kokoro* and *kotoba*. In addition, he introduces the *rikugi*, a group of six Chinese terms which denote six styles or rhetorical modes of verse. By Tsurayuki's time, the precise meanings of these categories were obscure even to the Chinese; nevertheless, he translates them into Japanese as best he can in the following manner:[4]

soeuta	the indirect style
kazoeuta	the enumerative style
nazuraeuta	the figurative style
tatoeuta	the metaphorical style
tadagotouta	the correct style
iwaiuta	the eulogistic style

Unfortunately, the example poems presented by Tsurayuki do not always fit these designations, and commentators have struggled with them ever since. In large part, the application of these traditional Chinese terms to native Japanese poetry represents an attempt by Tsurayuki to enhance the status of *waka*. It is important to note that these are descriptive, not normative, categories, which enumerate objective qualities of the poems as rhetorical entities.

In the intervening years, other treatises were composed which enumerate poetic styles; most notable is the *Wakatei jisshu*, dated 945 and traditionally attributed to Mibu no Tadamine. It presents ten styles. Several of these are derived from the *rikugi*, but others are innovative; for example, one of the four which represent aesthetic ideals is the "style of suggestive overtones (*yojōtei*)," which comes to figure prominently in later aesthetic developments. However, there is no discernible principle which unifies the ten categories. Again, they seem to have been borrowed from a variety of Chinese sources, without being truly assimilated.

In contrast, the writings of Kintō represent an important advance in *waka* criticism. In addition to his dominant role in the compilation of the *Shūishū*, Kintō assembled the *Wakan rōei shū*, a widely-circulated anthology of Chinese and Japanese verse, and composed a short but influential treatise, the *Shinsen zuinō*. For our purposes, however, most important of all is his *Waka kuhon*, "The Nine Varieties of *Waka*."

This work contains examples of superior poems to emulate, divided into nine categories. A short definition is presented for each variety, followed by two *waka* as illustration. For example, the first (and most exalted) category is described:

The Highest of the High   Here the words are wondrous and the emotion has suggestive overtones *(Kore wa kotoba tae ni shite amari no kokoro sae aru nari)*.

Haru tatsu to   Just because we say
Iu bakari ni ya   "Spring has come,"
Miyoshino no   Are the hills of fair Yoshino

> Yama mo kasumite This morning covered in spring mist?
> Kesa wa miyu ran
>
> (SIS I:1, Mibu no Tadamine)
>
> Honobono to   Dimly, dimly,
> Akashi no ura no   As dawn breaks in the morning mist
> Asagiri ni   At Akashi Bay,
> Shimagakure yuku   How I long for that boat
> Fune o shi zo omou As it departs, island-hidden.
>
> (KKS IX:409, anonymous; traditionally attributed to Kakinomoto Hitomaro)[5]

The subsequent levels, presented in descending order of quality, are:

Upper Level, Medium Grade	The appearance is beautiful with suggestive overtones (*Hodo uruwashikute amari no kokoro aru nari*)
Upper Level, Low Grade	The conception is not deep but there are interesting features (*Kokoro fukakaranedomo omoshiroki tokoro aru nari*).
Middle Level, High Grade	The diction and conception are fluid; interesting. (*Kokoro kotoba todokōrazu shite omoshiroki nari*).
Middle Level, Medium Grade	Nothing outstanding, nothing bad; an appropriate style is realized (*Suguretaru tokoro mo naku waroki tokoro mo nakute aru beki sama o shireru nari*).
Middle Level, Low Grade	Somewhat thoughtful conception (*Sukoshi omoitaru tokoro aru nari*).
Lower Level, High Grade	At least one point of interest (*Wazuka ni hitofushi aru nari*).
Lower Level, Medium Grade	Not completely ignorant of the sentiments [appropriate for poetry] (*Koto no kokoro muge ni shiranu ni mo arazu*).
Lower Level, Low Grade	The diction is awkward; nothing which pleases (*Kotoba todokōrite okashiki tokoro naki nari*).

It is important to note that the individual categories are not given descriptive names; instead, they are divided into three groups of three—high, middle, and low—which in turn are subdivided into high, middle, and low rankings. In fact, these divisions, and the title of the work itself, are borrowed from a Buddhist typology which defines nine levels of rebirth in the Western Paradise of Amida, the Buddha of Infinite Light. It is expounded in the *Kan muryōju kyō*, one of the major sutras of the Chinese Pure Land tradition.

In the sutra, the *kuhon* are defined as nine distinct varieties of salvation attainable by believers in Amida's Original Vow. The level appropriate for a given individual is determined by his accumulated karma, degree of faith, and stage of spiritual practice. For example, a person of the highest category exhibits the "three seeds" of sincerity, profundity, and resolve; he has a compassionate heart, abstains from killing any living being, observes the precepts, recites the Mahayana sutras, and contemplates the Three Treasures (Buddha, Dharma, and Sangha). When such a person makes a vow of faith in Amida's saving power, his final rebirth in the Western Paradise is confirmed within seven days. At the time of death he experiences a vision of the descent of Amida and His attendant bodhisattvas; he is then transported upon a diamond throne to Amida's realm, where he immediately awakens to the principle of "non-birth." A believer of the next category ("upper level, medium grade") is not quite so diligent in his devotions: he does not recite the sutras, for example. Nevertheless, he does comprehend the import of the scriptures, believes in the law of karma, and possesses complete mental tranquility. Consequently, at the time of death he experiences the descent of an assembly of arhats (saints in human form), a blissful encounter to be sure, but less rewarding than a vision of Amida Himself. In the space of a single night a lotus blossom opens, and the believer will never again embrace deluded views; his final awakening to the principle of non-birth will occur after "one minor kalpa"[6] has elapsed.

As one might expect, then, virtuous conduct and diligent religious practice ensure the quickest and most satisfying results. However, the doctrine of nine levels is not merely a prod to stimulate meritorious behavior; it also offers solace to persons of lesser qualification, who are assured of eventual salvation. For example, even an individual of the ninth category, who has committed the gravest of sins and not heeded the Dharma during his lifetime, may win rebirth in the Pure Land in the distant future by calling Amida's name ten times with sincerity at the time of death. Within twelve "major kalpas," a lotus will bloom, and for the first time he will experience *bodhicitta*, the aspiration to enlightenment.

What, then, are the implications of the *kuhon* system for the art of poetry? At first glance, the application of this Buddhist terminology seems almost gratuitous. There are no obvious cognates between the nine levels of rebirth and the nine categories of poetry; we are tempted to dismiss the use of the term *kuhon* in the title as mere ornamentation. However, I would argue that the implementation of this nine-tiered structure represents a revolution in *waka* criticism which would influence developments in Japanese poetry for many centuries.

First of all, in contrast to the mere cataloging of objective styles we find in Tsurayuki's Kana Preface and such works as the *Wakatei jisshu*, a *hierarchy* of poetic styles is presented, with gradations of perceived artistic merit. Through the ranking of the eighteen example poems, the enumerated stylistic categories are transformed from descriptive to normative entities; they appear in order of absolute value, from the highest to the lowest. Furthermore, the absence of descriptive names for these styles allows Kintō to utilize a coherent set of criteria for all nine categories. For the most part, he employs the traditional terminology of *kokoro* and *kotoba*. However, in contrast to Tsurayuki, who criticizes the conception or expression of individual poems on an *ad hoc* basis, Kintō presents a clearly delineated hierarchy of *kokoro/kotoba* configurations. At the higher levels, a balance between elegant diction and "interesting" content is advocated, which produces a "beautiful" overall effect. Despite his general preference for balance, however, it is clear that Kintō considers emotional content to be more central to poetry than pleasing expression: several of the lower ranks have merit because, even though the expression may be flawed, the underlying conception is interesting. Furthermore, the two highest ranks have "*kokoro* in abundance"—the "suggestive overtones" which Kintō prizes above all else.

The Buddhist model of nine levels can also be interpreted as a paradigm for the experience of learning the art of poetry. When read in reverse order, from lowest to highest, the nine levels represent progressive stages of accomplishment. Just as the Buddhist practitioner evolves, presumably over the span of many lifetimes, from a sinner who experiences a glimmer of faith at the end of his life to an accomplished renunciate who obeys the precepts unremittingly, so a poet passes through many phases of practice, observing various rules of composition as he endeavors to master his art. Judging from the *Waka kuhon*, this process might first involve an emphasis on composing *waka* which embody appropriate "poetic sentiment," progress to the attainment of a fluid balance between emotion and expression, and culminate in the style of suggestion, in which emotion overflows the boundaries of stated poetic conceit. In this sense, the *Waka kuhon* is the first work of Japanese poetics to utilize the Buddhist concept of *shugyō*, or spiritual self-cultivation, as a paradigm for the practice of poetry. In addition, by adopting this particular Buddhist model, in which even the lowest category of believer will win eventual salvation, Kintō implies that even inferior poems which "have awkward diction and nothing pleasing about them at all" still have merit; apparently there is value simply in utilizing the thirty-one syllable form.

Of course, it is possible to posit more than formal connections between the *kuhon* typology and Kintō's aesthetic ideals. Although the style of "suggestive overtones" predates explicit Buddhist influence, as we have seen, it is difficult to overlook the strong resonance between this ideal and the Buddhist world view, which interprets our conventional experience of everyday reality to be illusion. Just as spiritual discipline and mental concentration produce a transcendent vision of Amida not perceivable by the senses, so can the mastery of diction and expression generate emotional reverberations beyond the explicit meaning of the verse itself. In Kintō's two example poems, this effect is caused by the mystery of synchronicity: the confluence of the utterance that spring has arrived and the presumed arisal of mist in distant Yoshino, and the paradox of the departing boat which grows dimmer as the sky brightens, receding like a dream. Furthermore, in both poems the object of the speaker's emotion lies beyond his immediate perceptual field, a correlative of the indistinct emotional afterimages which linger just beyond the boundaries of the reader's lucidity. In my view, a taste for such poetic effect may have first appeared before the adoption of the *shugyō* paradigm for the art of poetry, but as the Buddhist attitudes implicit in this paradigm were assimilated, its emergence as a major aesthetic principle was almost inevitable. This style of suggestion so prized by Kintō, of course, subsequently developed into the *yūgen* ("mystery and depth") ideal featured in the medieval poetics of such figures as Shunzei and Kamo no Chōmei (1156?-1216).

After Kintō's time, the influence of Buddhist enumerative models upon Japanese poetics became more pronounced, and their implementation more sophisticated. The Pure Land system we have investigated is fairly straightforward: there are nine stages of increasing merit, and nine corresponding levels of reward. Other typologies within the Chinese Buddhist tradition are more complex. For example, the Hua-yen School[7] often utilizes sets of ten categories; one such grouping is the ten stages of faith in the career of a bodhisattva. As before, these stages represent a centripetal process, whereby an individual attempts to achieve ever higher levels of purification and wisdom through a prescribed set of religious practices. However, along the way, he experiences a realization that these gradations are an illusion: that the joyous mind of the beginner at the initial moment of faith is equivalent to the enlightened mind of a Buddha. At this moment, the discrete stages of accomplishment conflate, as the differentiated categories are experienced as interdependent and interpenetrating. In this sense, the enumerated categories are not rigid ontological distinctions, but rather a heuristic device which self-destructs at an appropriate time.

In the critical writings of the Nō dramatist Zeami (1364?-1443), we find a similar shift to more internalized, psychological models of enumerated style. This change reflects the primary objective of Zeami's treatises: the transmission of the internal experience of artistic praxis to his successors, rather than the evaluation of an extant body of work. For example, in his *Kyū-i*, a work which contains extensive allusion to Zen texts, Zeami also utilizes a nine-tiered structure. However, in contrast to Kintō, he makes an explicit distinction between the absolute ontological value of the nine ranks—which are also presented in the order of highest to lowest—and the proper pedagogical order, which is *not* simply from lowest to highest.[8] Furthermore, once the highest levels have been mastered, the actor freely performs all styles, high and low, shattering the previously learned hierarchy of value.

A detailed analysis of these later developments in medieval aesthetics is beyond the scope of this study. In conclusion, I would simply like to emphasize the importance of Kintō's contribution. While he is often characterized as a bland poet and a timid anthologizer, his adoption of a Buddhist typological model in the *Waka kuhon* was a formal innovation of great conceptual power. As a result, Japanese poetry incorporated a focus on certain aesthetic ideals and notions of poetic praxis which came to dominate in later ages.

NOTES

1. William R. LaFleur, *The Karma of Words* (Berkeley: Univ. of California Press, 1983) 80-106.
2. For example, in Konishi Jin'ichi, *Michi: chūsei no rinen* (Tokyo: Kōdansha, 1975).
3. Konishi Jin'ichi, *A History of Japanese Literature* vol. I (Princeton: Princeton UP, 1984) 57.
4. The English equivalents for the *rikugi* are from Helen McCullough, trans., *Kokin Wakashū* (Stanford: Stanford UP, 1985) 4-5.
5. The text used is found in Hisamatsu Sen'ichi and Nishio Minoru, ed., *Karonshū, nōgakuronshū,* (Tokyo: Iwanami shoten, 1961) 31-34.
6. A kalpa is defined variously in different Buddhist traditions. It is best thought of as one life-cycle of a universe—i.e., an inconceivably long period of time.
7. The teachings of the Hua-yen School, which derive from the *Avatamsaka Sutra,* are often described as the highest achievement of Chinese Buddhist thought. Perhaps the most famous Hua-yen doctrine is the notion of "All in One, One in All, All in All," which suggests that not only are the absolute and relative aspects of reality interdependent and mutually-defining, but all phenomenal existences are interdependent and equally reflected in every individual phenomenal existence, like the jewels of Indra's Net.
8. In the text of the *Kyū-i,* Zeami recommends that students begin with the middle levels of "realistic" portrayal and graceful beauty, then proceed to the higher levels of transcendent effect; only at that point should the more "vulgar" roles of the lower levels be attempted.

NATIONAL AND COMPARATIVE LITERATURE IN JAPAN

John T. Dorsey, Nihon University

One of the most natural tendencies in comparative literature is ultimately one of the most limiting: placing one's own country at the center of the literary world. This tendency is natural because one is most likely to study and understand the literature written in one's native tongue. Moreover, it can be plausibly argued that if one does not understand one's own literature, one cannot understand that of a foreign country. In *Comparaison n'est pas raison*, however, René Étiemble makes a solid case against literary nationalism in the West, in particular against this tendency in French comparative literature, but ironically, the more conservative trends in the French school of comparative literature have been the most influential in Japan.[1] The books on comparative literature which Étiemble criticizes were translated into Japanese, and a number of influential comparatists in Japan studied at the Sorbonne. Paul Van Tieghem's *La Littérature Comparée*, for example, has been translated *twice* into Japanese.[2] The translations of a number of other Western comparative literature textbooks limit themselves to American and Western European Literature, with particular emphasis on French and German literature.[3] As a result of these "influences" there is a tendency in Japan to limit comparative literature to the foreign relations of Japanese literature in textbooks, curricula, journals, and conferences, with the result that what we have is, essentially, comparative Japanese literature: the comparison of *our* national literary heritage, *kokubungaku*, with that of outsiders, usually from the West.

While the tendency to focus on one's own national literature is natural, it is limiting for a number of reasons, well known to comparatists, but perhaps worth calling to mind now and again. First of all, it divides the world of literature into two camps: native and foreign, or put more primitively, into *mine* and *yours*. This fundamental division is never really breached, no matter how similar we find each other's literature. In a sense, it was because of this limitation that comparative literature was founded: to give a broader perspective to the study of literature which had been so bound up with the history and culture of particular nations that the existence of masterpieces in a foreign tongue seemed to be an impertinence.

Unfortunately, however, early writings in comparative literature focused on what may be called import-export relations, what one of my teachers used to call the balance of literary trade. According to this cultural wealth-of-nations outlook, the nation with the most exports, usually France, would be considered, or more accurately, would consider itself, great. And so this allegedly international field of study was used to prove the value and cultural worth of one's literature by its reception or marketability abroad. The ideal situation seemed to be that of those countries which were able to absorb foreign influences without contamination while spreading enlightenment abroad.

Nevertheless, the indisputable quality of such exports as Goethe, the Mercedes Benz of German literature, and Shakespeare, the Rolls Royce of English literature, was grudgingly acknowledged: that is to say, these authors were acknowledged as "universal" geniuses who perhaps had no real nationality. And we even find complaints about the balance of trade such as those made by critics who deplore the fact that Goethe has not done as well in the literary markets of England and America as Shakespeare has in the lands of the German tongue.

In the case of Japan, the notion of *our* language, *our* literature and *our* culture in comparison and more often in contrast to *yours* is particularly strong, and the myth of Japanese uniqueness is quite alive in academic circles, including, of course, the world of comparative Japanese literature.[4] One of the first problems facing Japanese comparatists who adhered to the free market theory of literary relations was the fact that Japanese literature was not so readily exportable. Early studies focussed on the Meiji period (1868-1914) when the Japanese market was deluged with foreign literature from different countries and different ages all at the same time.

On the other hand, studies of the reception of Japanese literature or culture abroad were and still are accepted with some uneasiness. First of all, these exports were made almost entirely through translations. Second, the choice of works seemed arbitrary, that is to say, foreigners read whatever they could get their hands on: *The Tale of Genji*, assorted Nō plays, and various haiku. These translated works would often be retranslated from one foreign language into another and then adapted in various ways. Third and most important, the conviction that only Japanese could understand Japan or appreciate Japanese culture would show its face every now and then. Behind the humble stance that Japanese literature was not marketable abroad (and here the analogy of car sales falls completely apart, if it did not do so when I slyly omitted mentioning the case of French cars), there was a certain confidence and pride in the uniqueness of things Japanese, which was very reassuring: *we* are able to understand and master *your* culture, but . . .

Cultural smugness can also be seen in studies which show that although *real* Japanese writers may be infatuated with the sexy but unfaithful and perhaps diseased and perverted West for awhile, they always return to their roots. Another variation of this trend of thought may be seen in those studies which aim at correcting the enthusiasm with which early comparatists traced sources, influences, and reception. Such studies maintain that similarities with foreign works of literature are not sufficient proof of influence, that the same traits exist in Japanese literature. A number of these studies are correct in their findings, but the subtext is often the uniqueness of Japanese literature: *we* had the first novel, the first psychological novel, the first realistic novel, the first stream-of-consciousness novel, etc. Recently, such generalizations have been challenged, but they are still commonly held in Japanese literature studies and also in its stepsister, comparative Japanese literature.[5]

In practice, the tendency to focus on Japanese literature in Japanese comparative literature has resulted in a plethora of studies on the Meiji period, studies which are almost exclusively concerned with source, influence, and reception in the narrowest sense: *jijitsu kankei,* or to go back to the French source, *les rapports de fait.* First of all, there are numerous, detailed studies on Japanese authors who read foreign works and were influenced by them, or adapted or translated them. Typically, one goes directly to the private libraries of the Japanese writers, which are often preserved in universities and research centers, and lists what each writer read, when he read it, and what notes, if any, he made in the margins of the book. Then one scours his works for similarities. Next, there are comparative studies on Japanese authors who studied abroad and were presumably influenced by foreign culture, including a visit to the Eiffel Tower, the Louvre, or the Champs Elysées. Then there are studies which focus on foreigners who came to Japan, providing detailed descriptions of their travels, table manners, and writings.

The tendency to focus on the Meiji period is natural in the sense that the Meiji period was clearly one of international cultural exchange. Nevertheless, the same names appear again and again, as we learn what happened to this or that *Japanese* author on his journey to the West, or how this or that *foreign* author appreciated or failed to appreciate the uniqueness of Japanese culture during his residence in Japan or when he adapted Nō or haiku in translation to Western drama and poetry. The principle names in comparative Japanese literature are still Natsume Sōseki, Mori Ogai, and Japan's favorite American, Lafcadio Hearn.[6]

The problem with this overemphasis on the Meiji period is that Meiji literature is simply one fifty-year section of Japan's twelve-hundred-year literary tradition. We may question whether the Meiji novel, or the novel for that matter, is truly representative of a literary tradition which has been dominated by the lyric. Furthermore, those works of Japanese literature which stand in closest relation to the West are not necessarily the best or the most representative, and comparisons with Western works often focus on the less significant aspects of a work. We have all heard similar criticisms from our colleagues in the various national literature departments. Be that as it may, for these and other reasons, professors of Japanese literature generally steer clear of comparative Japanese literature. To fill this gap, Japanese professors of English, French or German language and literature write what are essentially "comparative" studies of Japanese literature by venturing beyond their field of specialization into that of their native tongue. Recently, however, professors of Japanese literature who happen to know a second language (and some who do not) have occasionally descended to the world of comparative Japanese literature in order to set the record straight.

As we have seen, then, although the tendency to place one's own national literature at the center of the literary world is a natural starting point in literary studies, it is ultimately incompatible with comparative literature because it places too much emphasis on the national character of a work, because it separates, in order to compare, and because it amounts to nationalism rather than internationalism in literary studies.

Let us discuss now a number of proposed solutions to this problem. One suggestion is that we should broaden the field of Japanese comparative literature by studying comparative culture. The proponents of this position argue that since Japanese and Western literatures are so different it is necessary to study the cultural backgrounds of the works, including history, philosophy, social structure, military organization, industry, economics, law, and religion, not to mention fine arts. To those of us who are alarmed by the steadily expanding universe of comparative literature, however, this may seem an unwanted development. The addition of comparative culture may seem to many, as it does to me, a crossing of disciplinary boundaries. I think that it is about time that we recognize the limits of our ever-expanding field before we end up as specialists in comparative studies or worse (on the lines of thematology, genology, narratology, and scientology), as professors of comparatology.

Another proposal is to pursue regional studies. It is suggested that since Western comparative literature developed from national to European, to European-American, and then to East-West literary studies, Japanese comparatists should first pursue literary relations within Asia. Perhaps the transition from *kokubungaku,* the study of Japanese literature, to East-West relations was too abrupt. There is much to support this idea. First of all, just as in the West, relations between classic and modern literature and the study of medieval literature in general were for a long time excluded from comparative literature, so most periods of Japanese literature have been virtually ignored. Literary relations with China and Korea have been relegated to Japanese, Chinese or Korean literature specialists. Buddhism has been left to the Buddhists. And the study of literary relations in Asia has simply not been pursued, in part because the relations were taken for granted, as they were in Europe between Latin and Renaissance literature, but also, I believe, because of a reluctance to acknowledge Asian sources for and influences on Japanese works, something which would obviously undermine the idea of the uniqueness of Japanese literature. In all fairness, I should add that I have also heard expressed the opposite but equally nationalistic view that *everything* in Japan is derivative. This kind of literary trade friction brings us back to the early days of comparative literature when exports and imports, sources, intermediaries, and influences were carefully measured in the literary commodities market. Recently, in fact, there has been a movement to study Asian literary relations, and this is a welcome development.

Another solution is to concentrate on rapprochement studies using traditional methods of comparative literature, that is, the study of genres, themes, periods, and theory without regard to place of national origin or to historical or factual relations. It is true that such studies may at first yield searches for tragedy and the epic in the East and haiku, Nō, and kabuki in the West. Again, looking for the Renaissance in Japan is not much different from looking for the Edo period in America. Especially working with genre, we may begin with some concept of the historical novel or the short lyric or comedy, but we must be prepared to alter this concept, change the name, in fact, as we proceed. Even within Europe, for example, there has been much disagreement over what constitutes a particular genre. For example, if we define *Bildungsroman* strictly on the basis of Goethe's *Wilhelm Meister,* we will be left with nothing but German examples. But if we approach the genre from even the point of view of other European literary traditions we must modify the concept. Period concepts, too, are of course subject to redefinition. Wellek and Warren have pointed out, for example, that the distinction between Elizabethan and Jacobean literature is fine for English literature but, from a European viewpoint, the term Elizabethan literature is more useful.[7] The well-studied Meiji period, for example, could be studied as an international literary period in relation to America, Germany, France and Italy: an age of the novel, of the new country, of urbanization.

The conflict between national and comparative literature is, of course, not limited to Japan—it is an issue all comparatists face. I think that the idea of East-West literary studies itself is an advance over Japanese-Western comparative literature. But this advance will, of course, disappear if we continue to discuss Chinese-Western, Japanese-Western, and Indian-Western literary relations separately, focusing on individual national literatures in the context of vague notions of East and West. We should try to achieve internationalism in comparative literature by putting aside the national origin of the works at hand and concentrating on problems which "transcend linguistic and national boundaries," as the founders of comparative literature wrote in their textbooks. Unfortunately, comparative literature without national boundaries has been considered a challenge to the concept of national literature. Some early scholars of comparative literature tried to justify the new discipline by maintaining that it would not conflict with, but would actually complement, national literature studies because it would point out what was uniquely French or German or American in literary works by comparing them with the works of "foreign" nations. Perhaps it is now time to place more emphasis on common points, especially in the field of East-West studies, where it is much easier to point out differences and where the tendency to conclude that East is East is still commonplace.

NOTES

1 In "Sur le renouveau du comparatisme en Chine populaire," *Comparative Literature Studies* 24.1 (1987): 2, Étiemble notes that he originally wrote this work for a Japanese audience and that it was initially published in Japanese.

Moreover, he delivered much of its material in a lecture in French at Tokyo University.
2 Van Tieghem's 1931 introduction to comparative literature was introduced to Japan in 1934 in an article by Nogami Toyoichirō, translated into Japanese by Ota Sakitarō in 1943 and by Tomita Hitoshi in 1973.
3 In addition to the French examples, other textbooks which have been translated into Japanese and which I have used in class are: Wellek and Warren's *Theory of Literature*, Weisstein's *Einführung in die vergleichende Literaturwissenschaft*, Stallknecht and Frenz's *Comparative Literature: Method and Perspective*, and Auerbach's *Mimesis: The Representation of Reality in Western Literature*.
4 A recent book by Peter N. Dale, *The Myth of Japanese Uniqueness* (London and Sydney: Croom Helm and Nissan Institute for Japanese Studies, University of Oxford, 1986), discusses this problem in detail, focusing on the pseudo-academic *nihonjinron*, which, the author claims, is a body of criticism "characterised by three major assumptions or analytical motivations. Firstly, they [the authors of *nihonjinron*] implicitly assume that the Japanese constitute a culturally and socially homogeneous racial entity, whose essence is virtually unchanged from prehistorical times down to the present day. Secondly, they presuppose that the Japanese differ radically from all other known peoples. Thirdly, they are consciously nationalistic, displaying a conceptual and procedural hostility to any mode of analysis which might be seen to derive from external, non-Japanese sources. In a general sense then, the *nihonjinron* may be defined as works of cultural nationalism concerned with the ostensible 'uniqueness' of Japan in any aspect, and which are hostile to both individual experience and the notion of internal socio-historical diversity" (introduction, n.p.).
5 Shunsuke Kamei, for example, presented a paper at the Fifth International Comparative Literature Conference at Tamkang University (proceedings to be published in the *Tamkang Review*) in which he outlines the influence of Chinese culture on Tanizaki Jun'ichirō and then challenges the idea that Tanizaki "turned his back on the West" in his maturity in order to devote himself to writing "classic" Japanese literature.
6 The amount of research conducted on Lafcadio Hearn in Japan will no doubt astound Americans, but it is a burgeoning industry with new studies released every year on the life, thoughts, teachings, and writings of this foreigner who loved Japan.
7 René Wellek and Austin Warren, *Theory of Literature* (New York: Harcourt Brace, 1949).

VI. DOMINATION, DECOLONIZATION, AND DICHOTOMY

THE CONTEXT OF DECOLONIZATION AND THE POETICS OF PLAGIARISM

> Dr. Johnson to an aspiring writer: "Sir, your work is both new and interesting. Unfortunately, the interesting parts aren't new, and the new parts aren't interesting."
>
> Boswell, *Life of Johnson*

Marilyn Randall, Queen's University

The thorny question of what is literary, that is to say, what is both new and interesting, has in recent years been laid aside. Structuralist attempts to define a "language of literature" have come to nought, sabotaged by their own presupposition that the literary essence of language can be identified as a specific concatenation of surface linguistic features. Most of these features, as both the traditional and new wave structuralist critics have shown, exist in more or less frequent occurrence in many types of discourse. With the wane of structuralist poetics, the notion of literariness itself has passed almost into oblivion, as the inadequate immanent definitions of literariness have yet to be replaced by any contending theories. Indeed, the very term "literariness" is somehow passé, evoking a formalist heritage which has largely been supplanted by larger social and institutional domains of concern, and where literariness is seen as a behavioral phenomenon, relatively indifferent to form and language.

In resurrecting the notion of literariness, I intend first of all to emphasize my own indebtedness to a formalist critical tradition, and also to enrich the theoretical content of the term by injecting into it considerations which transcend the textual boundaries defined by the structuralist principle of immanent significance.

The strategy which I propose would be to introduce a pragmatic attitude into the analysis of literature, specifically with respect to attempted definitions of the nature of literariness. Pragmatic principles would define *literature* as a communicative event evolving between the *text* and its *users* in a particular communicative *context,* where *literary* defines not a uniquely textual phenomenon, but the dynamic relation among these three elements.

The problematic element of the foregoing description—both for linguistic and literary pragmatics, is the component labeled *context*: in pragmatics, the term covers a seemingly unlimited extension of elements, difficult to define, but somehow crucial to communication (understanding). The operative component of context in linguistic definitions seems to be "mutual knowledge"—that is, the information set presumed by all participants to be common to each. The content of this mutual knowledge can be propositional or formal, referring to general world knowledge and to discursive rules and conventions respectively.

In considering the potential pragmatic function of literary context, we are confronted by an apparent anomaly: the literary text seems to be precisely that type of discourse which is distinguished by its autonomy from many contextual constraints, and where the notion of mutual knowledge seems precarious at best. It follows from this anomaly, that an aspect of the specificity of literary communication must reside in the way and degree to which the literary text communicates its own contextual information, guaranteeing the degree of mutual knowledge necessary not only for the understanding of the text, but for the understanding of the text as *literary*. It is my contention that the context specifically relevant to literary understanding is that governing linguistico-literary conventions and presuppositions.

I propose a definition of context which links the semiotic level of textual strategies, which I will call *conventions,* to the pragmatic level of literary knowledge, called *presuppositions.* Reader's presuppositions governing definitions of literariness exist prior to contact with individual texts—they participate to a greater or lesser degree in the communal institutional spectrum of what is admissible as literary. The text defines its position relative to this spectrum of presuppositions on an axis ranging from absolute conformity to absolute rupture. The literary text theoretically demonstrates an optimal position between the two poles, a position which necessarily varies according to cultural determinants.

In contemporary, that is, 20th century, poetics, the esthetic preference seems to tend towards an ideal of *rupture* as a positive value defining literariness. Linked to the romantic value of *originality,* it is the transgression of esthetic conventions and their attendant presuppositions which seems to characterize both art and critical judgments about what is artistic.

However, the valorization of originality in art has led to an impasse of which much contemporary, namely, "post-modern," art has become self-conscious. On the one hand, originality, in the guise of rupture, is a continuing if somewhat repressed value. On the other, contemporary esthetics recognizes, or rather proclaims the impossibility, of this submerged presupposition. This double-bind situation is especially apparent in the post-modern esthetic, where pastiche, collage, intertextuality and other ancient forms of repetition, imitation and derivation constitute the foundation of a "new" esthetics of rupture.

I want to pose the esthetic question of literariness from a pragmatic point of view by considering the fortunes of two texts which seem to exemplify the contemporary double-bind which simultaneously demands rupture and construes its impossibility. The pragmatic approach to the problem of literariness will take into consideration not only textual evidence but also the contextual presuppositions solicited or generated by semiotic strategies. Conventional textual strategies are semiotic signalling devices which work to guarantee a minimal requisite level of mutuality between text and reader contexts.

The esthetic double-bind to which I referred is roughly that described by Sam Johnson, but with a modern twist: the "new" or original is simultaneously prescribed and proscribed. In an era where there is nothing new under the literary sun, strategies of repetition, reminiscent of Renaissance forms like the cento and the florilège, fulfill the requirement of rupture by transgressing the fundamental esthetic law of originality. The rupture of convention has, in other words, evolved into the *convention of rupture*.

The two texts that I have chosen, *Trou de mémoire* by Hubert Aquin and *Le Devoir de violence* by Yambo Ouologuem, are both, within and beyond the bounds of their cultures (Québecois and French African respectively), institutionally acclaimed examples of literariness. Ouologuem's text, heralded as the first authentic African novel, won the Prix Renaudot in 1968. *Trou de mémoire*, the "first truly Québecois novel," was awarded a similar distinction, the Governor General's Award in Canada in the same year.

But a paradox surrounds the success of both texts. In the case of Aquin, an avowed anti-federal political commitment caused him to refuse the reward proffered by an institution that his revolutionary project purported to abhor. In Ouologuem's case, the novel created a scandal when its publication in English revealed extensive "plagiarism" of Graham Greene's *It's a Battlefield*. Tipped off to the possibility of plagiarism, critics did not take long to discover that this "authentic" African text actually read like a rewrite of André Schwartz-Bart's novel, *Le Dernier des Justes*.

Hubert Aquin was active in the revolutionary, quasi-terrorist separatist movement that shook Canada in the late 60s and early 70s. Promoting the independent statehood of Quebec, Aquin's activism led him to be arrested, interned, and later expelled from Switzerland. He was linked to a group of young intellectuals whose mandate was the political and cultural *decolonization* of Quebec. Inspired by the decolonialist theories of Memmi, Fanon and Berque,[1] these artist-politicians strove to realize the indigenous history, character, and culture that two centuries of English domination threatened to assimilate. Aquin and his co-revolutionaries promoted a socio-political rejection of the dominant colonial ideology through their art, explicitly adopting an anti-literary mode designed to transgress the conventions and presuppositions governing institutional esthetic judgments. Paul Chamberland, a Québecois poet declares:

> To write means therefore to write badly, because it is a matter of reflecting bad living. It is good writing which is the lie, it is correctness which is the aberration, it is purity of style which is, here and now, meaningless. Today I vomit this aseptic verbiage which has been proposed to me as a model of writing, this gilded delirium which opens the wounds of my people, and commits treason against them.[2]

The paradox here, of course, is that the project is doomed to failure: success means recuperation by the institution which moves the marginal and the disruptive into the center creating a norm out of an intended aberration. And Aquin's text is aberrant. Without belaboring the outline of a complex, even incoherent plot, it is fair to say that the text breaks diegetic and narrative conventions in an incorrigible fashion. The critical search for underlying or transcendental unity is anticipated in the text, and even forms part of the fictive editor's fruitless search for coherence through the stratagem of the anamorphosis metaphor. But, as the fictive author declares:

> Look no further, and above all don't rack your brains to explain my recitative or try to understand the framework of this plot which I myself am vainly trying to understand before I assemble it.[3]

Like so many other of Aquin's cryptic fictive elements, it is necessary to take this reading directive seriously—it is an explicit warning that the critical project of re-establishing coherence is being intentionally flouted. Among the other esthetic taboos that Aquin intentionally transgresses is the most serious of all—that of plagiarism. This strategy is overt by means of at least two conventions—its thematization, whereby the characters discuss the problem of plagiarism and inauthenticity as an aspect of the text being written; and secondly, by means of fictive footnotes which demonstrate the intertextual nature of the text by their references to a vast body of other texts, for the most part real, which support and form part of the erudition and argument of the text. The culmination of the overt indications of plagiarism is its actual practice on a covert level, of which the most pointed example appears in a discussion of Renaissance art and the technique of anamorphosis, the distortion of perspective in a painting which renders the object obscure until restored by projection in a mirror, or by a change in the viewer's point of view. The plagiarized work is *Anamorphoses ou perspectives curieuses* by Jurgis Baltrusaitis.[4]

I would like to leave Aquin's work momentarily to turn to a discussion of a second text, Yambo Ouologuem's *Bound to Violence*. The controversy surrounding the charges of plagiarism, fought within and without the pages of the *Times Literary Supplement,* concerned not only the establishment of the fact of plagiarism, but stimulated, more interestingly perhaps, a lively discussion about questions of literary and esthetic value, and their relations to authenticity and originality. The same questions, in fact, which are explicitly posed in the pages of Aquin's cryptic text.

The two texts demonstrate a marked difference in the nature of their plagiaristic tendencies, and in their objects. First of all, Ouologuem's plagiarism appears more intentionally covert, not leaving possible surface clues and traces as in Aquin's case. Secondly, the objects of Ouologuem's plagiarism, if one accepts the term, are contemporary novels, not a relatively obscure, however well-known in art critical circles, Renaissance art theory text. The third outstanding difference is the effect of the plagiarism. In Aquin's text, although the presence of Baltrusaitis' text is generally recognized, the extent of the actual plagiarism has not been examined. Pat Smart mentions without elaboration that Aquin quotes Baltrusaitis "inexactly and without naming him."[5]

It is not likely, however, that this revelation would cause a scandal, and it would certainly not affect the esthetic fortunes of the text. In Ouologuem's case, the outrage was general, and many editors chose to expurgate the contentious passages from the text. But for all their differences, it is rather the similarities which concern me, the implications of which I would like to explore. In particular, I would like to inquire into the esthetic and social ramifications of this plagiaristic art, and to pose the question of its significance in terms of its emergence in two post-colonial societies.

The decolonization movement in Quebec, adopted by Aquin and others, produced many marginal works which were not accepted into the canon. In an effort to express the alienation and loss of identity experienced by a colonized people, literary conventions were intentionally and irrevocably broken: an esthetics of failure was even adopted, which recognized the paradox of the literary revolutionary project. A sympathetic critic declares:

> And if by chance (for it is not always so) the work is a failure, [these writers] triumph: What a lie it would be to express failure by a success.[6]

Aquin explicitly shares this view, and even speaks in his diary of *failure*, personal, national, and literary, as being somehow the perverse but native motivation behind his own writing. To this end, his work defies many novelistic conventions, and it is a matter of opinion whether or not their subsequent canonization constitutes the failure or the success of this "poetics of failure." One thing is apparent, however: Aquin, by perpetrating the literary crime of plagiarism, has succeeded in passing off as authentic, literary, and original, a text partly composed of stolen, non-literary material.

In Ouologuem's case, the discovery of his plagiarism potentially jeopardized the book's literary merit, although his defenders point out that the "plagiarisms" are in fact no different than other literary imitations which have long been an accepted literary practice, a "stylistic technique to further the purposes of the novel."[7]

In attacking Ouologuem, the anonymous *Times Literary Supplement* critic remarks: "Or is M. Ouologuem on to something: a style of literary imperialism intended as a revenge for the much chronicled sins of territorial imperialists."[8] The intended sarcasm may contain more truth than its author would like. Seth Wolitz suggests a touch of occulted racism in the accusations of plagiarism, for the "authentic African novel" which borrows heavily from European sources is criticized as being somehow neither authentic nor African.[9] Although Eric Sellin himself cites Ouologuem's claims that his novel is "not traditional," is written with "references to international examples" and is "not just an African novel,"[10] Sellin epitomizes the attitude charaterized by Wolitz, according to whom "some western critics, by naiveté or by obsession, commend the authenticity of the new African literature when it exploits only traditional African sources."[11] This injustice, Wolitz goes on to argue, denies the essential reality of a contemporary Africa created by the assimilation of Western traditions imposed by those very colonial forces which continue to "ghettoize" the African by valorizing only traditional folklore.

It is probably true that much of Ouologuem's success came from the self-proclaimed indigenous nature of the book. It is written largely in the oral story-telling style of the *griots* (traditional poet and musician), it borrows heavily from traditional tales and histories, is luridly savage in its depiction of violence and perverse sex, and responds in this way to the occidental taste for the exotic—the "real" Africa. The irony, of course, is that the *real* Africa is precisely the one that the West rejects in the form of accusations of plagiarism. Formed by Western values and culture, modern African writers are, as Wolitz points out, as literate and as steeped in Western literary and cultural knowledge as are their Western critics.

Critical judgments aside, it is interesting to look at the simple presence of a "poetics of plagiarism" in two texts emanating from a decolonial situation. One scholar of literary quotation, S. Morawski, claims that the practice of quotation increases notably during periods of cultural crisis or revolution, or when a culture is dominated by an oppressive force, like the church, or presumably, we can add, the effects of colonization.[12] From this perspective, the *Times Literary Supplement*'s ironic remark takes on a ring of truth. But how exactly would such a poetics of plagiarism effect this alleged revenge for the "sins of territorial imperialism"? Presumably Baltrusaitis, Greene, and Schwartz-Bart are not the most appropriate targets for such a revenge, and, in any case, as Ouologuem himself points out, literary and other forms of imitation are often intended as "a kind of homage."[13] Similarly, the passages from Baltrusaitis, which are mostly technical descriptions of anamorphic art, have the quality of encyclopedia entries, free from the ideological overtones that would make them suitable objects for reprisal.

From a literary pragmatic perspective, it is perhaps more reasonable to view the alleged crime of plagiarism as an attack against larger and more powerful forces than individual authors, or even against a literary heritage. If the practice is evaluated in terms of the *presuppositions required to generate the accusation of plagiarism,* we see that this form of repetition, distinguished from others perhaps only by the epithet which determines its criminality, is the reverse of cultural values such as *individual identity, originality,* and *authenticity.*

These presuppositions are supported by strong literary conventions which even their transgression has not dispelled. The 20th century revolution breaking down conventions such as the stable narrative voice continues to stimulate critical attempts to rationalize apparent incoherences into coherence, revealing the continued control of the ideal of identity. In Aquin's work, the central problem of the Québecois personal and national identity generates the breakdown of narrative identity and leads to an incorrigible narrative incoherence. On the thematic level, loss of identity is linked to questions of the absence of history through loss of memory, and the problem of multiple identities is seen as an effect of over-determination by the imposition of foreign histories on the authentic one. In other words, a national identity crisis leads, as Fanon has already indicated, to a cultural profession of borrowing, imitation, and repetition of the products of the dominant culture.[14]

According to Aquin, the colonized writer is condemned to practise imitation: his history is written in advance. In decolonial theory as adopted by the Québecois writers, the necessary phase preceding liberation is the recognition by the colonized of their lamentable condition, which contrasts strongly with the forms of evasion and desire for assimilation characterizing the preceding phase. *Trou de mémoire* is clearly an expression, not of the final triumph of the colonized, but of the previous phase. It is an attempt to assume the absent or multiple identity. Plagiarism is a strategy proclaiming this negative identity in a criminal mode, effecting a crime against literary conventions and the presuppositions of identity, originality and authenticity on which they depend—qualities of which the colonized is deprived. The transgression is thus both social and literary: the overdetermined cultural identity produces a textual *métis*, the assimilation of the "other" being metaphorically projected onto the text.

I would suggest that, generated in an analogous socio-cultural climate, Ouologuem's text functions in the same way. In *Lettre à la France nègre*, published in the same year as *Bound to Violence*, Ouologuem addresses an open letter "aux pisse-copie Nègres d'écrivains célèbres" ("to hack nigger-writers of famous authors") where he ironically advises black writers to stick to the mystery or detective novel, which is, incidentally, the form chosen by Aquin for *Trou de mémoire*.[15] Ouologuem proposes a formula for producing an infinite number of assembly-line type novels by juggling in any order a number of passages stolen from major mystery writers. For demonstration purposes, Ouologuem provides a number of these passages, rated according to their quotient of humor, suspense, violence, eroticism, etc. Explicitly advocating a kind of wholesale plagiarism, Ouologuem points out the infinite possibilities available to the hack writer of second-rate fiction, the fate that he imputes to the majority of black writers. It is not coincidental that a form of this very strategy appears in the pages of Ouologuem's "literary" novel. The transgression is therefore not only the plagiarism itself, but moreover the success of the novel in which it appears, and its target—not detective fiction, however great, but "serious" literature. What appears as a rhetorical joke in the context of Ouologuem's essay, becomes a crime in the context of the literary text.

If Aquin's text has not been condemned as plagiaristic, it is perhaps, on the one hand, an effect of the explicitation of the possibility of the practice (plagiarism needs an intention to hide) or, on the other, because the object of the plagiarism does not impinge on the territory of the dominant culture. The increased criminality of Ouologuem's plagiarism compared to Aquin's, both in the more covert way it is perpetrated and in the more severe censure it received, corresponds perhaps to the more extreme historical situation of colonization as suffered by the Black African people whose history Ouologuem is writing and of which he is a product.

NOTES

1. Albert Memmi, *Portrait du colonisé* (1957; Montréal, Les Editions de l'étincelle, 1972); Frantz Fanon, *Les Damnés de la terre* (Paris: Editions Maspero, 1961); Jacques Berque, *Le dépossession du monde* (Paris: Seuil, 1964).
2. Paul Chamberland, "Dire ce que je suis," *Parti pris* 2.5 (1965): 35.
3. Hubert Aquin, *Blackout*, trans., Alan Brown (Toronto: Anansi, 1974).
4. Jurgis Baltrusaitis, *Anamorphoses ou perspectives curieuses* (Paris: Oliver Perrin, 1955). (See appendix).
5. Hubert Aquin, *Agent double* (Montréal, Les Presses de l'Université de Montréal, "Lignes Québecoises," 1973) 90.
6. André Brochu, "La Nouvelle relation écrivain-critique," *Parti pris* 2.5 (1965): 56.
7. Quoted by K.W., "In Defence of Yambo Ouologuem," *West Africa* 2875 (21 July 1972): 941.
8. *Times Literary Supplement* 5 May 1972: 525.
9. Seth Wolitz, "L'art du plagiat," *Research in African Literatures* 4.1 (1973): 130-134.
10. Eric Sellin, "Ouologuem's Blueprint for *Le Devoir de violence*," *Research in African Literatures* 7.2 (1971): 119.
11. Wolitz 134.
12. S. Morawski, "The Basic Functions of Quotation," *Sign, Language and Culture* (The Hague: Mouton, 1970) 690-705.
13. Quoted by K.W., *West Africa* 941.
14. Fanon 166.
15. Yambo Ouologuem, *Lettre à la France négre* (Paris: Editions Edmond Malis, 1968).

APPENDIX: Aquin and Baltrusaitis

Compare the following passages. The **bold** type indicates elements in the Baltrusaitis text that have been deleted by Aquin. The < > indicate additions made by Aquin. The two ambassadors

> sont représentés grandeur nature devant **une table ou plutôt** un rayonnage <re>couvert d'un tapis oriental. **Derrière eux tombe un rideau de soie.** Le pavement est une dallage de marbre incrusté reproduisant la mosaïque du sanctuaire de Westminster **exécuté au temps d'Henri III.** Dinteville est **d'une carrure robuste accentuée encore par** <vétu d'>une large veste fourrée à manches bouffantes. **Il porte à son cou l'Ordre de Saint-Michel.** Le poignard qui pend à son côté indique son âge: il a vingt-neuf ans. (*Trou de mémoire* 130; *Anamorphoses* 58).
>
> <Hans> Holbein <a> lui-même **aurait** exécuté vers 1517 deux crânes sur l'extérieur d'une dyptique<,> avec deux jeunes garçons. Le symbole de la <m>Mort y apparaît lorsqu'on referme le volet, <tandis que,> dans la figuration des **deux** <A>ambassadeurs, <le symbole de la mort

… devient évident—d'une évidence funèbre—> lorsqu'on se déplace. (*Trou de mémoire* 132; *Anamorphoses* 65).

En arrangeant la succession des deux images indépendantes, Holbein ne les a pas dissociées. (*Trou de mémoire* 132; *Anamorphoses* 65).

Another type of plagiaristic repetition, this time much closer to the use by Ouologuem of Greene and Schwartz-Bart, involves the rewriting of a scene by echoes, rather than by direct copying. Here the **bold** type indicates the repeated discourse.

Trou de mémoire 133:

> Alors commence **le deuxième acte: le visiteur,** repu des apparences infinitésimales du portrait mystérieux, **se retire par la porte de gauche, la seule issue** de cet enclos. Alors, juste avant de franchir le seuil et de quitter cette chambre obscure, il **jette un dernier regard,** furtif, **sur le tableau et comprend** d'un seul coup son double sens: le **distancement visuel** s'estompe la figure des "Ambassadeurs" et révèle la **"figure cachée"**.

Anamorphoses 65:

> Déconcerté, **le visiteur se retire par la porte de gauche, la seule ouverte,** et c'est **le deuxième acte.** En s'engageant dans le salon voisin, il lève la tête pour **jeter un dernier regard sur le tableau,** et c'est alors qu'il comprend tout: le **rétrécissement visuel** fait disparaître complètement la scène et apparaître la **figure cachée.**

SALMAN RUSHDIE'S *MIDNIGHT'S CHILDREN*: MODELS FOR STORYTELLING, EAST AND WEST

K. J. Phillips, University of Hawaii

Salman Rushdie's novel *Midnight's Children,* published in 1980, generously mixes eastern and western sources. As a Moslem Indian writing in English, Rushdie is likely to mention Ali Baba and the forty thieves on one page and Superman comics on the next. The narrator might compare lovers to stars in the Bombay film industry, to the Hindu god Krishna and his milkmaid Radha, to Romeo and Juliet, or to Katharine Hepburn and Spencer Tracy. For his primary eastern sources, Rushdie returns frequently to both *The Arabian Nights* and the Hindu epics of India, *The Ramayana* and *The Mahabharata.* And, as I will mainly argue here, he extensively alludes to the 18th-century British novel *Tristram Shandy* by Laurence Sterne: not so openly as to his eastern models, but just as pervasively.

These eastern and western influences have actually been reverberating back and forth for centuries. Laurence Sterne, for example, acknowledges Cervantes' *Don Quixote* as one of his great teachers. The narrator of *Don Quixote,* in turn, claims that he is merely transmitting the story as he heard it from an Arabic author, one Cid Hamete Benengeli. Of course, attributing Don Quixote's story to an Arabic author is all a hoax, to imitate the way a medieval narrator of romance will refer to a previous minstrel from whom he heard the tale. But Cervantes' parody reminds us that Arabic forms did, in fact, influence the development of courtly love and medieval romance in the first place. And so, from Arabic love poetry to European romance to Spanish picaresque, on to the British 18th-century novel, and back to India's *Midnight's Children,* we have come full circle, showing a fertile interplay from east to west and from west to east.

Rushdie's immediate written sources have one thing in common: the representation of a reader-figure in the text. Rushdie's narrator, Saleem, supposedly reads his pages aloud to a robust and practical young woman, Padma, modeled in part on the Hindu goddess Lakshmi, deferentially crouched at Vishnu's feet. The Hindu epics and *The Arabian Nights* both represent listeners in the text, recalling a time when storytellers delivered these tales orally. Instead of an anonymous, omniscient narrator addressing a page, one named character talks to another named character who stands in for us—even if these personages disappear for long stretches of narration. *The Bhagavad Gita,* for example (which is part of *The Mahabharata*), starts out with a series of speakers: a king asks his teacher what happened, and the teacher recounts how a prince approached his guru, then tells the king how Krishna replied when Arjuna inquired why he should fight.[1]

Another such frame situation with a listener-figure occurs in *The Arabian Nights,* where Scheherazade tells the tales of a thousand and one nights to King Shahryar. Rushdie's narrator, Saleem, calls himself a Scheherazade.[2] There is a similar sexual attraction between listener and teller—Padma to Saleem and Shahryar to Scheherazade. More importantly, there is a serious purpose underlying both *Midnight's Children* and *The Arabian Nights,* despite their humor and frivolity. *The Arabian Nights* starts out with a sober claim: "Praise be to [Allah] who hath made the histories of the Past an admonition unto the Present."[3] We might not believe this pious pose, since *The Arabian Nights* are so bawdy. Entertainment, not didacticism, is clearly one of their chief functions. But the frame situation in *The Arabian Nights* does introduce a non-frivolous urgency: Scheherazade keeps talking to forestall future violence. She talks so that her new husband will not kill her nor any successors, the way he has already murdered more than a thousand previous brides. Rushdie, too, while aiming to amuse us, has an urgent social purpose. He condemns political betrayal of the ideals of Indian independence and tries to heal some of India's sectarian violence.

The presence of a listener whose comments are imagined might seem to be particularly eastern, as in the examples from *The Gita* and *The Arabian Nights.* But actually Rushdie could also model the conversations between Saleem and a listener- or reader-figure on *Tristram Shandy.* Sterne addresses his pages to a "Sir" and a "Madam," and he makes up whole paragraphs in which they quibble with him about his style. Padma may derive her outspoken objections less from her polite eastern models than from her more fastidious western prototype in Sterne's "Madam."

I would like to spend the rest of this paper showing the influences from *Tristram Shandy* to *Midnight's Children* and the differences between them. Both Saleem and Tristram start out to tell their autobiographies but cannot even work their way up to the birth of the apparently indispensable subject until well over a hundred pages into their books. Rushdie and Sterne delay the births for several reasons. One is simply to tease us and keep us reading. A second reason for postponing the birth of the main character is to give witness to the difficulty of getting any story told: delay testifies to the limitations of language in encompassing the intractable details of life. But in *Midnight's Children* this postponement has an additional thematic importance. Saleem, born on a midnight in 1947 just as India becomes a nation, takes a long time arriving because India too was long in gaining its independence from England.

It takes such a long time to tell about Saleem's confusing tangle of possible fathers and mothers because every contemporary Indian possesses a mixed cultural heritage. Let me review some of the candidates for Saleem's family tree. It turns out that his nurse switched him with another child in their cradles (a time-tested folk tale motif from around the world), so Saleem's father is not the Moslem who raised him. His father is a low-caste Hindu entertainer who goes by the British nursery rhyme name Wee Willie Winkie. But no, Wee Willie Winkie is not Saleem's father after all, because the last Britisher in India, one William Methwold, cuckolded Winkie. This adultery is thematically appropriate, Rushdie implies, because Britain was in India illegitimately. So our hero Saleem has a British father: "Oh no," Padma protests, "an Anglo-Indian!" Rushdie's own Anglo heritage shows in the very language, English, he uses for this book; and if Methwold is Saleem's father, Laurence Sterne is Rushdie's.

Rushdie reveals his kinship to Sterne in both subject matter and technique. Besides a narrator who cannot get born into his own autobiography, common subjects include noses (much discussion of noses), the possible impotence of major characters (constant sexual innuendo, in fact, attached to any topic at all), and a mysterious widow whose story is teasingly announced in both books long before we hear it.

There are also common strategies besides the hypothetical conversations between narrator and listener. First, self-conscious narrators in both Rushdie and Sterne comment on their own techniques. Second, the narrators announce topics but then endlessly avoid them, tantalizing us with clues whose meaning we can scarcely grasp. Third, the narrators recapitulate, at breakneck speed, lists of topics already covered. Fourth, the narrators create humor but, particularly in *Midnight's Children,* also infuse it with social criticism. Fifth, they both link trivial actions performed by characters with historical events. For example, Saleem acquires a silver bicycle which, he claims, enables him "to ensure the partition of the state of Bombay."[4] And sixth, both pursue what Rushdie calls "matter of fact descriptions of the . . . bizarre, and their reverse, namely heightened, stylized versions of the everyday."[5] Some critics associate Rushdie's method here with that of Gabriel García Márquez or Günter Grass, calling the method "magical realism."[6] But Rushdie himself traces this kind of double vision—reality as fantastic, fantasy as concretely detailed—to the Hindu view of the world as illusion, or Maya: we're all "lost in Brahma's dream," Saleem tells Padma.[7]

Rushdie chooses this double method because history after independence has been so incredible. Could West Pakistani soldiers really believe their indoctrination to hate Hindu vegetarians? Yes. Could these soldiers really have been flown, not to India, but to East Pakistan and ordered to kill other meat-eaters, Moslems like themselves? Yes. Did the soldiers really carry out such preposterous orders? Yes, they did. When reality is so nightmarish, realism yields to surrealism to depict it.

Obviously I cannot discuss all these common topics and techniques in depth, so I'll just give you my "chapter on noses," as Sterne might say, and then some of the parallels the authors draw between mundane fictional events and history.

You would be surprised how much time the narrators spend talking about noses. Saleem is Snotnose, Sniffer and Ganesha (after the elephant-headed god). His "Ganeshnose" proves to Saleem's satisfaction that he is related to his Moslem grandfather, who lost his faith when he bumped his enormous beak on a clod of earth treacherously hidden under the prayer mat. But, of course, Saleem is not related biologically to that grandfather at all, and the nose is Methwold's, a Cyrano de Bergerac monstrosity from some French ancestor. Saleem's nose comes from the West, all right, not so much from France as England, since Saleem's nose is a sign of paternity to Tristram. Tristram's family has always favored big noses, and they worry when his is squeezed during birth, since they think it now gives poor promise of future virility. Moreover, Tristram claims that "the excellency of the nose is in a direct arithmetical proportion to the excellency of the wearer's fancy."[8] In a kind of sniff in the direction of Sterne, Rushdie has Saleem first acquire his fancifully grand telepathic powers from the shock of sneezing, after snuffling a pajama cord up his nose while hidden in a washing chest. Both authors relate sexuality to writing, as a kind of excess creativity.

If Rushdie affectionately nods toward Sterne with the case of the creative nose, he follows him in relating history to everyday events for a much more serious purpose than Sterne had in mind. Sterne reminds us of history when Tristram's Uncle Toby builds model fortifications in his kitchen garden to mimic sieges and battles of early 18th-century European wars.[9] Just as Uncle Toby maneuvers his makeshift battering rams, Saleem moves pepper pots around a dinner table to simulate a military coup in Pakistan. Nevertheless, there's a world of difference between Sterne's kitchen garden and Rushdie's dinner table. First, Uncle Toby builds *after* the battles, and he aims only for some small "quirk of improvement."[10] Saleem, on the other hand, supposedly moves pepper pots *before* the coup, and he claims to *create* history—though all unwittingly, as an eleven-year-old boy.

Second, the authors' purposes in alluding to history are much different in scale, if not in kind. Sterne does intend some satire, but his mild manner heals all stings before they can take effect. Mentioning the fashionable Louis XIV in connection with extravagantly painted war machines, even when the narrator denies any slur on the "prancing" king, does bring a doubt about the ruler to our minds.[11] Sterne implies that the great powers, Louis XIV and William III, are nothing more than boys in their mentality. Uncle Toby's hobby horse, his obsessive fashioning of model fortifications, does, then, satirize war to some extent. Its perpetrators have arrested their own development in decidedly adolescent needs. But overall I don't think that Toby's games damage the real enterprise of war in our minds all that much. Uncle Toby is just too likeable, so that Sterne's book produces the odd effect of making weapons seem not so much juvenile, after all, as really harmless.

Rushdie produces the opposite effect entirely, despite his humor. He is truly satirizing governments, not just joshing them. The one critic I found who mentions Rushdie's use of Sterne's highly self-conscious novel says the influence proves that for Rushdie "the business of writing" is all important. "Imagination" surpasses mere "side issues" like history and politics.[12] Such an interpretation could not be more wrong. Imagination and storytelling provide spice for his "chutneyfication" of the past, but history supplies the substance, and Rushdie is not about to deny himself or us our nourishment.

True, Saleem's constant warnings to his devoted Padma that he will never be able to sleep with her hint that Saleem wonders if he might be impotent to change history too. He might be fated to inherit passively from his century. Rushdie makes an important metaphoric meaning for impotence, then, lacking in Sterne's book. In *Tristram Shandy,* when a window sash falls on the child Tristram as he happens to be urinating out the window, Sterne writes entire elliptical chapters on the extent of Tristram's injury—mere circumcision or more—probably just because Sterne thinks the details will titillate us. But when Rushdie creates a hushed-up genital injury for Saleem, it turns out to be the excessive result of Prime Minister Indira Gandhi's forced sterilization program in the mid 1970s. Rushdie wants seriously to criticize that particular program and, more generally, the state of emergency, vote buying, censorship, and imprisonment of political foes that formed the larger context for the forced sterilizations. The Gandhi regime operated literally on coerced citizens;[13] metaphorically it extirpated hope and blighted the promise of independence.

Indira Gandhi turns out, in fact, to resemble the colonizer alarmingly. Rushdie dwells on the "Widow" Gandhi's light and dark hair on either side of a center parting, whereas he had earlier claimed that the Britisher Methwold fascinated women by his meticulous hair parting. Since the Indian Prime Minister and the colonizer look practically like twins, Rushdie implies that it is not only the British who can oppress India.

Because Rushdie can point out these excesses, he does not just inherit from history passively after all. He does not lapse into the apathy of his character Saleem, who unquestioningly follows orders to track down East Pakistanis. Rushdie seriously accepts the admonition of *The Arabian Nights* to remember the past. Writing about the past becomes itself a form of potency. It turns out that Saleem, for all his physical problems, can claim a son, as Scheherazade surprises us by having borne three children sometime during her storytelling: Saleem adopts the offspring of the person with whom he was switched in the cradle. He then tells his story to this son, to Padma, and to us, his eastern and western audience. Rushdie implies that if we listen to him and then act on what we hear, rejecting the bigotries and violence of the past, we too can bequeath (retell) "morality, judgment, and character," as Rushdie says, to our sons and daughters.[14]

NOTES

1. Swami Purohit, trans., *The Gospel of the Lord Shri Krishna: The Bhagavad Gita* (New York: Vintage-Random, 1977) 4-10.
2. Salman Rushdie, *Midnights' Children* (New York: Avon, 1980) 4, 22.
3. Richard Burton, trans. *The Arabian Nights' Entertainments,* ed. Bennett A. Cerf (New York: Modern Library, 1959) 1.
4. Rushdie 216.
5. Rushdie 261.

6 Rudolf Bader, "Indian Tin Drum," *The International Fiction Review* 11 (Summer, 1984): 75-83.
7 Rushdie 253.
8 Laurence Sterne, *The Life and Opinions of Tristram Shandy, Gentleman,* ed. James A. Work (Indianapolis: Bobbs-Merrill, 1940) 233.
9 Sterne 212.
10 Sterne 446.
11 Sterne 446.
12 Keith Wilson, *"Midnight's Children* and Reader Responsibility," *Critical Quarterly* 26 (Autumn, 1984): 35. Rushdie himself mentions Sterne in an interview, *"Midnight's Children* and *Shame," Kunapipi* 7 (1985): 2.
13 Kai Bird, "Indira Gandhi Uses Force: Sterilization in India," *The Nation* 222 (19 June 1976): 747-49; Donald P. Warwick, "Compulsory Sterilization in India," *Commonweal* 103 (10 Sept. 1976): 582-85.
14 Rushdie 252.

"DIFFERENCE THAT KILLS" / DIFFERENCE THAT HEALS: REPRESENTING LATIN AMERICA IN THE POETRY OF ELIZABETH BISHOP AND MARGARET ATWOOD

Deborah Weiner, University of Hawaii

The notion of difference appears at the intersection of many contemporary discourses: political, cross-cultural, postmodernist, feminist.[1] Here I will look at contrasting notions of difference in the work of two major poets: Elizabeth Bishop (1911-1979) and Margaret Atwood (b. 1939). Their many similarities include a sharp, ironic intelligence, experimentation with a variety of poetic techniques and voices, continuing poetic growth throughout their careers (both moving from a more distanced stance to greater openness) and many shared poetic themes. Yet their poems representing Latin America—a place very different from their Canadian homeland—reveal strong contrasts not only in the way they construct the other and constitute difference but also in the consequences for each poet's epistemology, aesthetics, and ethics.

I present these contrasts not to valorize Atwood over Bishop (I think both are excellent poets), but to draw attention to what I feel are some serious consequences of Bishop's way of thinking that Bishop herself seemed eager yet unable to avoid. Reasons for the contrasts between them could include their different life stories, social status, and historical contexts. They were born nearly thirty years apart. Bishop lost both parents and then was taken from her beloved grandparents and village at age seven; she spent part of her childhood as an invalid. Atwood's family is still intact; she spent summers exploring Canada's backwoods—her father was a government entomologist. However, my purpose here is not to speculate on causes but to examine effects. Setting up a sharp dichotomy between the two poets inevitably distorts as well as clarifies (as I will argue here). Yet it may prove useful to look at the contrasts between them, first briefly in overview, then in detail within the poems.

While Bishop often sees difference in terms of binary oppositions, hierarchically ranked as superior or inferior, with clear separation between self and other and between active and passive, Atwood sees both similarity and difference within and between herself and the other, turning a shifting and multifaceted glance on a shifting and multifaceted world, a world with which she reciprocally interacts.[2] Atwood writes in "True Stories," the title poem of the 1981 collection I will be using here, "The true story lies / among the other stories, / a mess of colours, like jumbled clothing."[3] And in "Mushrooms," "Here is the handful / of shadow I have brought back to you: / this decay, this hope, this mouth- / ful of dirt, this poetry."[4] While Atwood can see in the same place both dirt and poetry, and thus maintains, alongside decay, her sense of hope, Bishop seems trapped by a conceptual system, analyzed by Cixous, which emphasizes either/or judgements, in which difference is either a threat—"O difference that kills"[5]—or dissolves into synthesis: "life/death, right/wrong, male/female / —such notions would have resolved, dissolved, straight off / in that watery, dazzling dialectic."[6] In this system of binary oppositions she thus risks ending up either on the negative side or nowhere.[7] As Bishop faces these two equally unsatisfactory alternatives within herself, her picture of what is outside of her becomes correspondingly distorted. Later I will come back to how the system works within, but first I will consider the consequences for the epistemologies of each poet as they represent Latin America.

Both Bishop and Atwood present complexities of a place neither sees as wholly different. Bishop clearly loves Brazil, where she lived from age 40 to 61. Much of her best work was written in Brazil or is about it, and she generously helped Brazilian writers gain a North American hearing. Her poems describing the place focus on its differences from North America, its lushness and overabundance. For example, "Song for the Rainy Season" depicts her garden

> where blood-black
> bromelias, lichens,
> owls, and the lint
> of the waterfalls cling,
> familiar, unbidden.[8]

Other poems celebrate local characters: "Manuelzinho," "The Riverman," "The Burglar of Babylon." Yet she risks some of the dangers, pointed out by Said in *Orientalism*, of a Western view that sees the non-Western world as exotic, separate, different: e.g., the dangers of romanticization of difference and of pretended disinterest while observing the other from a privileged position. Bishop herself is not unaware of some of these dangers. In "Arrival at Santos" she mocks the tourist's "immodest demands for a different world, / and a better life, and complete comprehension / of both at last, and immediately."[9] And "Questions of Travel" asks,

> Is it right to be watching strangers in a play
> in this strangest of theatres?
> What childishness is it that while there's a breath of life
> in our bodies, we are determined to rush
> . . . . .
> To stare at some inexplicable old stonework,
> inexplicable and impenetrable,
> at any view,
> instantly seen and always, always delightful?[10]

The answers remain ambiguous: "but surely it would have been a pity / not to have seen the trees along this road, / really exaggerated in their beauty, / not to have seen them gesturing / like noble pantomimists, robed in pink."[11] And she ends with a final question: *"Should we have stayed at home, / wherever that may be?"*[12] Bishop here adopts the familiar modernist stance of precise observation from a position different from (and implicitly superior to) what is observed.

Atwood's picture of Latin America seems at first sight far harsher than Bishop's.[13] Many of her poems on Latin America aim at getting people to take heed of political violence and exploitation in the region, poems such as "A Conversation," "The Arrest of the Stockbroker," "Torture," and "French Colonial." In "Notes Towards a Poem That Can Never Be Written," responding to political critiques of the poet as privileged observer, Atwood begins with a look at the country observed—"This is the place / you would rather not know about"—and ends up by looking at the home of the observer as well:

> In this country you can say what you like
> because no one will listen to you anyway,
> it's safe enough, in this country you can try to write
> the poem that can never be written,
> the poem that invents
> nothing and excuses nothing,
> because you invent and excuse yourself each day.
>
> Elsewhere, this poem is not invention.
> Elsewhere, this poem takes courage.
> . . . . .
> Elsewhere you must write this poem
> because there is nothing more to do.[14]

In other poems, like "Landcrab I," "Landcrab II," "One More Garden," "Postcard," "Petit Nevis," and "Dinner," when Atwood is actually describing the place or the people, she seems to make a special effort to shun romanticization and to acknowledge her own presence and interests, as in the glaringly unpretentious way she depicts "One More Garden" where, "on bare feet, fishbelly-white, I wince / over stubble & around / sheepshit, to hang the wash."[15] The last stanza begins "I should throw my gold watch / into the ocean and become / timeless."[16] The title and tone of dry mockery seem aimed at undercutting the stereotypical view of a South Seas Island paradise where time stands still. But what does she offer in its place? When Atwood describes a scene with people in "Dinner," she begins with a jaundiced view of a

> Dining room: tinsel festoons,
> gold stars, hibiscus grown from plastic.
> . . . . .
> The tapedeck groans about love[17]

But then she argues against taking up a superior stance:

> *I love you,* whines the soprano.
> It's the same song, and mine is
> also. Why sneer at those ancient
> rhythms, constant and constantly
> broken, our cut feet move to?[18]

The rhythms are both endless and fragmentary; we keep moving despite cut feet, despite having been hurt where we move, in motivation, in our desire. She ends up claiming kinship as she answers her question, "Why sneer . . . ?"

> Unless you need
> nothing. That whisper
> and thud is the undertow
> of all this filagree · heartbeat · the same
> desire and greed.[19]

As if to say, don't sneer at the tasteless decor, don't sneer at the tawdriness of our needs, don't sneer at poverty. We all share "the same desire and greed." No one is exempt: "unless you need nothing." Atwood's admission of shared need (instead of pretended disinterest) serves as a bridge between people otherwise very different.

To sum up, Atwood sees people and places as both different and similar, while for Bishop people and places are often either one or the other. The problem for Bishop's epistemology is the distortion caused when any elements that contradict the dominant side of the opposing pair become invisible.

This contrast in epistemologies corresponds to contrasting aesthetics; here I want to look briefly at the way their notions of difference operate aesthetically in their poetic structures. In the poem just looked at, "Dinner," Atwood begins by focusing on differences between the speaker's implied aesthetic judgement and the locals' taste, but ends by affirming similarities. In the poem's middle, the soprano's "whine" undercuts the otherwise direct and strong affirmation of love. There are no clear sectional hierarchies or boundaries.

Bishop's sections, however, tend to contrast starkly. In "Song for the Rainy Season," the poet uses her home and garden's wetness and overabundance to figure fulfillment in love, building to a central affirmation of openly expressed intense joy, very rare in Bishop's work. But the possession of such riches leaves her vulnerable to overwhelming loss, and in mid-stanza the poem's mood shifts abruptly and totally from joy to despair:

> darkened and tarnished
> by the warm touch
> of the warm breath,
> maculate, cherished,
> rejoice! For a later
> era will differ.
> (O difference that kills,
> or intimidates, much
> of all our small shadowy
> life!)[20]

It ends with a description of the same place parched and loveless: "the several waterfalls shrivel in the steady sun."[21]

Expressions of intense joy are rare in Atwood's poetry also. One example is "Flying Inside Your Own Body." The first stanza rises from "Your lungs fill & spread" to

> your heart is light too & huge
> beating with pure joy, pure helium.
> The sun's white winds blow through you,
> there's nothing above you,
> you see the earth now as an oval jewel,
> radiant & seablue with love.[22]

But the second and final stanza immediately contradicts this image of transcendence. It begins, "it's only in dreams you can do this. / Waking, your heart is a shaken fist" and ends, "you try & try to rise but you cannot."[23] Whereas Bishop's poem moves from total rejoicing to total destitution, Atwood undercuts both the first stanza's transcendence by calling it only a dream and also the end's harsh landing down below by asserting an unbroken desire to rise.

In Bishop's "Santarém," the contrast between center and end is even starker.[24] The poem begins with a look back "after—how many years?" at "that conflux of two great rivers"

> with everything gilded, burnished along one side,
> and everything bright, cheerful, casual—or so it looked.
> I liked the place; I liked the idea of the place.[25]

The phrase "everything gilded . . . along one side" sums up the way the dichotomization we have been looking at powerfully affects her vision: "everything" she sees is divided and only "one side" appears briefly to shine. This emphasis on one side's shining seems to reflect unconsciously the traditional alignment of binary pairs in which only the male side represents light and sun. She observes the place carefully to use it for her purposes, to create her "idea of the place." Although she seems to undercut the validity of her view with "or so it looked," her purpose is not to go beyond mere appearances but to use them as the substance of her art, to create from them a "sublime" moment by precise observation.[26]

A similar moment appears in an Atwood prose poem "Instructions for the Third Eye," which explains how this moment may be reached. It moves from everyday reality through the grotesque and painful to a sudden radiant vision: "One day you will wake up and everything, the stones by the driveway, the brick houses, each brick, each leaf of each tree, your own body, will be glowing from within, lit up, so bright you can hardly look."[27] Where for Bishop everything shone only on one side, reflecting the sun, here everything glows from within; where Bishop sees the shining outside herself at a remote place she travels to and must leave, here it includes "your own body" and just happens by surprise one day at home. Atwood continues: "You will reach out in any direction and you will touch the light itself." The light is there outside, in any direction, and also within; she can touch it.

Bishop in contrast touches and takes one object from her place of golden union, "an empty wasp's nest," "small, exquisite, clean matte white," an object emblematic of her own aesthetic. The last stanza then sharply differs from the rest as she is forced to leave that perfect place and face its opposite:

> Then—my ship's whistle blew. I couldn't stay.
> Back on board, a fellow-passenger, Mr. Swan,
> Dutch, the retiring head of Philips Electric,
> really a very nice old man,
> who wanted to see the Amazon before he died,
> asked, "What's that ugly thing?"[28]

Her "exquisite" nest is the old man's "ugly thing." The poem emphasizes absolute dichotomies: between that perfect place and elsewhere, between her "idea of the place" and whatever else it might be for others including those who live there, and between her own refined aesthetic sensibility and the old man's lack of taste.

It might be tempting to ascribe the difference between Bishop's scenes of intense union and Atwood's mixed, antiromantic approach to Latin America to the fact that Bishop grew deeply attached to Brazil over a 21-year residence while Atwood was merely a visitor, except that Atwood's poems about her Canadian homeland, which she deeply cares for, show a comparably mixed approach. Her poem "Damside" is comparable to "Santarém" in that rivers in both poems evoke similar traditional associations with time and destiny. In "Damside" the speaker and another person walk beside a river that is "brown"

> and not something you'd drink
> unless you thought you were dying.
>
> If this were a poem I'd trust the river,
> kneel and cup my hands
> around its liquid ice, its ozone-
> blue. If this were a poem you'd live forever.[29]

These lines deny the traditional eternizing conceit, that poetry can grant immortality, at the same time they offer it. Both poems bring up ideas of eternity at their centers, yet Atwood with these lines at the same time also undercuts the traditional trust in a timeless succession of readers. It is as if she asks whether we can claim to be creating "poems" like those of the past 3,000 years or so if we cannot take for granted the survival of our own species let alone of our civilization. Yet she does not despair, and unlike Bishop who ends with an unbridgeable gap between her view and the other's (the old man's), Atwood at the end offers the other a chance to share some hope in what is there for both of them:

> As it is, I can offer you
> only this poor weather:
> my chilled hands, the fragments
> of a noon in early spring,
> an east wind which includes
> both of us, and the stained river,
> a prayer, a sewer, a prayer.[30]

Despite the setting's bleakness it includes traditional metaphors for rebirth: spring, an east wind, the river. The last line forms a kind of postmodern sandwich, a sewer between two prayers, emblematic of Atwood's characteristic stance—facing the worst head-on while hoping for something better. As she once put it in a talk reprinted in *Second Words*:

> Writing, no matter what its subject, is an act of faith; the primary faith being that someone out there will read the results. I believe it's also an act of hope, the hope that things can be better than they are. If a writer is very lucky and manages to live long enough, I think it can also be an act of charity. It takes a lot to see what is there, both without flinching or turning away and without bitterness. The world exists; the writer testifies. She cannot deny anything human.[31]

Atwood's struggle to see "what is there," to "testify," is at the core of the contrasts we have been looking at in epistemology, in aesthetics, and also in ethics. The three cannot really be separated. Atwood's espousal of writing as an act of faith, hope, and charity suggests that her ethics are grounded in Christian tradition, but whatever their source, her poetry's ethical stance and tone differ from those of Bishop. Earlier I mentioned that Bishop risks ending up either on the negative side or nowhere, and that facing this unsatisfactory choice inside herself distorts her view of what is outside. Now let us look at the inner picture and how it affects ethics.

While a dichotomized stance causes distortions and resulting limitations in perception that can hamper men and women alike, the costs hit women harder, because woman is defined as inferior in a conceptual system created by men. Bishop was obviously aware of these costs, but she apparently saw no alternative to the system which mandated a clear divide between inferior and superior. Within it, she tried two strategies of mitigation. On the one hand she could try to escape the problem entirely, either by a synthesis as in "Santarém," or by becoming asexual (as Joanne Feit Diehl argues) and thus denying the existence of the most undeniably hierarchized couple of all the opposing pairs, according to Cixous the one couple that forms the blueprint for all the others.[32] But strategies of trying to split off and control parts of oneself usually backfire, requiring more and more energy drained off from positive accomplishment. As she said in an interview, "sometimes I think if I had been born a man I probably would have written more. Dared more, or been able to spend more time at it. I've wasted a great deal of time."[33] On the other hand she could try to get onto the superior side, like a man to assume a position of mastery and possession, but this position brings fears of losing control, losing possessions. In "One Art" she writes "I lost two cities, lovely ones, and vaster / some realms I owned, two rivers, a continent."³⁴ However ironic or self-mocking the tone, she here lays claim to all of South America! In a late poem she hints at the high costs of such losses in her past, "a yesterday I find almost impossible to lift."³⁵

For Atwood, loss cannot be as absolute because possession was not absolute. In "Petit Nevis" she calls her beloved "extra, / a mistake, something found: / a gift, a contradiction. / I've been away from you / too long for comfort, not long enough / for safety."³⁶ The contrast with "One Art" is clear. Bishop tries to "master" the "disaster" of loss by framing it in the strict structure of the villanelle, to prove that her art, "One Art," has control over her needs and lacks.³⁷ It ends: "The art of losing's not too hard to master, / though it may look like (*Write* it!) like disaster."³⁸ Atwood, in contrast, sees art not as a means to mastery but as something more reciprocal. In the talk quoted earlier, she compares the writer's struggle to Jacob's wrestling with the angel: "The encounter with language is a struggle in which each side is equally active . . . . [W]e hope that if we receive the blessing it will not be for ourselves alone."³⁹ For her the blessings as well as the risks are to be shared. Love is a risk, but one that cannot be controlled; she writes of falling in love: "free fall / is falling but at least it's free. . . . I wish I knew whether you'll catch or watch."⁴⁰ The only security is in isolation: "Safety would be / this island."⁴¹ She suggests that it is exactly the attempt to take control, to hold on, that can destroy what it tries to grasp: "If I reach my hands into you, will you vanish?"⁴²

Atwood's resistance to the urge to dominate (in herself or in others) extends beyond her art and her relations with other people to include relations even with another species, for instance, the landcrab. Both poets were drawn to identify with that shy, hard-shelled creature that moves sideways and waves around its eyes. In "Strayed Crab," Bishop looks only for similarities between herself and the crab, appropriating the crab's voice to draw a sharp distinction between the proper and the excessive: "I am making too much noise," says the crab.⁴³ Atwood in "Landcrab I" sees the crab as both similar and different, "a piece of what / we are, not all."⁴⁴ In "Landcrab II" she goes further, trying to imagine what the crab perceives though not speaking for it: "I smell the pulp / of her body, faint odour / of rotting salt, / as she smells mine, / working those martian palps: / seawater in leather."⁴⁵ This relation between speaker and crab is two-sided, not under the human's control. Respecting the crab's separate existence, Atwood explicitly tries to avoid appropriating the other: "you're no-one's metaphor."⁴⁶ By refraining from appropriation and dichotomization, Atwood minimizes the risk of harm to self or other, of despair or exploitation, though she does not claim absence of such risk: as she says to the crab, "I'm up to scant harm," not none.

In contrast, Bishop tends to appropriate what is similar or to separate herself from what is different. Therefore the differences she focuses on are usually conceptual and outside herself, as in the contrast between the proper and the excessive in "Strayed Crab," or between her view of transcendent union in

"Santarém" and the old man's view, whereas Atwood threads her way between difference and similarity in a landscape where the worst dangers are physical as well as conceptual and could originate inside as well as out, external dangers like torture or political and personal oppression, or internal ones like failure to resist that oppression.[47] Yet in facing these dangers she does not constitute them as clearly different and separate from herself, nor does she define the other as wrong, herself as right. And it is here that Atwood points to epistemology's effect on ethics. In "Torture" she describes a woman's face sewn shut:

> It doesn't matter where
> this was done or why or whether
> by one side or the other;
> such things are done as soon
> as there are sides[48]

It may be relatively easy to condemn torture and taking sides, but it is harder to acknowledge a measure of kinship even with the side of the torturers, as Atwood does in a poem on Nazis when she symbolizes our potential for evil as "the / long bone lying in darkness / inside my right arm: not / innocent but latent."[49] Kristeva similarly suggests we replace scapegoating of the other with "the analysis of the potentialities of *victim/executioner* which characterize each identity, each subject, each sex."[50]

It is as passive victim that Bishop sometimes constitutes herself. In "Song for the Rainy Season,"[51] with its sharp contrast between love and loss discussed above, when Bishop uses rain as a metaphor for love, the change from rainy to dry is like the weather, beyond human agency. Atwood's poem "Nothing" uses a comparable metaphor; it begins, "Nothing like love to put blood back into the language."[52] Its last line verbally performs, with chiasmus, a small replica of the reciprocity of being *both* passive and active at once: "What touches you is what you touch."[53]

By shunning the hierarchized binary oppositions that distort Bishop's view of Latin America, Atwood may or may not see it more nearly "as it is," but at least she is less likely to project onto it her preconceptions. Atwood may forego some of the "classical" elegance and "mastery" which won Bishop high praise from the likes of Robert Lowell and Harold Bloom, but in undoing neat dichotomies between similarity/difference, inferior/superior, self/other, Atwood gains thereby abundant energy, a tough hope, greater reciprocity in relations, and a less "pure" but stronger and more resilient affirmation:

> Here is the handful
> of shadow I have brought back to you:
> this decay, this hope, this mouth-
> ful of dirt, this poetry.[54]

NOTES

1. To investigate contemporary notions of difference in political, cross-cultural discourse, see Edward Said, *Orientalism* (New York: Pantheon, 1978); in postmodernism, see Jacques Derrida, *Writing and Difference*, trans. Alan Bass (Chicago: Univ. of Chicago P, 1978); in feminism, see Helene Cixous, "Sorties: Out and Out: Attacks/Ways Out/Forays," *The Newly Born Woman*, Helene Cixous and Catherine Clement, trans. Betsy Wing (Minneapolis: Univ. of Minnesota P, 1986) 63-132, and Julia Kristeva, "Women's Time," *The Kristeva Reader*, ed. Toril Moi, trans. Alice Jardine and Harry Blake (Oxford: Blackwell, 1986) 187-213.
2. According to Sherrill E. Grace, "Atwood identifies human failure as acquiescence in those Western dichotomies which postulate the inescapable, static division of the world into hostile opposites: culture/nature, male/female, . . . victor/victim" (Sherrill E. Grace, "Articulating the 'Space Between': Atwood's Untold Stories and Fresh Beginnings," *Margaret Atwood: Language, Text, and System*, eds. Sherrill E. Grace and Lorraine Weir [Vancouver: Univ. of British Columbia P, 1983] 5). Atwood offers "a system embodying dualities, but dualities understood as mutually interdependent aspects of a continuum of relationship, functioning dialectically and modelled upon natural processes" (Grace 13).
3. Margaret Atwood, *True Stories* (Toronto: Oxford UP, 1981 and New York: Simon and Schuster, 1981) 11.
4. Atwood, *True Stories* 93.
5. Elizabeth Bishop, *The Complete Poems, 1927-1979* (New York: Farrar, Straus, Giroux, 1983) 102.
6. Bishop 185.
7. Joanne Feit Diehl points to largely the same evidence as I do to make a very different argument: using Harold Bloom's theoretical model with its emphasis on agonistic struggle, on the sublime as growing out of humiliation and loss, and on the value of autonomy for the individual, Diehl valorizes those qualities in Bishop which I see as most problematic. See Joanne Feit Diehl, "At Home With Loss: Elizabeth Bishop and the American Sublime," *Elizabeth Bishop*, ed. Harold Bloom (New York: Chelsea House, 1985) 175-88.
8. Bishop 101.
9. Bishop 89.
10. Bishop 93.
11. Bishop 93-94.
12. Bishop 94.
13. In "An End to Audience?" Atwood responds to those who accuse her of being too negative: "I doubt that there's a writer in Canada who is asked more often, 'Why are you so pessimistic?' . . . What I usually say to them is, *What you think is pessimistic depends very largely on what you believe is out there in the world.* I myself think that compared to reality I'm a reincarnation of Anne of Green Gables" (Margaret Atwood, *Second Words: Selected Critical Prose* [Boston: Beacon, 1984] 349).
14. Atwood, *True Stories* 70.
15. Atwood, *True Stories* 16.
16. Atwood, *True Stories* 17.
17. Atwood, *True Stories* 24-25.

18 Atwood, *True Stories* 25.
19 Atwood, *True Stories* 25.
20 Bishop 102.
21 Bishop 102.
22 Atwood, *True Stories* 47.
23 Atwood, *True Stories* 47.
24 Diehl writes, "for Bishop, the Sublime poem must begin and end in loss"; for Diehl "hers is a loss equivalent to restitution" of a world that is "anomalous, isolated, yet sublimely defiant" (Diehl 187-8).
25 Bishop 185.
26 Diehl argues that in "Santarém" "Bishop describes an alternative Eden, one that . . . [creates] a fusion that draws all power into the observing self." In this poem she "delineates the conditions that surround the Sublime moment (an experience she typically defines through travel, presence, and observation)" (Diehl 183).
27 Margaret Atwood, *Selected Poems II: Poems Selected & New 1976-1986* (Toronto: Oxford UP, 1986 and Boston: Houghton Mifflin, 1987) 105.
28 Bishop 187.
29 Atwood, *True Stories* 99.
30 Atwood, *True Stories* 99.
31 Atwood, *Second Words* 349.
32 In contrast to Cixous's argument that we need to become more aware of gender, and in any case cannot escape its influence, Diehl argues that "one finds in Bishop's poems a map of language where sexuality appears to yield to an asexual self. . . . Her poems are a kind of brilliant compensation, a dazzling dismissal of the very distinctions that might otherwise stifle her" (Diehl 178).
33 George Starbuck, "'The Work!': A Conversation with Elizabeth Bishop," *Elizabeth Bishop and Her Art*, eds. Lloyd Schwartz and Sybil P. Estess (Ann Arbor: Univ. of Michigan P, 1983) 329.
34 Bishop 178.
35 Bishop 181.
36 Atwood, *True Stories* 22.
37 According to Diehl, the title of "One Art" "conveys the implicit suggestion that the mastery sought over loss in love is intimately related to the control she maintains in her poetry" (Diehl 178).
38 Bishop 178.
39 Atwood, *Second Words* 348.
40 Atwood, *True Stories* 28.
41 Atwood, *True Stories* 22.
42 Atwood, *True Stories* 27.
43 Bishop 140.
44 Atwood, *True Stories* 13.
45 Atwood, *True Stories* 14-15.
46 Atwood, *True Stories* 15.
47 Grace argues that "beginning with the dominant Western system of hierarchical dichotomies which support economic and class structures and encode a society's political, cultural, and psychological values, [Atwood] continually explores the evils of that system, forcing her readers to recognize their blindness and responsibility" (Grace 13).
48 Atwood, *True Stories* 50.

49 Atwood, *True Stories* 62.
50 Kristeva 210.
51 Bishop 101-102.
52 Atwood, *True Stories* 26.
53 Atwood, *True Stories* 26.
54 Atwood, *True Stories* 93. I would like to thank the members of the feminist theory group with whom I read Cixous and Kristeva for the stimulating exchange of ideas, and the following for encouragement and helpful criticism of drafts: Gayle Fujita, Electa Arenal, and Cristina Bacchilega. Any inadequacies that remain are my own.

ABOUT THE EDITORS

Cornelia N. Moore is a Professor of German and Dutch and Associate Dean of the College of Languages, Linguistics and Literature at the University of Hawaii. She was the Director of the Conference, entitled *Comparative Literature East and West: Traditions and Trends*, held in January 1988 in Honolulu, of which this volume contains the selected papers. She has published extensively on the development of literature for and by women.

Raymond Moody is an Associate Professor and Chair of the Division of Spanish and Portuguese at the University of Hawaii. As such his research spans two continents: Europe and South America. Among his many interests are computer-related instruction and he is the author of a soon-to-be published textbook in Portuguese that takes full advantage of the newly developed technology in language teaching.

Stafford Library
Columbia College
10th and Rodgers
Columbia, MO 65216